C0-DXD-713

101 Best *Vegan* RECIPES

Copyright © 2020 Moseley Road Inc.

All rights reserved. No part of this publication may be reproduced, distributed, or transmitted in any form or by any means, including photocopying, recording, or other electronic or mechanical methods, without he prior written permission of the publisher, except in the case of brief quotations embodied in critical reviews and certain other noncommercial uses permitted by copyright law.

MOSELEY ROAD INC.

International Rights and Packaging

22 Knollwood Avenue

Elmsford, NY 10523

www.moseleyroad.com

President Sean Moore

Editorial and art director Lisa Purcell

Editor Finn Moore

Production director Adam Moore

Cover designers Dawn Wilkins. Adam Moore

Printed in China

ISBN 978-1-62669-203-9

20 19 18 17 16 1 2 3 4 5

101 Best *Best* VEGAN RECIPES

Easy to prepare plant-based meals

SANDRA RUDD

mri
Moseley Road, Inc.
Elmsford, New York

CONTENTS

BREADS & MUFFINS
White Sandwich Loaf.................15
Whole-Wheat Loaf 16
Lavender-Lemon Cornbread 19
Scones..........................20
Cranberry Scones..................21
Nutty Berry Lemon-Poppy Bread.... 23
Banana Bread 24
Barmbrack 27
Matcha Pistachio Muffins 28
Blueberry Muffins.................31
Green Spinach Muffins 32
Pumpkin Muffins..................35
Cauliflower Pizza Crust.............36
Eggplant & Olive Pizza 39

SOUPS, STARTERS & SNACKS
Vegetable Broth 42
Vegetable Soup....................43
Easy Carrot Potato Soup 45
Quick & Easy Miso Soup 46
Mushroom Miso Soup 47
Cream of Mushroom Soup 49
Tomato Soup.....................50
Kale Potato Soup 53
French Onion Soup 54
Potato & Corn Chowder 55
Roasted Asparagus Soup 57
Lemon & Rosemary Barley Soup.....58
Spinach & Cannelini Soup...........61
Gazpacho........................62
Chilled Cucumber & Mint Soup 63
Red Beet Gazpacho 65
Roasted Beetroot Hummus 66
Sweet Potato Toast with Beetroot Hummus & Roasted Chickpeas 69
Baba Ganoush....................70
Guacamole.......................71
Roasted Eggplant Rolls with Spinach Hummus..............72
Melon & Arugula Salad with Watermelon Vinaigrette........75
Baby Spinach, Plum & Walnut Salad with Honey Mustard Dressing...........76
Curried Roasted Cauliflower Dip.....78
Hot & Sweet Cauliflower Bites.......79
Cauliflower Hot Wings..............81

MAIN COURSES & SIDE DISHES
Tofu Breakfast Scramble with Spinach & Tomatoes...........84
Mexican Quinoa Salad with Chili Lime Dressing 87
Avocado & Roasted Sweet Potato Salad with Spinach & Chickpeas 88
Zucchini Spiral Noodles with Basil Pesto Salad Bowl..........91

Air-Fried Falafel 92
Falafel, Tomato & Cucumber Salad . . . 94
Lentil Loaf with Barbeque glaze 95
Pumpkin Lentil Curry 96
Red Lentil & Bulgur Wheat Patties . . . 98
Red Lentil Dal 99
Peanut Stew 101
Stuffed Sweet Potato with Arugula, Olives & Guacamole 102
Hasselback Potatoes 103
Chana Masala 105
Aloo Gobi 106
Sesame Cauliflower 109
Pad Thai 110
Brussels Sprouts & Kabocha Squash Quinoa Salad 113
Open-Faced Beetroot Hummus Sandwich with Pomegranate & Corn Salsa 114
Bruschetta with Beetroot Hummus, Chopped Nuts & Microgreens 116
Avocado-Pomegranate Sweet Potato Toast 117
Tomato & Avocado Toast 118
Roasted Brussels Sprouts, Pecan & Cranberry Quinoa Salad 120
Spring Veggie Risotto 123
Ratatouille 124
Quinoa with Broccoli, Mushrooms & Spinach 127
Tabbouleh Salad 128
Teriyaki Tempeh Bowl 129
Barbeque Tempeh Skewers 130
Basil Pesto 132
Tagliatelle Pasta with Spinach Pesto & Green Peas 133
Eggplant Meatballs 135
Beetroot Burgers 136
Sweet Potato Burgers 139
Potato Pancakes 140

DESSERTS & SWEETS

Whipped Coconut Cream 144
Whipped Aquafaba Topping 145
Dalgona Matcha Latte 147
Matcha Green Tea Brownies with White Chocolate Drizzle 148
Chocolate Hummus 151
Mint Chocolate Avocado Pudding . . . 152
Nutty Chocolate Mousse 153
Cocoa Banana-Avocado Pudding 154
Carob & Date Balls 157
Dark Chocolate Truffles 158
Chia Pudding 161
Blue Spirulina Chia Pudding 162
Layered Peach Pudding 165
Berry Mousse 166
Old-Fashioned Tapioca Pudding 168
Mango Tapioca Parfait 169
Pumpkin Spice Pudding 171
Apple Crumble 172
Maple Walnut Baked Apples 175
Grilled Apple with Nutty Cinnamon & Honey Drizzle 176
Strawberry Freezer Pie 179
Tri-Layered Freezer Cake 180
Minty Cucumber, Green Tea & Lime Popsicles 183
Fruit Puree Popsicles 184
Piña Colada Popsicles 187
Orange Granita 188

Alphabetical List of Recipes 190
Photo Credits 192

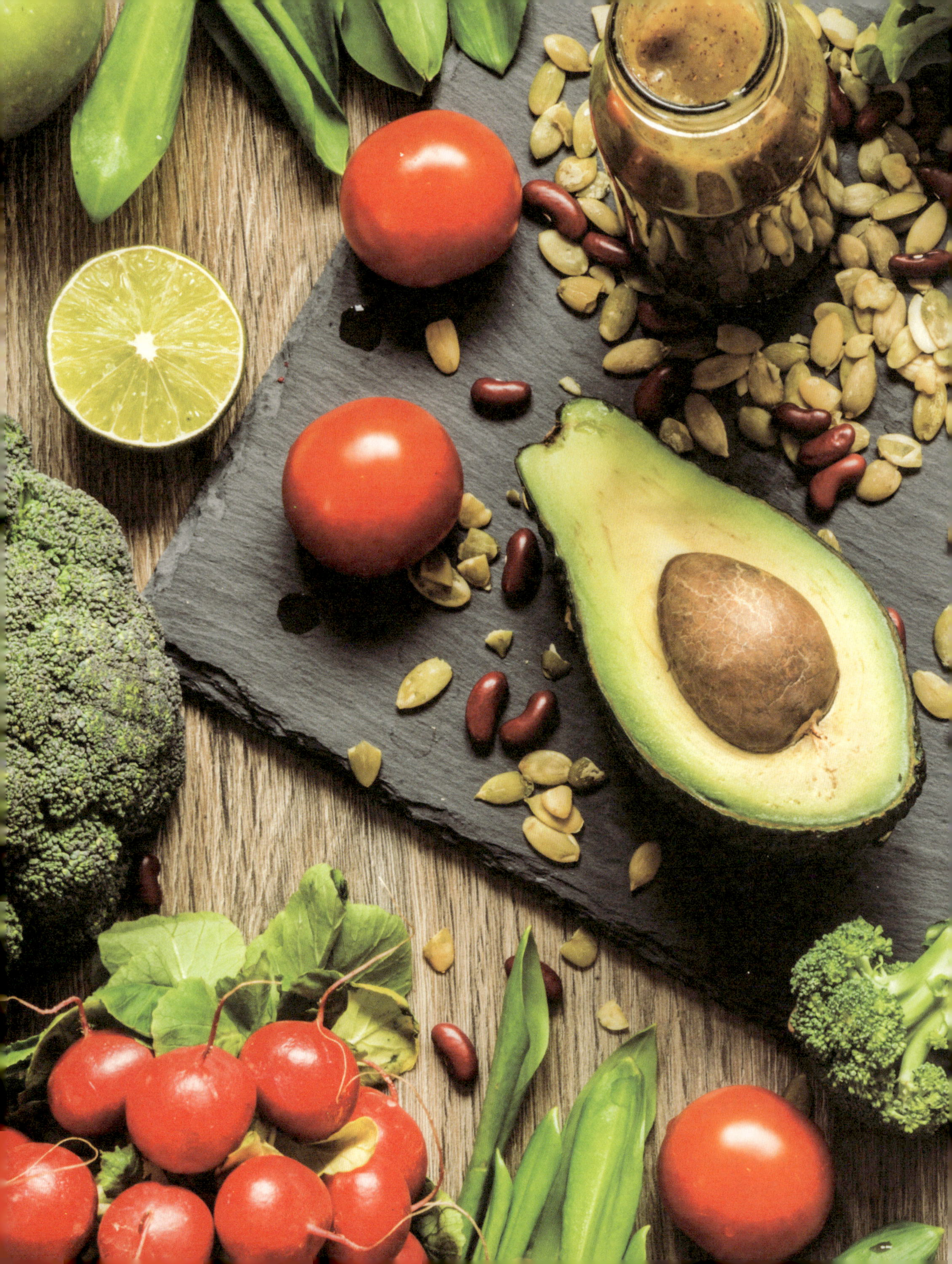

THE VEGAN PANTRY

STOCKING YOUR KITCHEN

Keep some key ingredients stocked so that you can put together healthy and delicious vegan recipes. The following lists can give you an idea of the kinds of foods that will come in handy.

LEGUMES

From soups to desserts, legumes feature in many vegan recipes. These versatile—and inexpensive—foods are the main protein source in a vegan diet. They are also low in fat and contain lots of fiber and micronutrients.

Keep both dried and canned varieties around. Canned chickpeas (also known as garbanzo beans) will also supply you with a source of aquafaba, the liquid left in the can. Aquafaba can act like a binder, such as an egg will, and it can be whipped to make a dessert topping.

Here are just a few:
- adzuki beans
- black beans
- black-eyed peas
- fava beans
- flageolet beans
- chickpeas (garbanzo beans)
- edemame
- kidney beans
- lentils (green, red, black)
- lima beans (also known as butterbeans)
- pinto beans
- peas (split and whole)
- red beans
- white beans (cannellini, navy, Great Northern)

GRAINS & FLOURS

Protein and fiber-rich grains make a great base for a filling meal. They are also used to bind other ingredients, such as in veggie burgers and loafs. If you need gluten-free, there are many kinds to choose from. Be sure to check the label.
- amaranth (gluten-free)
- barley
- basmati & jasmine rice (gluten-free)
- black rice (gluten-free)
- brown rice (gluten-free)
- buckwheat groats (gluten-free)
- bulgar wheat
- farro
- millet (gluten-free)
- oats (steel-cut, rolled, or quick—can be gluten-free)
- quinoa (gluten-free)
- tapioca (gluten-free)
- wheat berries
- white rice (gluten-free)
- wild rice (gluten-free)

Flour forms the base of some of our favorite foods, from breads to brownies. It also thickens sauces. Be sure to refrigerate flour once you have opened the package. For most recipes, you can switch out the called-for flour for what you have on hand, or substitute a gluten-free option if it isn't indicated in the ingredient list.
- all-purpose flour (regular or gluten free)
- almond flour (gluten-free)
- almond meal (gluten-free)
- buckwheat flour
- chickpea flour (also knowns as garbanzo bean, besan, or gram flour) (gluten-free)
- cornmeal, grits, polenta (gluten-free)
- oat flour (gluten-free)
- semolina
- spelt flour
- whole-wheat flour (regular and pastry)

PASTAS

Pasta is a great base for so many flavorful sauces and can be added to soups and salads to make them both more filling and tastier. These days, there are high-protein varieties, as well as veggie pastas. Look for couscous, too, which is made from semolina,

- brown rice pasta (gluten-free)
- couscous
- quinoa pasta (gluten-free)
- rice noodles (all sizes) (gluten-free)
- soba noodles (gluten-free)
- spelt pasta
- whole-wheat pasta

NUTS AND SEEDS
These are versatile ingredients: they can be sprinkled on salads and sandwiches, ground into flour or made into butters, or simply eaten as a tasty snack. Look for raw or toasted, with no salt.

- almonds
- Brazil nuts
- cashews
- chia seeds
- flaxseed meal
- hazelnuts
- hemp seeds
- peanuts
- pecans
- pistachios
- poppy seeds
- pumpkin seeds (pepitas)
- sesame seeds (white or black)
- sunflower seeds
- walnuts

DRIED FRUITS
Another staple that can be enjoyed as a simple snack or used as a recipe ingredient or topping. They are rich in fiber and nutrients, but are high in sugar and calories, so use sparingly.

- apples
- apricots
- bananas
- coconut flakes
- cranberries
- currants
- dates
- figs
- goji berries
- mango
- peaches
- pears
- prunes
- raisins

SWEETENERS
There are many kinds of sweeteners, including basics like pure cane sugar and maple syrup.

- cane sugar (including white granulated, brown, demerara, turbinado (raw), and confectioner's)
- coconut sugar
- coconut nectar
- date sugar
- dates
- honey
- maple syrup
- monkfruit
- stevia

HERBS AND SPICES
Herbs and spices are what give a recipe its signature flavor. There are so many to choose from, and a well-stocked pantry will feature a plethora of them. Spices are usually dried and ground, but for herbs, use fresh when possible,

- allspice
- basil (fresh or dried)
- bay leaves
- caraway seeds
- cardamom
- cayenne
- chili powder
- cilantro (fresh or dried)
- cinnamon
- cloves
- coriander
- cream of tartar
- cumin
- curry
- fennel seeds
- garam masala
- garlic powder
- ginger (fresh and ground)
- herbs de Provence
- Italian seasoning
- lavender
- lemon pepper

- marjoram
- mustard powder
- nutmeg
- old bay seasoning
- oregano
- onion powder
- paprika (sweet or smoked)
- parsley (fresh or dried)
- peppercorns
- pumpkin pie spice
- red pepper flakes
- rosemary
- sage
- salt (sea, Himalayan pink, or kosher)
- summer savory
- tarragon
- thyme
- turmeric
- vanilla (extract and beans)
- white pepper
- za'atar

OILS & FATS

Fat is an essential part of a healthy diet, but it should be used sparingly. Light oils are best for baking because they don't add their own flavors. Seed and nut oils will add a nutty flavor and are great for stir-fries and Asian recipes. For sautéing, use any olive oil, but for dressings, extra-virgin is best. For sandwiches or muffins, there are many vegan buttery spreads available.

- coconut oil
- grapeseed oil
- olive oil (light or extra-virgin)
- nut oils (walnut, hazelnut, pistachio, and others)
- sesame oil (regular and toasted)

VINEGARS

Vinegar lifts the taste of many dishes and also forms the base of salad dressings.

- apple cider vinegar (unfiltered)
- balsamic vinegar (white and dark)
- champagne vinegar
- red wine vinegar
- rice vinegar
- white wine vinegar

CONDIMENTS

A well-stocked kitchen will include a wide assortment of condiments. Check labels to be sure dressings, dips, sauces, spreads, and toppings are truly vegan.

- almond butter
- chili paste
- coconut butter
- fruit jams, preserves, and jellies (100% fruit)

CHEF'S TIPS

Plan ahead and craft your own mixtures for recipes that call for a blend of herbs and spices. Play with the ingredients and quantities, adjusting them until you find the right balance for your tastes. Here are options for two of the most common blends. For each, measure out all ingredients into a small bowl, and then whisk together until well combined. Store in an airtight container for up to 6 months.

Pumpkin Spice Blend
Version 1
4 teaspoons ground cinnamon
2 teaspoons ground ginger
1 teaspoon ground cloves
½ teaspoon ground nutmeg

Version 2
3 tablespoons ground cinnamon
2 teaspoons ground ginger
2 teaspoons nutmeg
1½ teaspoon ground cloves
1½ teaspoon ground allspice

Italian Seasoning
Version 1
2 tablespoons dried basil
2 tablespoons dried marjoram
2 tablespoons dried oregano
2 tablespoons dried rosemary
2 tablespoons dried thyme

Version 2
2 teaspoons dried sage
1 tablespoon dried basil
1 tablespoon dried marjoram
1 tablespoons dried oregano
1 tablespoon dried rosemary
1 tablespoon dried thyme

- hot sauce
- mustard (whole grain, and Dijon)
- sriracha
- tahini
- tamari (or soy sauce)
- vegan buttery spread

CANNED, BOTTLES & PACKAGED GOODS

These are easy and convenient foods to have around. Fresh may be best, but when time is an issue, these save a lot of energy, allowing you to throw together a quick meal. Refrigerate canned and bottled goods after opening. Many packaged goods will keep in the cupboard, but some, such as flour, should also go in the fridge after opening.

- apple sauce (unsweetened)
- arrowroot flour
- baking powder
- baking soda
- beans
- bouillon cubes
- breads
- chocolate chips
- cocoa nibs
- cocoa/cacao powder
- coconut cream
- coconut milk (full fat and light)
- cornstarch
- curry paste
- enchilada sauce (green or red)
- espresso (instant)
- green chilies (fire roasted)
- hemp protein powder
- lemon juice
- lime juice
- matcha powder (green tea and yerba mate)
- mirin
- mushrooms (dried, such as shitakes)
- nori wraps/sheets
- nutritional yeast
- olives (green or black)
- pepperoncini
- popcorn kernels
- potato starch
- rice paper sheets
- salsa
- spirulina powder (blue or green)
- sun-dried tomatoes
- tapioca flour
- tomato paste
- tomato sauce
- tomatoes (dices or whole)
- tortillas (corn or whole wheat)
- vegetable broth base
- wakame (sea kelp)

REFRIGERATOR ITEMS

From milk to miso, there are a few items to have at the ready for any recipe. And be sure to keep a selection of frozen fruits in the freezer.

- nondairy milk (almond, cashew, hemp, oat, rice, soy, and among others)
- nondairy yogurt
- miso
- tofu
- tempeh

PRODUCE

Be sure to keep long-lasting produce on hand. There are plenty of vegetables that can last for up to 2 weeks, so you can have them when needed. Some, such as root vegetables and onions, are best kept in a cool, dry place, with very little light.

- apples
- bell peppers (red, green, and yellow)
- brussels sprouts
- cabbage (red and green)
- carrots
- celery
- citrus fruits
- garlic
- onion
- pomegranates
- potatoes
- shallots
- sweet potatoes
- tomatoes
- winter squash (acorn, butternut, kabocha, red kuri, spaghetti, and pumpkin, and others)
- yams

FRESH FRUIT AND VEGETABLES

This category is truly at the heart of vegan eating. The list of these is nearly endless, with a wealth of fruits, such as berries, stone fruit, and summer melons, and vegetables, such as leafy greens and crucifers. Look for local in-season produce whenever you can.

CRANBERRY SCONES (*see page 21*)

BREADS & MUFFINS

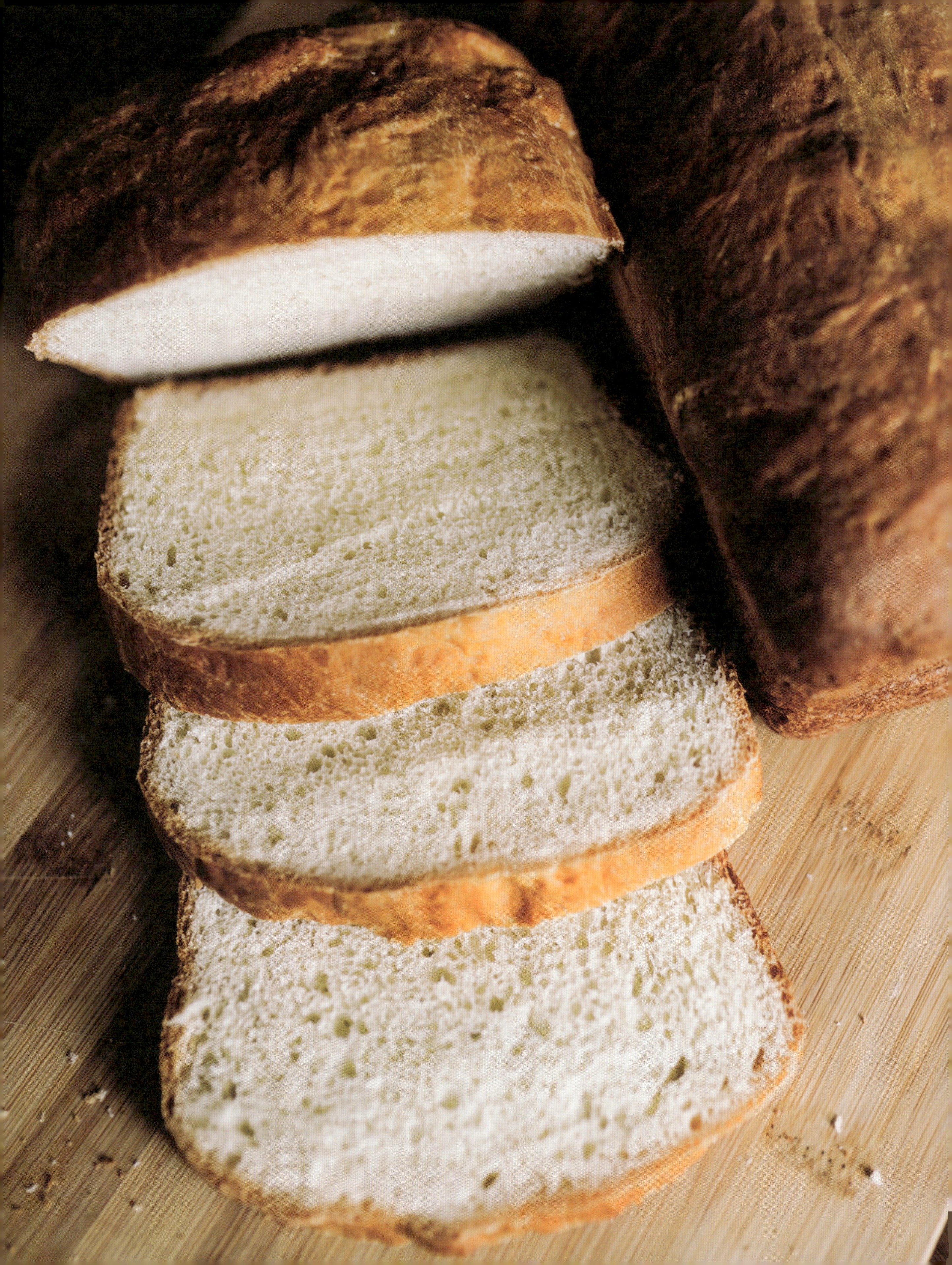

WHITE SANDWICH LOAF

This basic bread makes a great base for grilled and toasted sandwiches.

YIELD: 1 LOAF · PREP TIME: 1.5 HOURS · COOK TIME: 40 MINUTES

INGREDIENTS

½ cup (120mL) warm water

1 tablespoon raw sugar or 2 tablespoons maple syrup

1 tablespoon active yeast

½ cup (120mL) warm almond milk

2 tablespoons oil

3 cups (360g) organic bread flour or all-purpose flour or unbleached white flour

1¼ teaspoon salt

DIRECTIONS

- To proof the yeast, mix water, sugar, and yeast. Let sit for 5 minutes or until frothy.
- In large bowl, add the flour and salt, and mix well.
- Add the yeast mixture, oil, and warm almond milk to the flour-salt mixture, and then knead for about 8 minutes or until you have a soft, smooth non-sticky dough. Use more water or flour if needed.
- Spray water on top, and cover the bowl with a towel, and let the dough rise until doubled in size (about an hour and a half).
- Remove the dough from the bowl, punch it down, and then shape into a loaf.
- Place in a parchment-lined 8½ x 4½–inch (20 x 11-cm) bread pan. Spray top with water, and then spray oil or dust with flour.
- Cover lightly with a towel, and let rise for about 10 to 40 minutes, or until doubled in size.
- While the dough is rising, preheat the oven to 375°F (190°C).
- When the dough has risen, bake in the oven for 30 to 40 minutes.
- Remove the bread from pan, and cool completely.

CONTAINS

GLUTEN

SUGAR

FREE FROM

NUTS

METHOD

OVEN BAKE

CHEF'S TIPS

- To reduce browning, cover the top of the loaf in the last 5 minutes of baking.

WHOLE-WHEAT LOAF

This hearty loaf adds a fiber boost to sandwiches when just sliced fresh or when toasted.

YIELD: 1 LOAF · PREP TIME: 30 MINUTES · COOK TIME: 40 MINUTES

INGREDIENTS

- 4 cups (480g) whole-wheat flour
- 1 packet (11g) or 1 tablespoon instant yeast
- ½ teaspoon salt
- 2 teaspoons maple syrup
- 2 cups (480mL) warm water

DIRECTIONS

- To proof the yeast, mix water, sugar, and yeast. Let sit for 5 minutes or until frothy.
- In large bowl, add the flour, yeast, and salt, and mix well.
- Stir the maple syrup in the warm water, and then add to the dry ingredients.
- Mix (don't knead) until you have a sticky dough. Use more water or flour if needed.
- Transfer to a greased 9 x 5-inch (23 x 13-cm) bread pan.
- Cover lightly with a towel, and let rise for about 20 minutes, or until doubled in size.
- While the dough is rising, preheat the oven to 390°F (200°C).
- When the dough has risen, bake for 40 minutes.
- Remove the bread from pan, and cool completely.

CONTAINS
- GLUTEN
- SUGAR

FREE FROM
- NUTS

METHOD
OVEN BAKE

CHEF'S TIPS

- You can replace the maple syrup with agave nectar or other vegan syrup sweetener.
- This bread will keep for a day or two in a closed container, but you can still make delicious toast for a couple days after.

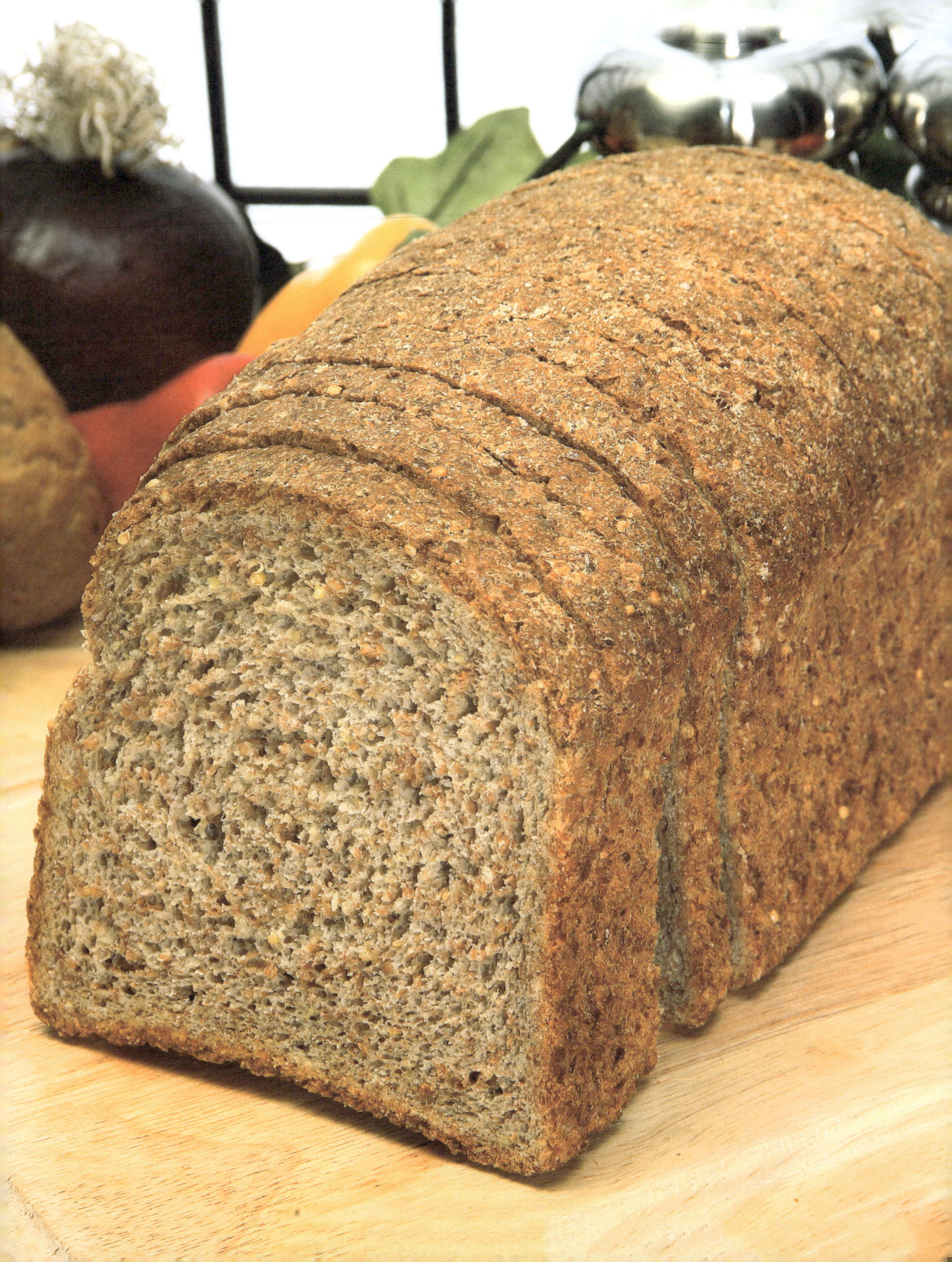

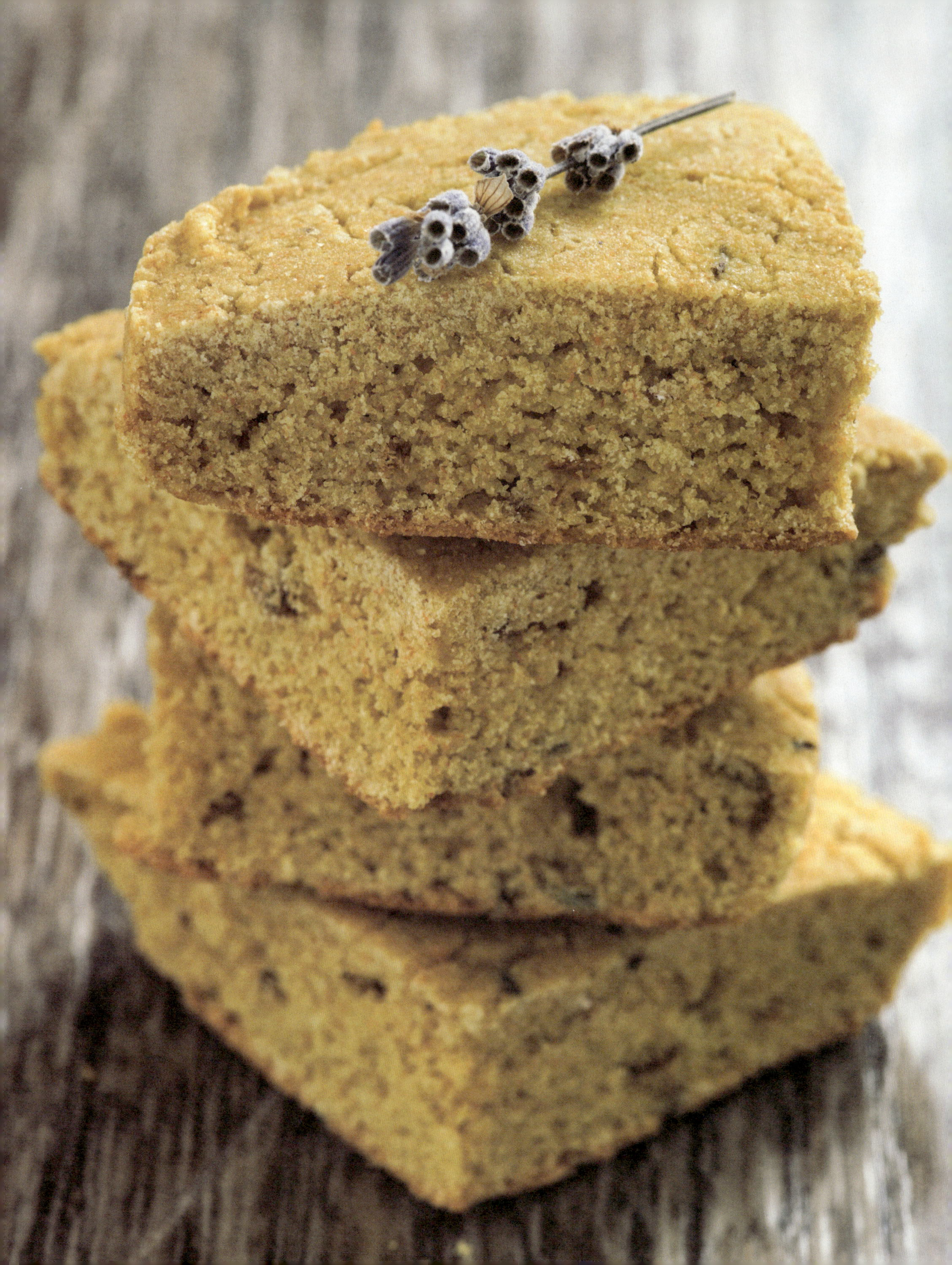

LAVENDER-LEMON CORNBREAD

Use this moist and sweet cornbread as a base for a summer berry dessert, or enjoy a square as a snack.

YIELD: 1 LOAF · PREP TIME: 5 MINUTES · COOK TIME: 25 MINUTES

INGREDIENTS

1¼ cup (140g) cornmeal
1 cup (120g) all-purpose flour
1 tablespoon baking powder
½ teaspoon salt
½ cup (100g) sugar
zest of 1 lemon
2 tablespoons freshly chopped lavender (leaves and flowers)
1 cup (240mL) nondairy milk
5 tablespoons extra-virgin olive oil

CONTAINS
- GLUTEN
- SUGAR

FREE FROM
- NUTS

METHOD
OVEN BAKE

DIRECTIONS

- Preheat your oven to 400°F (200°C), and lightly grease an 8 x 8–inch (20 x 20–cm) baking pan.
- In a large bowl, combine cornmeal, flour, baking powder, salt, sugar, lavender, and lemon zest. Mix using a fork to distribute the lavender and lemon zest.
- In a measuring cup, combine oil and milk.
- Gradually pour in the oil-milk mixture to the dry ingredients, and stir until just combined, being careful not to overmix.
- Pour the batter into the greased pan, and spread evenly with a spatula. Bake for 20 to 25 minutes, until a toothpick inserted into the center comes out clean.
- Let cool for at least 15 minutes, and then slice. Serve with your favorite summer fruit, plain, or with a vegan buttery spread.

CHEF'S TIPS

- For a chewier texture, you can add ¾ cup (130g) corn kernels (fresh, canned, or frozen) to the batter before baking,

SCONES

Serve these for breakfast, a snack, or a cream tea.

YIELD: 9 · PREP TIME: 40 MINUTES · COOK TIME: 20 MINUTES

INGREDIENTS

- 3 cups (360g) self-raising flour
- ½ teaspoon salt
- 1 teaspoon baking powder
- ½ cup (115g) vegan butter
- 4 tablespoons superfine sugar
- ¾ cup (180mL) nondairy milk
- 1 teaspoon vanilla extract
- 2 tablespoons lemon juice

DIRECTIONS

- Preheat oven to 430°F (220°C), and line a baking sheet with parchment paper.
- Sift the flour, salt, and baking powder into a large mixing bowl, add the vegan butter, and rub it in until the mix is crumbly.
- Add the caster sugar, and then slowly drizzle in the milk, vanilla extract, and lemon juice, and mix in, first with a spoon, and then just use your hands, just until it's combined and stays together.
- Roll out the dough on a lightly floured surface, flattening it to about ¾ inches (2cm). Dip a cookie cutter in flour, and then cut out 8 scones, and place them on the baking tray. Roll the leftover dough, cut out the final scone, and transfer to the baking pan.
- Brush the tops of the scones with milk, and bake for 15 to 20 minutes until the tops are golden brown.
- Serve warm with jam and Whipped Coconut Cream *(see* page 144) or Aquafaba Whipped Topping *(see* page 145).

CONTAINS
- GLUTEN
- SUGAR

FREE FROM
- NUTS

METHOD
OVEN BAKE

CRANBERRY SCONES

This vegan version of the British classic is soft on the inside and crispy on the outside, and studded with tart berries.

SERVES: 8 · PREP TIME: 10 MINUTES · COOK TIME: 15 MINUTES

CONTAINS
- GLUTEN
- SUGAR

FREE FROM
- NUTS

METHOD
OVEN BAKE

INGREDIENTS

- 1½ cups (180g) all-purpose flour
- 1⅓ cups (120g) fine oats
- 1 tablespoon baking powder
- ½ teaspoon salt
- 3 tablespoons coconut sugar
- ¼ cup (60g) apple sauce
- ¼ cup (60mL) oat milk
- 2 teaspoons apple cider vinegar
- 1 teaspoon vanilla extract
- ½ cup (115g) vegan butter, very cold and grated
- 1½ cups (150g) frozen cranberries
- 1 cup (150g) golden raisins

DIRECTIONS

- Preheat oven to 450°F (230°C), and line a baking sheet with parchment paper.
- Sift the flour, salt, sugar, and baking powder into a large mixing bowl, then add oats, and mix thoroughly.
- In a measuring cup, mix the apple sauce, milk, vinegar, and vanilla extract, and then pour it into the flour mixture along with the vegan butter. Mix until the dough is sticky. Toss the cranberries and raisins with 1 or 2 tablespoons of flour to coat, and then carefully fold them into the dough.
- Transfer the dough to the baking sheet, dust it with a little flour, and then gently shape into an 8-inch (20-cm) circle. With a sharp knife, cut into 8 equal slices, and sprinkle with coconut sugar. Bake for about 15 to 20 minutes until golden brown.
- Serve warm with a vegan buttery spread.

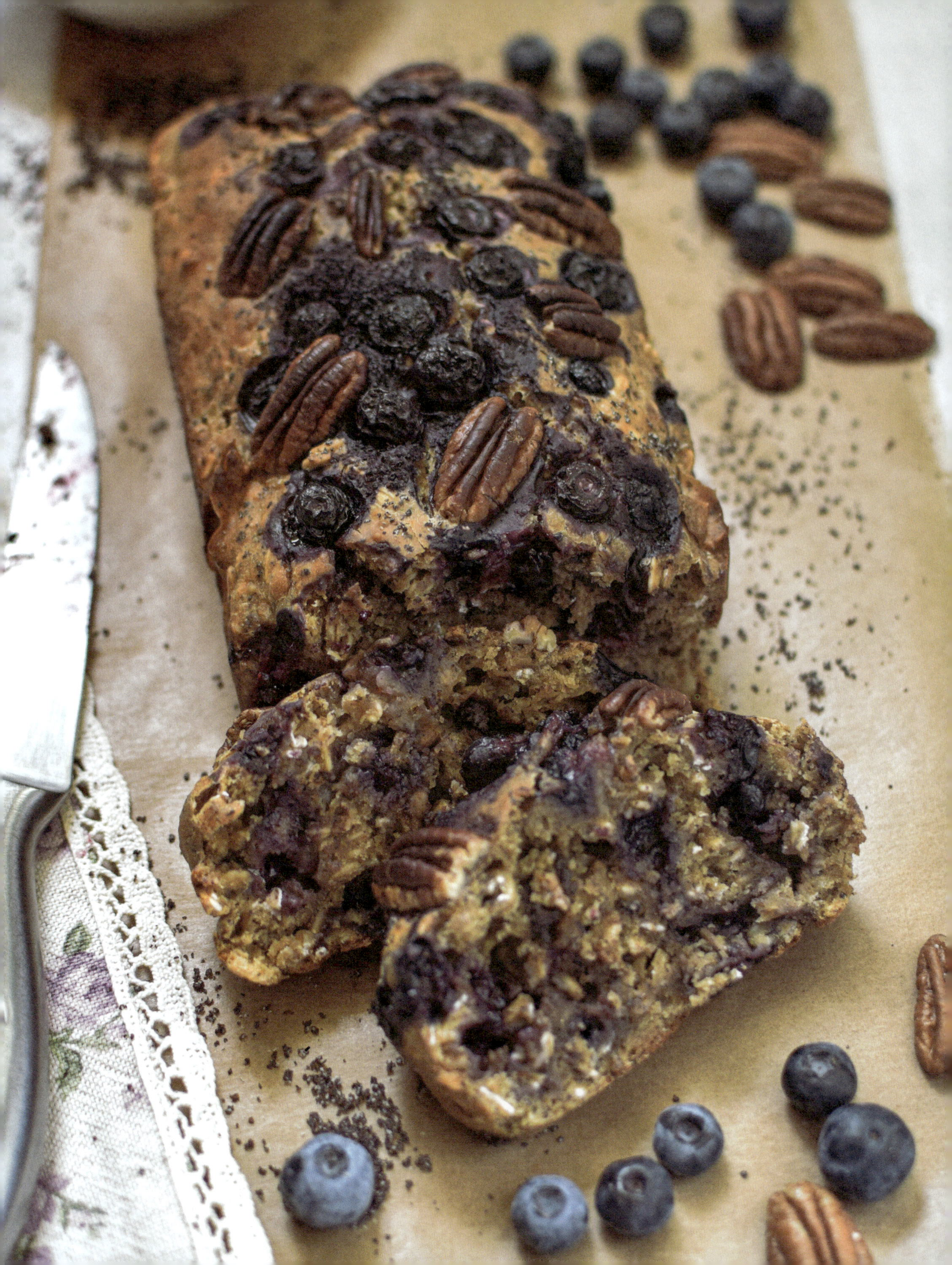

NUTTY BERRY LEMON-POPPY BREAD

Packed with blueberries and pecans, this poppy-seed bread gets a citrus zing from lemon juice.

YIELD: 1 LOAF · PREP TIME: 10 MINUTES · COOK TIME: 50 MINUTES

INGREDIENTS

- 1–2 large lemons
- ½ cup + 3 tablespoons (165mL) almond milk
- ¼ cup (60mL) canola oil
- 2 tablespoons unsweetened applesauce
- 1 teaspoon pure vanilla extract
- ¾ cup (150g) granulated sugar
- 2½ cups (300g) all-purpose flour
- 2½ teaspoons baking powder
- ½ teaspoon salt
- 1 tablespoon ground flaxseed
- 1 tablespoon poppy seeds
- 1 cup (100g) fresh blueberries
- ¼ cup (16g) pecans, halved

CONTAINS
- GLUTEN
- NUTS
- SUGAR

METHOD
ASSEMBLY

DIRECTIONS

- Preheat oven to 350°F (180°C).
- Reserving about 8 halves for garnish, coarsely chop the pecans.
- Zest the lemon until you have 1 tablespoon of finely grated zest, and then squeeze the zested lemon until you have 3 tablespoons of fresh lemon juice.
- Add zest and juice to a medium bowl, and then add the milk, oil, applesauce, vanilla, and sugar. Stir and then set aside.
- In a large bowl, add the flour, baking powder, salt, flaxseed, and poppy seeds, and mix well.
- Combine the wet lemon mixture with the flour mixture, stirring until well combined.
- Fold in the blueberries and chopped pecans.
- Grease a 8½ x 4½-inch (21 x 11–cm) bread pan, and pour in the batter. Top with reserved pecan halves, and bake for 40 to 50 minutes until the top is lightly browned and an inserted toothpick comes out clean.
- Remove the bread from the pan, and let cool completely.

BANANA BREAD

This easy vegan version of banana bread makes a delicious—and healthy—breakfast.

YIELD: 1 LOAF · PREP TIME: 15 MINUTES · COOK TIME: 60 MINUTES

INGREDIENTS

- 4 medium overripe bananas
- 2½ cups (225g) rolled oats, divided
- ½ cup (100g) coconut sugar
- ¼ cup (57g) nut or seed butter
- 2 tablespoons ground flaxseed
- 6 tablespoons water
- 2 teaspoons baking powder
- 1 teaspoon baking soda
- 2 teaspoons apple cider vinegar
- 1 teaspoon pure vanilla extract
- ½ teaspoon salt

CONTAINS
- GLUTEN
- NUTS
- SUGAR

METHOD

OVEN BAKE

DIRECTIONS

- Preheat oven to 350°F (180°C).
- In a small bowl, combine the ground flax with the water to form an "egg." Stir, and set aside for 5 to 10 minutes.
- Place 2 cups (180g) of the oats in a blender or food processor, and blend until they form a fine flour.
- Place the flour into a medium-sized bowl. Add the baking powder, baking soda, salt, and remaining oats. Mix well, and set aside.
- Peel 3 of the bananas, and in a separate, large bowl, mash them with a fork until they are as chunky or as smooth as you prefer.
- Add the nut butter, coconut sugar, apple cider vinegar, vanilla extract, and flax "egg" to the bowl. Mix well.
- Slowly incorporate the dry flour mixture into the wet banana mixture, stirring until the batter is smooth.
- Grease a 8 x 4-inch (20 x 10-cm) bread pan, and pour in the batter, smoothing off the top with a spatula. Peel the remaining banana, and press the halves lengthwise into the batter.
- Bake for 60 to 70 minutes, or until the top is golden brown and an inserted toothpick comes out clean.
- Remove from oven, let cool for 10 minutes in the pan, then remove from the pan and allow to cool completely before slicing.

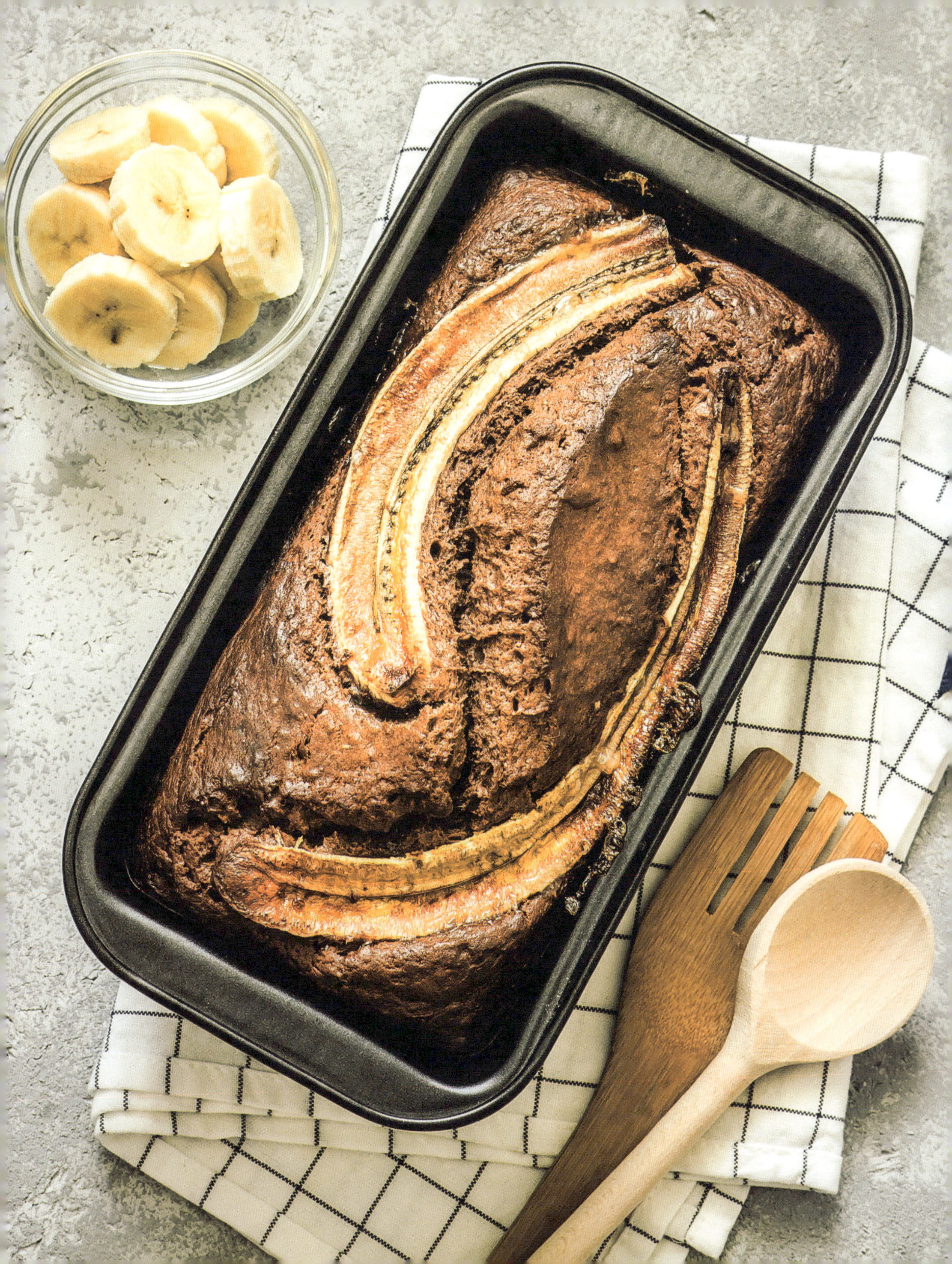

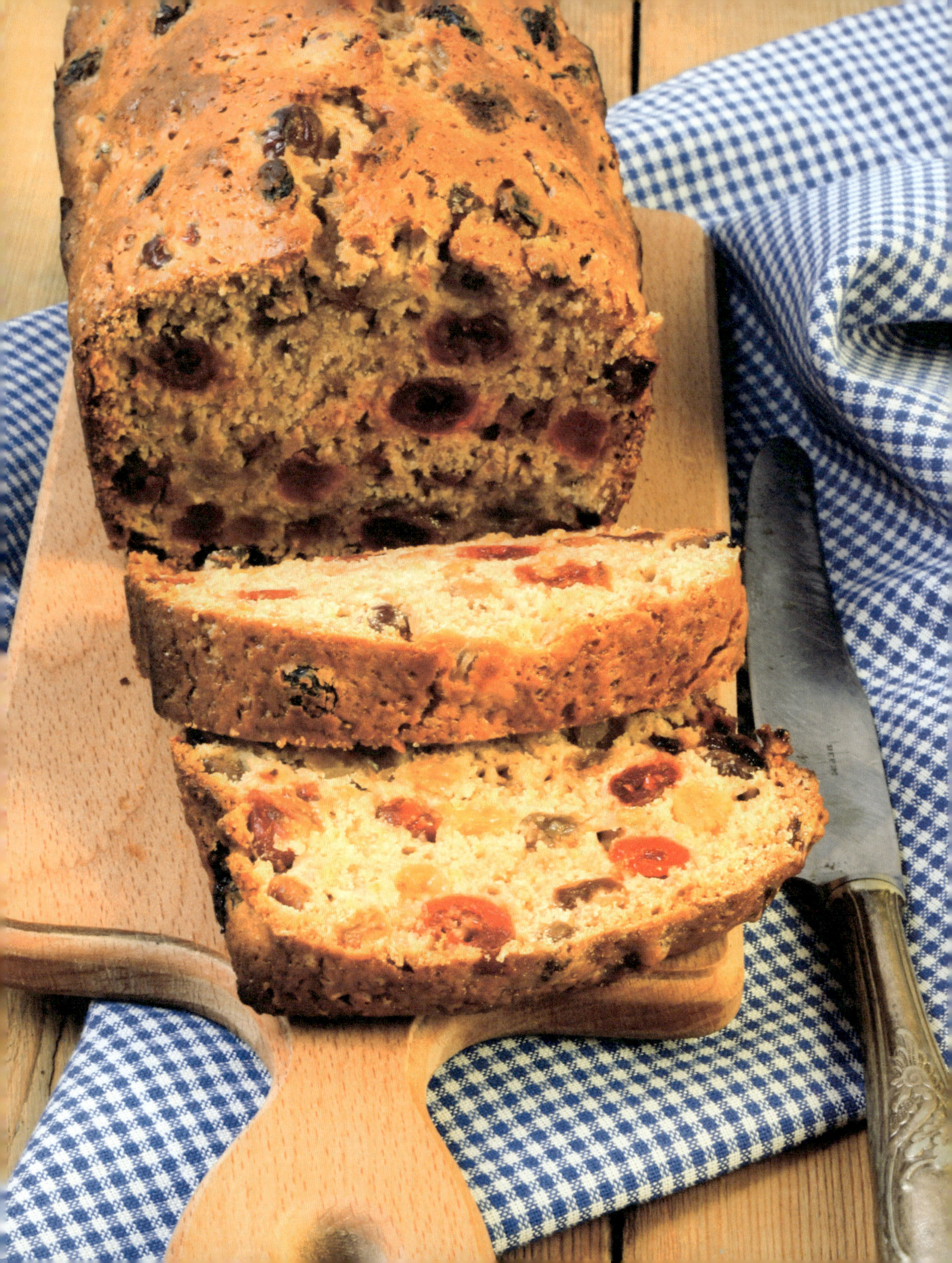

BARMBRACK

In Ireland, this tea loaf—studded with dried fruit and flavored with black tea—is often served at Halloween.

YIELD: 12 MUFFINS · PREP TIME: 55 MINUTES · COOK TIME: 1 HOUR

INGREDIENTS

1½ cups (225g) all-purpose flour

2 teaspoons baking powder

½ cup (105g) brown sugar, softened

½ large banana, mashed

1 cup (240mL) black tea, brewed

1 cup (300g) mixed dried fruits

¼ cup (60mL) nondairy milk

¼ teaspoon ground cinnamon

¼ nutmeg

¼ cloves

¼ ginger

pinch of salt

CONTAINS

- GLUTEN
- SUGAR

FREE FROM

- NUTS

METHOD

OVEN BAKE

DIRECTIONS

- Place the dried fruit in the cooled black tea, and soak for at least 4 hours.
- Preheat oven to 350°F (180°C).
- In a large mixing bowl, place the flour, salt, baking powder, sugar, and spices. Mix until well combined and all sugar lumps are broken up.
- Make a well in the center, add the mashed banana, and then add the milk.
- Strain the liquid from the tea-fruit mixture, and then pour into the bowl.
- Mix together the wet and dry ingredients until the batter is smooth. Add the fruits, and stir well.
- Line a 9 × 5-inch (23 × 13–cm) bread pan with parchment paper, and pour in the batter, smoothing off the top with a spatula. Bake for 40 minutes to 1 hour, or until a toothpick inserted in the middle comes out clean.
- Place in an airtight container and store in the refrigerator for 2 days, and then serve with vegan buttery spread.

MATCHA PISTACHIO MUFFINS

A topping of pistachios add a delightful crunch to these green tea muffins.

YIELDS: 12 · PREP TIME: 10 MINUTES · COOK TIME: 15 MINUTES-

INGREDIENTS

- 2 tablespoons ground flaxseeds
- ¾ cup (180 mL) unsweetened nondairy milk of your choice
- 1⅓ (160g) cups whole-wheat flour
- 2 teaspoons baking powder
- 1 tablespoon matcha powder
- 1 teaspoon lemon zest
- 1 teaspoon cinnamon
- ¼ teaspoon nutmeg
- ⅛ teaspoon salt
- ½ cup (113 g) vegan margarine, room temperature
- ½ cup sugar
- 2 teaspoons vanilla extract
- ½ cup (75g) pistachios, chopped

CONTAINS

- GLUTEN
- NUTS
- SUGAR

METHOD

OVEN BAKE

DIRECTIONS

- Preheat oven to 425°F (220°C), and line a 12-muffin tin with paper liners.
- In a small bowl, whisk together milk and flaxseeds, and them let sit for 10 minutes.
- In a medium bowl, combine flour, baking powder, matcha powder, lemon zest, cinnamon, nutmeg, and salt. Set aside.
- In a separate medium bowl, cream margarine, sugar, and vanilla. Stir in milk-flax mixture, adding a bit at a time.
- Add dry-ingredient mixture, about a third at a time, mixing well between additions.
- Spoon the batter into the muffin liners (about 1/2 cup each) and sprinkle with chopped pistachios.
- Lower the oven temperature to 375°F (190°C), and bake in the middle rack of the oven for 15 minutes, until lightly golden.
- Remove from the oven, and let sit in the tin for 2 to 3 minutes before transferring to a baking rack. Let cool completely.
- Sprinkle with matcha powder and chipped pistachios, and serve.

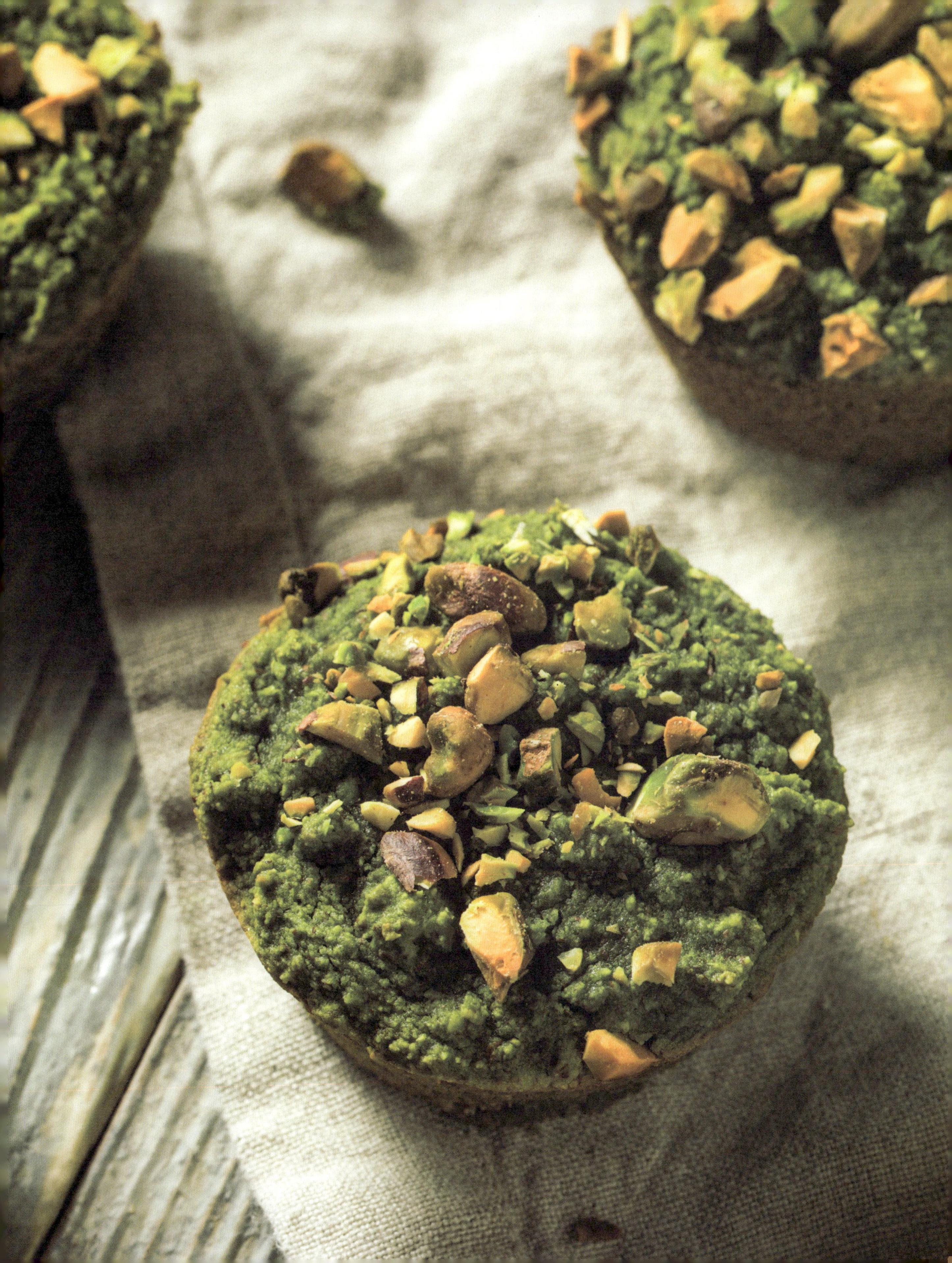

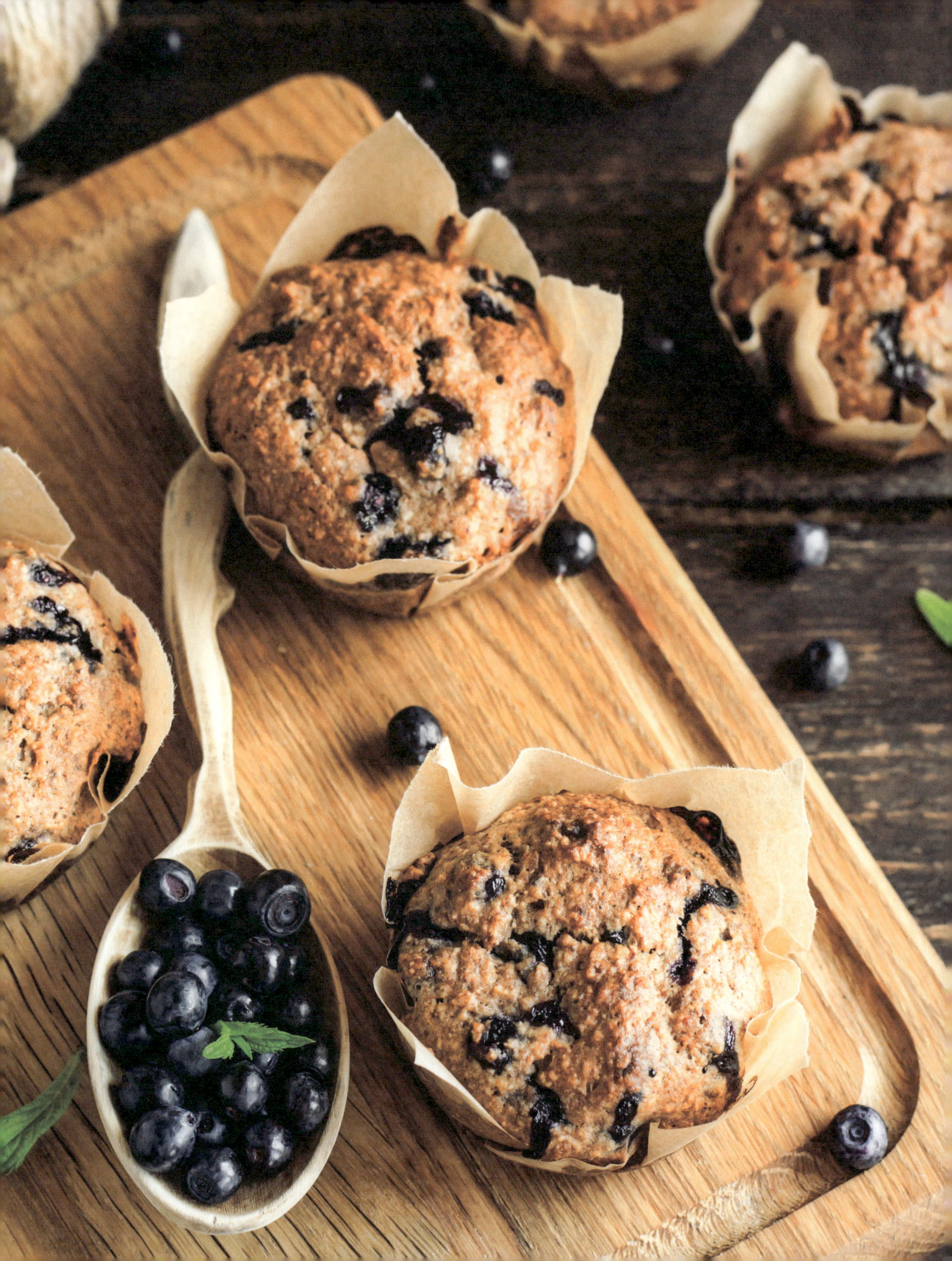

BLUEBERRY MUFFINS

Take a bite into these moist muffins to taste a refreshing hint of lemon and fresh, bright berry flavor.

YIELD: 12 MUFFINS · PREP TIME: 20 MINUTES · COOK TIME: 25 MINUTES

INGREDIENTS

1 cup (240 mL) soy milk

1 teaspoon apple cider vinegar

2 cups (240g) all-purpose flour

2½ teaspoons baking powder

¼ teaspoon baking soda

½ teaspoon salt

½ cup + 2 tablespoons (125g) granulated sugar

¼ cup + 2 tablespoons (90mL) canola oil

1 teaspoon vanilla extract

zest of 1 lemon

2 cups (200g) fresh blueberries

CONTAINS
- GLUTEN
- SUGAR

FREE FROM
- NUTS

METHOD

OVEN BAKE

DIRECTIONS

- Preheat oven to 375°F (190°C), and line a 12-muffin tin with paper liners.
- In a small bowl, combine soy milk and apple cider vinegar. Set aside to allow milk to curdle.
- In a separate bowl, combine flour, baking powder, baking soda, and salt. Set aside.
- In a large bowl, mix together sugar, oil, lemon zest, and vanilla extract. Add soy milk–vinegar mixture, and stir to combine.
- Stir in the dry ingredients. Avoid overmixing—a few lumps are okay. Gently fold in the blueberries.
- Spoon the batter into the muffin liners (about three-quarters full).
- Bake in the middle rack of the oven for 20 to 25 minutes, until a knife inserted in the middle comes out clean.
- Remove from the oven, and let sit in the tin for 2 to 3 minutes before transferring to a baking rack. Let cool completely.

CHEF'S TIPS

- You can store the muffins in an airtight container at room temperature for up to 5 days, or freeze them for up to 2 months.

GREEN SPINACH MUFFINS

With a cheerful, bright green color, these gluten-free muffins will tempt kids to eat a healthy breakfast.

YIELDS: 12–24 · PREP TIME: 10 MINUTES · COOK TIME: 30 MINUTES

INGREDIENTS

- 1 ripe banana
- ¼ cup + 3 tablespoons (105mL) water
- ¼ cup (57g) almond butter
- 1 tablespoon of ground flaxseed
- 1 teaspoon apple cider vinegar
- ¼ cup (60mL) honey
- 1–2 cups (225–450g) fresh baby spinach, loosely packed
- 1 cup (90g) rolled oats (certified gluten-free, if needed)
- ¼ teaspoon baking soda
- ¼ teaspoon ground cinnamon
- ½ teaspoon vanilla extract
- ⅛ teaspoon salt

CONTAINS
- NUTS
- SUGAR

FREE FROM
- GLUTEN

METHOD
OVEN BAKE

DIRECTIONS

- Preheat oven to 350°F (180°C), and line a 12-muffin tin or 24-mini-muffin tin with paper liners.
- In a small bowl, combine the ground flaxseed with 3 tablespoons of the water to form an "egg." Stir, and set aside for 5 to 10 minutes.
- Place the banana, water, vinegar, almond butter, egg, honey, spinach, rolled oats, baking soda, cinnamon, vanilla, and salt (in that order), in a blender or food processor, and blend until very smooth, stopping to scrape the sides as needed.
- Pour the batter into the lined muffin tin, and bake until the muffins rise and feel firm when pressed lightly in the middle, about 15 to 30 minutes, depending on the size of the muffin tin. The surface of the muffins may crack a bit.
- Remove from oven, and let cool for 30 minutes.
- Serve plain, with jam, or a vegan buttery spread.

CHEF'S TIPS

- You can store the muffins in an airtight container at room temperature for 24 hours, or you can store them in the refrigerator for up to a week.

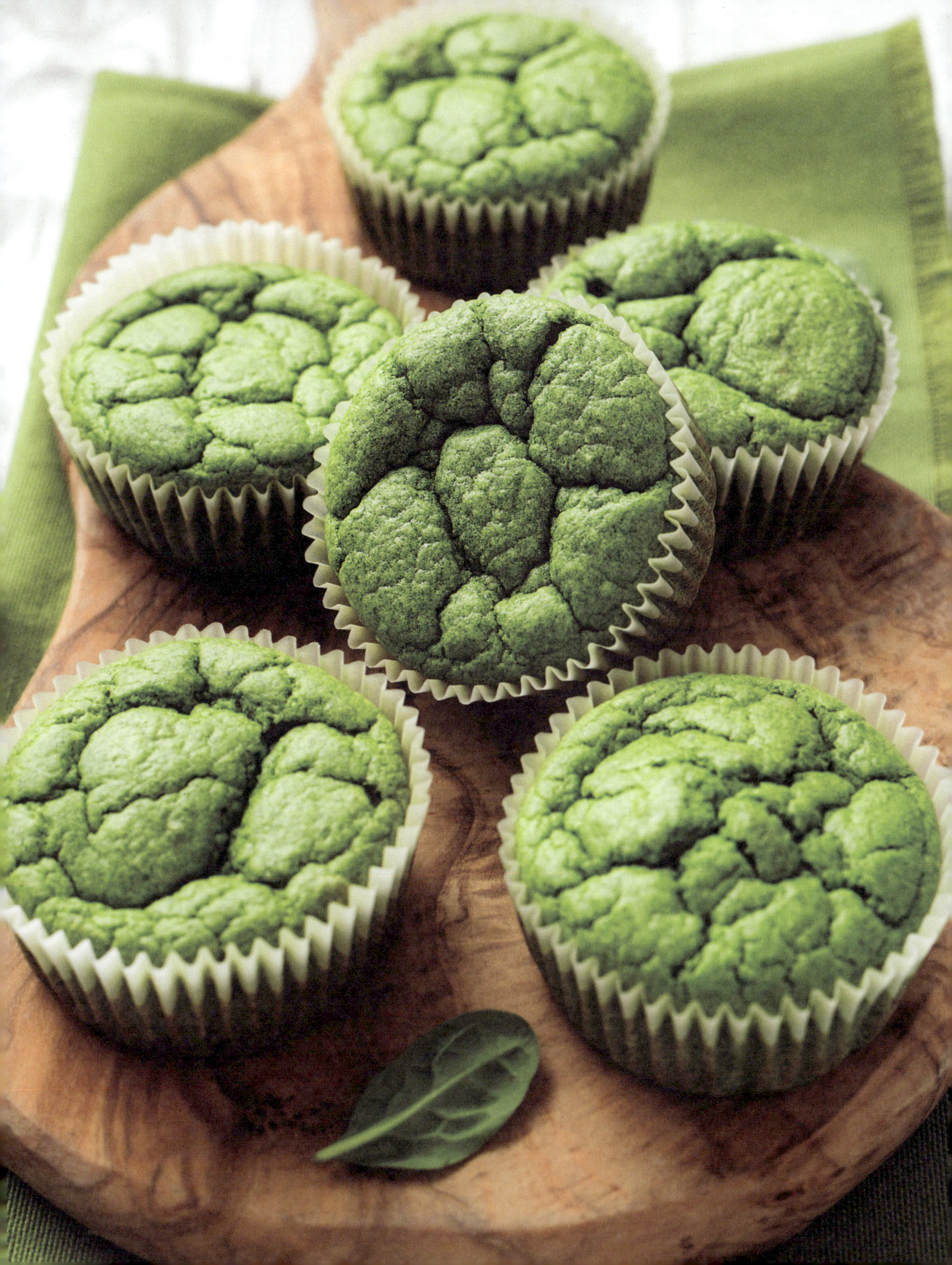

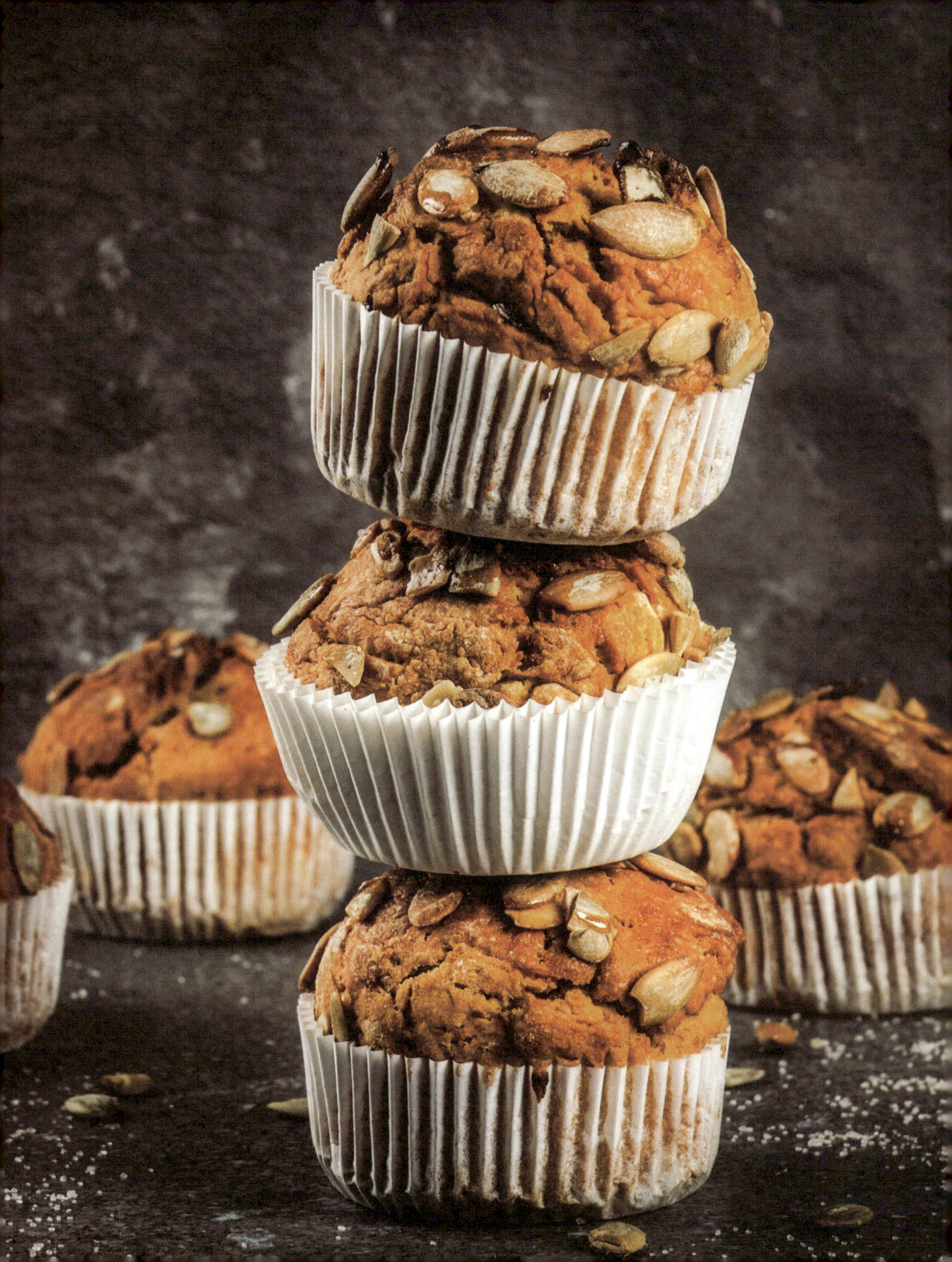

PUMPKIN MUFFINS

Serve these moist and yummy muffins for an autumn breakfast or brunch.

YIELD: 12 MUFFINS · PREP TIME: 15 MINUTES · COOK TIME: 30 MINUTES

INGREDIENTS

- 1 15-ounce (425g) can pumpkin puree
- 1 cup (240mL) almond nondairy milk
- 1 cup (200g) coconut sugar
- ¼ cup (56g) nut or seed butter
- 1 teaspoon pure vanilla extract
- 2½ cups (225g) quick or rolled oats
- 1 tablespoon pumpkin pie spice blend
- 1 tablespoon baking powder
- 1 teaspoon baking soda
- ½ teaspoon kosher or sea salt
- juice of ½ lemon (or 1 tablespoon apple cider vinegar)
- ¼ cup (40g) pumpkin seeds

CONTAINS
- NUTS
- SUGAR

FREE FROM
- GLUTEN

METHOD
OVEN BAKE

DIRECTIONS

- Preheat oven to 350°F (180°C), and line a 12-muffin tin with paper liners.
- Add the rolled oats into a blender or food processor, and blend until they form a fine flour, about 45 to 60 seconds.
- In a large bowl, combine the pumpkin puree, milk, coconut sugar, nut butter, and vanilla extract, stirring until a thick, even consistency forms.
- Add the blended oat flour, baking powder, pumpkin pie spice, and salt to the bowl, and mix well.
- Add the lemon juice, stirring until evenly combined.
- Spoon the batter into the muffin liners (about 1/2 cup each) and sprinkle some of the pumpkin seeds on top.
- Bake in the middle rack of the oven for 30 to 32 minutes, until fluffy and golden.
- Remove from the oven, and let sit in the tin for 2 to 3 minutes before transferring to a baking rack. Let cool completely.

CHEF'S TIPS

- You can store the muffins in an airtight container at room temperature for up to 5 days, or freeze them for up to a month.
- For homemade pumpkin spice blends, *see* page 9.

CAULIFLOWER PIZZA CRUST

Top this vegan, keto, and low-carb version of a pizza crust with your favorite toppings.

SERVES: 6 · PREP TIME: 15 MINUTES · COOK TIME: 35 MINUTES

INGREDIENTS

- ½ medium head cauliflower
- ¼ cup (60mL) water
- ⅓ cup (40g) all-purpose flour
- ¼ teaspoon garlic powder
- 1¼ teaspoon baking powder
- ½ teaspoon salt

DIRECTIONS

- Preheat oven to 450°F (230°C), and line a baking sheet with parchment paper.
- Steam cauliflower florets until they are soft and falling apart. Drain.
- Stir the garlic, baking powder, and salt into the flour.
- Let the cauliflower cool a bit, and then place it in a dish towel over a sink, and squeeze out as much moisture as possible. Place it in a bowl, and add the water. Mash and stir well. Stir in the flour mixture.
- Form into a ball, and place it on the baking sheet. Pat into a circle about ¼ inch (6mm) thick. Bake 25 minutes, or until lightly browned with crispy edges. Add toppings, and bake an additional 8 to 10 minutes. Allow to cool 5 minutes, slice, and serve.

CONTAINS
- GLUTEN

FREE FROM
- NUTS
- SUGAR

METHOD

OVEN BAKE

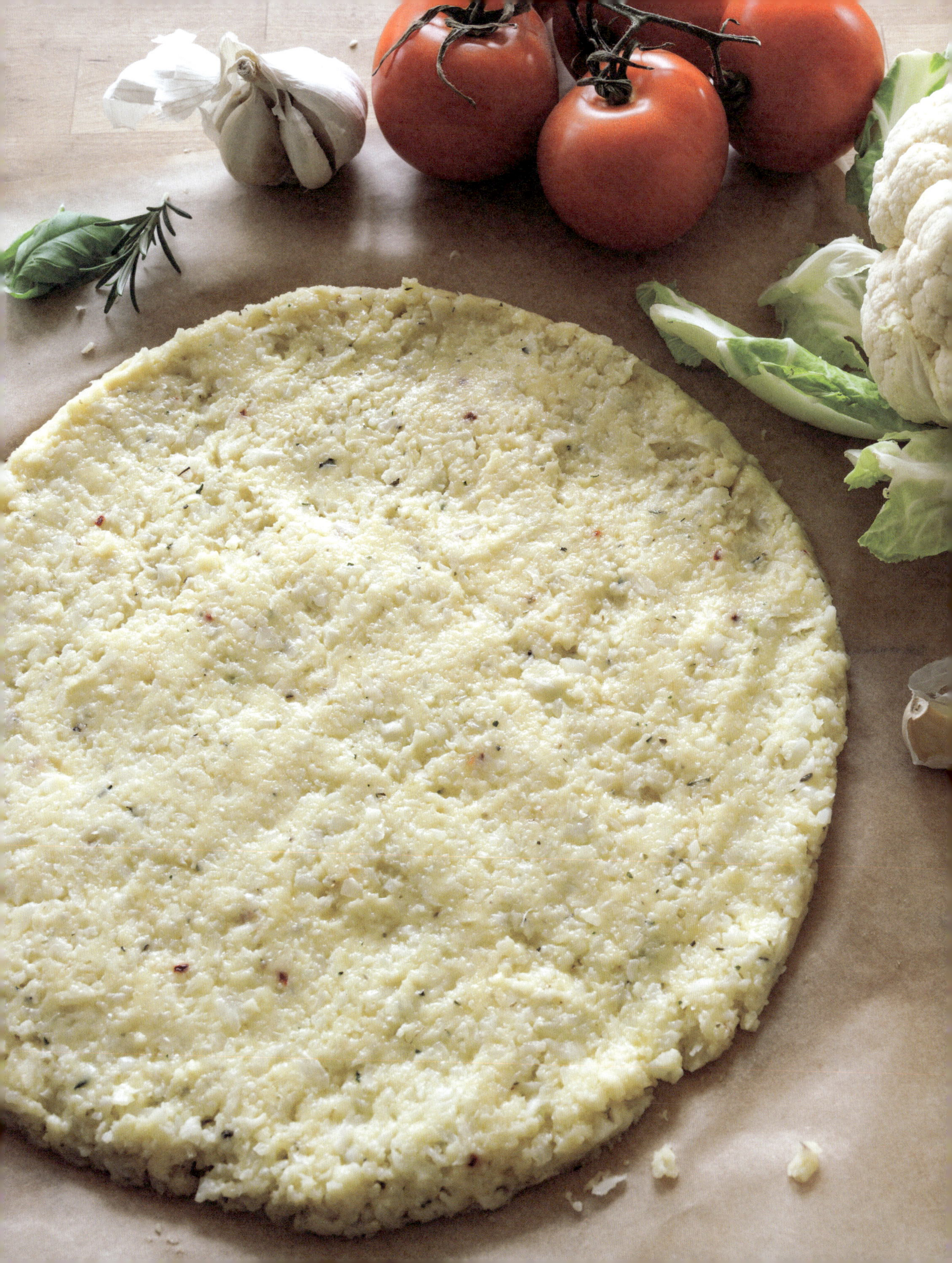

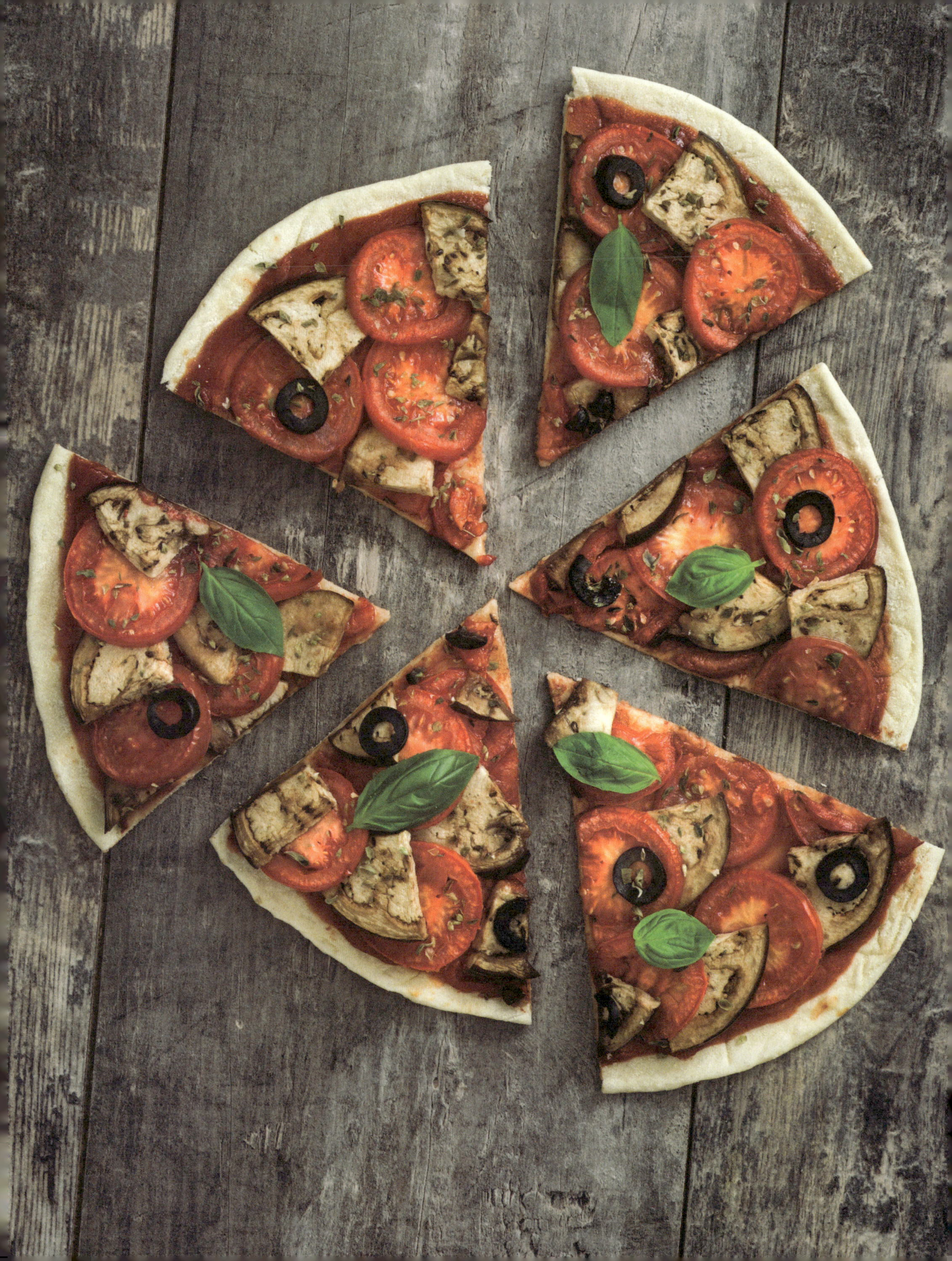

EGGPLANT & OLIVE PIZZA

This hearty pizza makes a great lunch or dinner. You can also use the crust recipe for the toppings of your choice.

SERVES: 4–8 · PREP TIME: 20 MINUTES · COOK TIME: 35 MINUTES

INGREDIENTS

- 1 tablespoon (10g) dry active yeast
- 1¼ cup (300 mL) warm water,
- 2–3 tablespoon sugar
- 3 cups (360g) gluten-free flour
- 1 teaspoon salt
- ½ teaspoon baking powder
- 4 tablespoons olive oil
- ½ cup (90g) black olives
- 3 tomatoes, sliced
- 1 eggplant
- ½ teaspoon oregano
- ½ teaspoon garlic powder
- fresh basil, for topping

DIRECTIONS

- Cut eggplant into bite-sized triangles, and arrange in a layer on a foil-lined baking sheet. Lightly brush both sides with 3 tablespoons of the olive oil, and season with salt. Broil 2 to 3 inches (50 to 75mm) from heat until golden brown and tender, about 3 to 8 minutes on each side.
- Preheat oven to 350°F (180°C), and line a baking sheet with parchment paper.
- In a small bowl, combine yeast and ¾ cup (180 mL) warm water. Let set for 5 minutes to activate. Sprinkle in 1 tablespoon of the sugar a few minutes in.
- In a separate bowl, combine flour, salt, baking powder and remaining sugar. Whisk until well combined. Make a well, and add the yeast mixture. Add the remaining olive oil and warm water. Stir until well combined.
- Form into a ball, and place it on the baking sheet. Pat into a circle about ¼ inch (6mm) thick. Bake 25 minutes, or until lightly browned. Add tomatoes, eggplant, and olive, and sprinkle with oregano and garlic powder. Bake an additional 8 to 10 minutes. Allow to cool 5 minutes, slice, garnish with fresh basil, and serve.

CONTAINS
SUGAR

FREE FROM
GLUTEN
NUTS

METHOD
OVEN BAKE

VEGAN RECIPES: BREADS & MUFFINS

GAZPACHO (*see page 62*)

SOUPS, STARTERS & SNACKS

VEGETABLE BROTH

Freeze leftover veggie scraps to make this broth that you can sip as is or use as a base in any soup recipe.

YIELD: 12 CUPS · PREP TIME: 5 MINUTES · COOK TIME: 50 MINUTES

INGREDIENTS

- 1 tablespoon olive oil
- 1 yellow onion chopped
- 3 cloves garlic, minced
- 12 cups (1 liter) water
- 2 bay leaves
- 1 teaspoon whole peppercorns
- ½ teaspoon salt, optional
- 1-quart freezer bag of vegetable scraps, such as the peels, skins, and trimmings of carrots, onions, herbs, broccoli, kale, squash, mushrooms, fennel, turnips, potatoes, or celery)

FREE FROM

- GLUTEN
- NUTS
- SUGAR

METHOD

STOVETOP

DIRECTIONS

- In a large soup pot, heat the oil over medium-high heat. When the oil is hot, add the onion and garlic and sauté for around 5 minutes until the onion turns translucent and begins to brown.
- Add the veggie scraps, water, bay leaves, peppercorns, and salt.
- Bring to a simmer, and then continue to simmer for about 45 minutes until the broth takes on a rich fragrance and color (which will vary, along with the taste, according to the vegetables used).
- Place a fine colander or cheesecloth over a large bowl or pot, and strain out the scraps and discard.
- Transfer the broth to airtight containers, and store for later use.

CHEF'S TIPS

- The broth will last a week in the refrigerator, or you can freeze it for up to 3 months.

VEGETABLE SOUP

This classic soup gets its flavor from Italian spices.

SERVES: 6 · PREP TIME: 10 MINUTES · COOK TIME: 35 MINUTES

INGREDIENTS

- 2 tablespoons extra-virgin olive oil
- 4 cloves of garlic, chopped
- 2 celery sticks, chopped
- 1 onion, chopped
- 2 medium potatoes, peeled and diced
- 2 large carrots, peeled and diced
- 1 cup (120g) frozen green beans
- 2 14-ounce (400g) cans crushed tomatoes
- 4 cups (960 mL) vegetable broth
- 1 tablespoon Italian seasoning
- ¼ teaspoon salt
- ¼ teaspoon freshly ground black pepper

FREE FROM
- GLUTEN
- NUTS
- SUGAR

METHOD
STOVETOP

DIRECTIONS

- In a large soup pot, heat the oil over medium-high heat. When the oil is hot, sauté the garlic, celery, and onion until golden brown, stirring occasionally.
- Add all the remaining ingredients, and bring to a boil. Reduce heat, and simmer, partially covered, for 30 minutes or until the potatoes and carrots are tender.
- Serve with a crusty bread.

CHEF'S TIPS

- For a homemade vegetable broth, see opposite page; for Italian seasoning blends, *see* page 9.

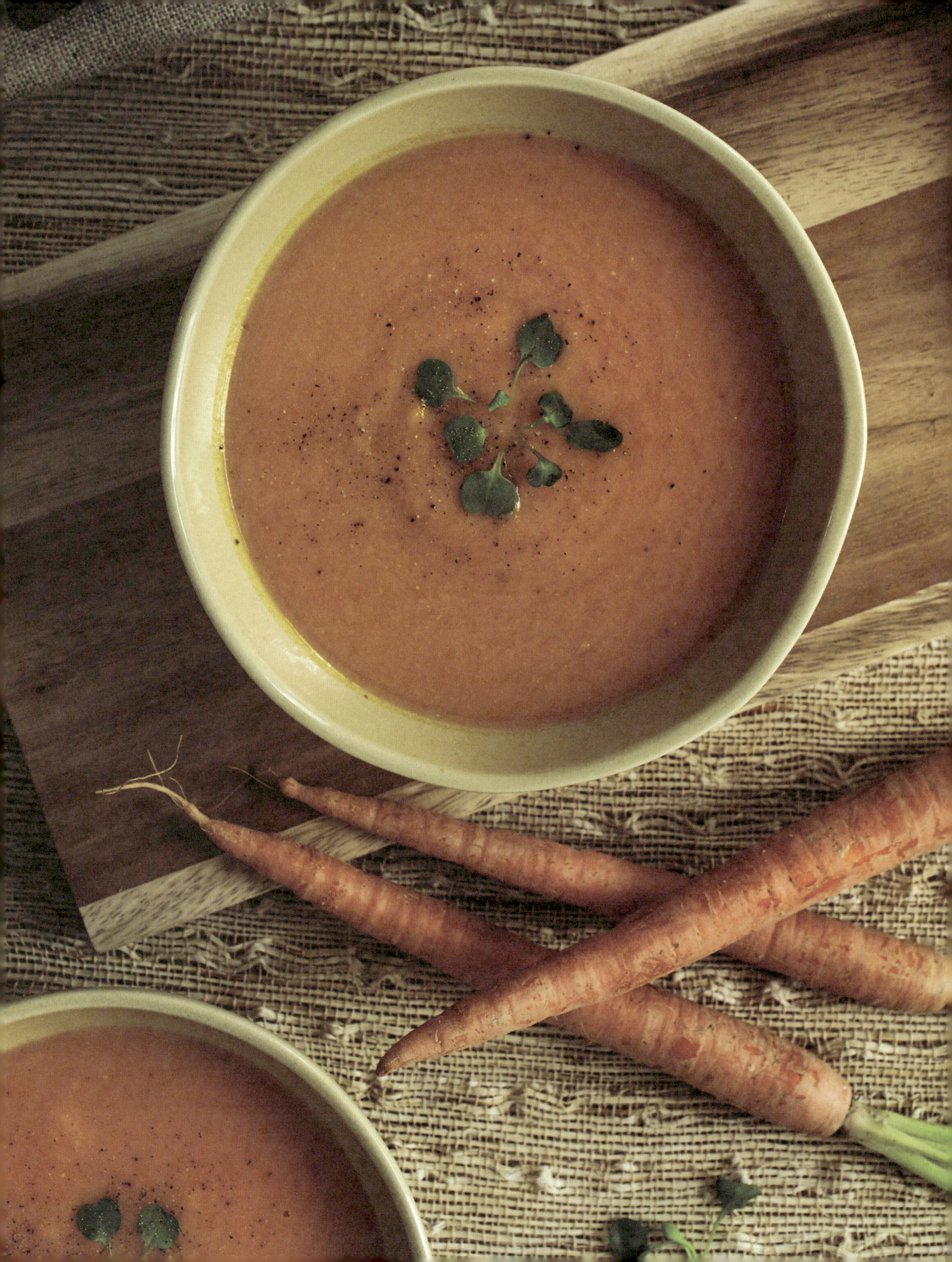

EASY CARROT POTATO SOUP

Sweet and white potatoes add depth to this simple recipe that results in a smooth veggie soup.

SERVES: 2–4 · PREP TIME: 10 MINUTES · COOK TIME: 35 MINUTES

INGREDIENTS

- 3 carrots, peeled and cut into small pieces
- 2 sweet potatoes, peeled and cut into chunks
- 2 celery stalks, chopped
- 3 medium russet potatoes peeled and cut into chunks
- 4 cups (960 mL) vegetable broth

DIRECTIONS

- Place the carrots, celery, sweet potatoes, and potatoes in a large soup pot, and cover with the vegetable broth (if necessary, add enough water so that the vegetables are completely covered by about an inch.
- Bring to a boil, and then reduce the heat. Simmer for 30 to 45 minutes, until the vegetables are cooked through and tender.
- In batches, transfer the mixture into a blender or food processor, and blend until smooth, adding more broth if necessary for a thinner consistency. Return all blended batches to the pot, and stir.
- Pour into bowls or cups, and serve.

FREE FROM

- GLUTEN
- NUTS
- SUGAR

METHOD

STOVETOP

BLENDER

CHEF'S TIPS

- For a homemade vegetable broth, see page 42.

QUICK & EASY MISO SOUP

You can whip up this simple version of the flavorful Japanese classic in just 15 minutes.

SERVES: 2–4 · PREP TIME: 10 MINUTES · COOK TIME: 10 MINUTES

INGREDIENTS

4 cups (960 mL) water

1 tablespoon dried wakame seaweed

3½ ounces (100g) soft tofu

2 green onions, trimmed and thinly sliced

3 tablespoons organic red miso paste

DIRECTIONS

- Pour water into a large saucepan, and bring to a boil.
- Add the seaweed, and cook over medium heat for about 5 minutes.
- Add the tofu, and stir, heating for another 5 minutes.
- While the soup heats, mix the miso paste with a bit of hot water in a small bowl, and whisk until smooth, and then add to the broth.
- Pour the soup into bowls, add the green onions, and serve immediately.

FIVE INGREDIENTS

CONTAINS
SOY

FREE FROM
GLUTEN
SUGAR

METHOD
STOVETOP

CHEF'S TIPS

- You can substitute other green veggies, such as bok choy or kale, for the seaweed.

MUSHROOM MISO SOUP

Meaty mushrooms add an earthy edge to the traditional miso soup recipe.

SERVES: 2–4 · PREP TIME: 5 MINUTES · COOK TIME: 5 MINUTES

INGREDIENTS

- 4 cups (960 mL) mushroom (or vegetable) broth
- 3 cups (225g) portobello or shitake mushrooms, thinly sliced
- 1 teaspoon grated fresh gingerroot
- 3 tablespoons organic red miso paste
- 4 teaspoons soy sauce
- 2 green onions, trimmed and thinly sliced
- ¼ teaspoon red chili flakes (optional)

DIRECTIONS

- Pour the broth into a large saucepan, and bring to a boil.
- Add the mushrooms and gingerroot, reduce heat to low, and simmer 4 minutes.
- Stir the miso paste and soy sauce together in a small bowl, and then add to the broth. Continue cooking for 1 minute more.
- Pour the soup into bowls, add the green onions, sprinkle with chili flakes (if desired) and serve immediately.

CONTAINS
- CHILIS
- SOY

FREE FROM
- GLUTEN
- NUTS
- SUGAR

METHOD

STOVETOP

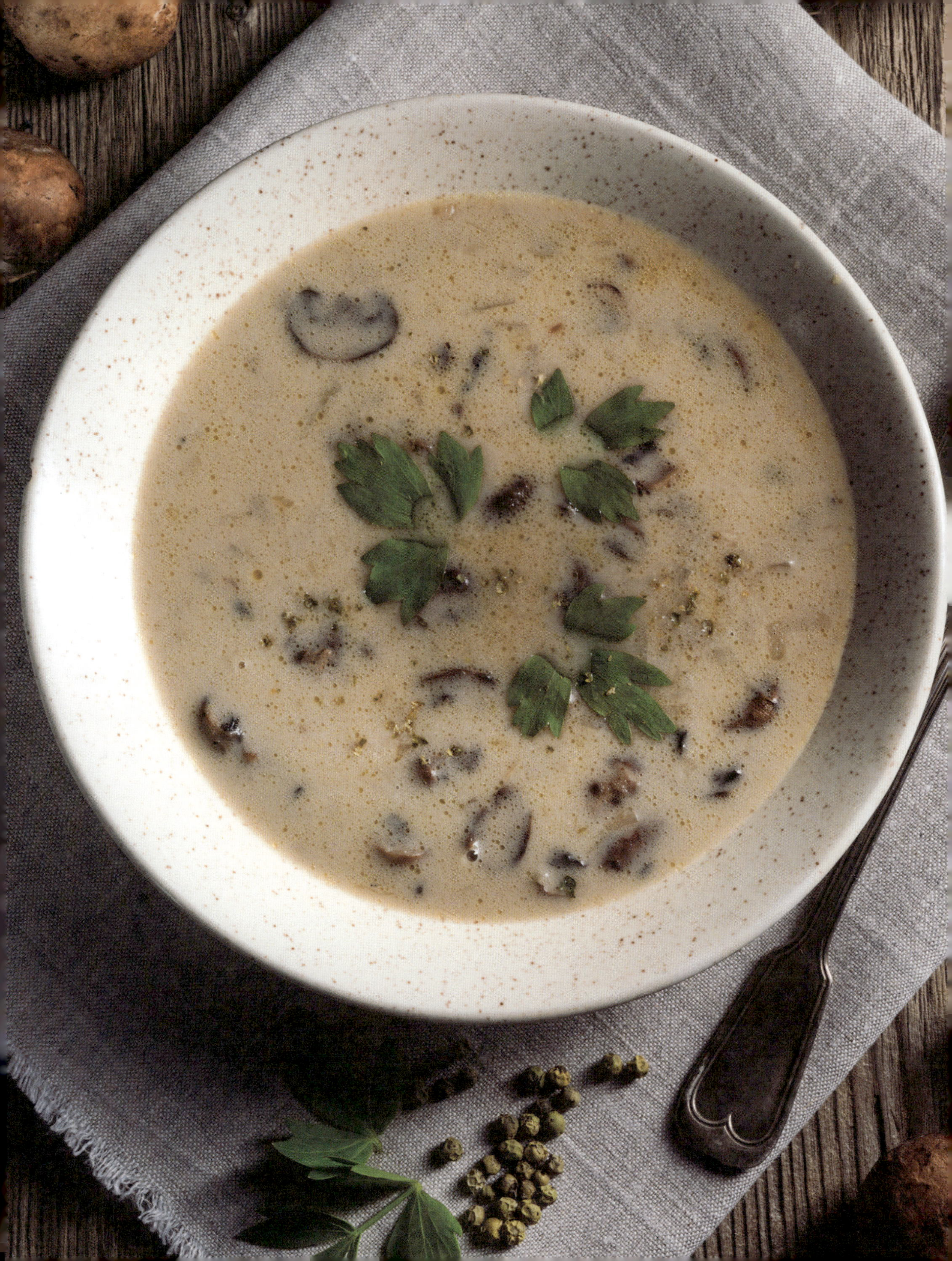

CREAM OF MUSHROOM SOUP

A bit of Balsamic vinegar brightens this easy vegan recipe that results in a smooth, creamy soup.

SERVES: 2–4 · PREP TIME: 10 MINUTES · COOK TIME: 35 MINUTES

INGREDIENTS

- 1 tablespoon olive oil
- ½ teaspoon balsamic vinegar
- ½ small onion, finely chopped
- 1 clove garlic, minced
- 2 portobello mushrooms
- 4 large cremini mushrooms
- 3 cups (720 mL) vegetable broth
- ½ cup (120mL) coconut milk
- 1 tablespoon cornstarch optional
- 1 bay leaf, dried
- ½ teaspoon parsley flakes optional
- ½ teaspoon salt (or to taste)
- ¼ teaspoon black pepper (or to taste)
- parsley, for garnish

FREE FROM
- GLUTEN
- NUTS
- SUGAR

METHOD
STOVETOP

DIRECTIONS

- In a soup pot, heat the oil over medium-high heat, and sauté the garlic and bay leaf, being careful not to burn the garlic. When the garlic starts to brown, add the diced onions, and sauté them until they turn translucent. Add some water if the bottom of your pot turns sticky and/or brown to prevent the garlic, onion, and bay leaf from burning.

- While the onions sauté, dice the mushrooms, add them to the pot, and let them sweat for a minute or two. Add in the balsamic vinegar.

- Add the vegetable broth, cover the pot, and bring mixture to a boil. When it starts boiling, reduce flame, and allow it to simmer for about 10 to 15 minutes.

- Scoop out a few tablespoons of the soup, and mix it with 1 tablespoon of cornstarch in a separate bowl. Make sure there are no lumps, and then pour back into the soup, allowing it to simmer for another minute or two.

- Turn off the heat, and add the coconut milk. Stir well. Add salt and pepper to taste.

- Pour into bowls or cups, sprinkle with parsley, and serve.

CHEF'S TIPS
- For a homemade vegetable broth, see page 42.

TOMATO SOUP

Italian spices give this classic an herbal kick. Serve as a vibrant starter or as a hearty lunch with crusty bread.

SERVES: 4 · PREP TIME: 10 MINUTES · COOK TIME: 40 MINUTES

INGREDIENTS

- 1 tablespoon coconut oil
- 1 onion, finely chopped
- 1 teaspoon fresh garlic, crushed
- 2 teaspoons fresh oregano (or 1 teaspoon dried)
- 2 teaspoons fresh basil (or 1 teaspoon dried)
- 2 tablespoon coconut sugar
- 10 to 12 whole tomatoes, peeled (or 2 14-ounce (400g) cans whole peeled tomatoes)
- 2 large potatoes, peeled and chopped into chunks
- 2 cups (480ml) vegetable broth
- Kosher salt, to taste
- black pepper, to taste

CONTAINS
- SUGAR

FREE FROM
- GLUTEN
- NUTS

METHOD
- STOVETOP
- BLENDER

DIRECTIONS

- In a large soup pot, heat the oil over medium-high heat. When the oil is hot, add the onion and garlic and sauté for around 5 minutes until the onion turns translucent and soft.
- Add the tomatoes, potatoes, sugar, and 2 cups of the vegetable broth. Bring to a boil, and then turn down heat. Simmer until all the ingredients are soft and thoroughly cooked (about 30 minutes).
- Using an immersion blender, blend the mixture until it is smooth and silky. Add salt and pepper to taste.
- Pour the soup onto bowls, sprinkle with a bit of dried basil and dried oregano and fresh, and serve.

CHEF'S TIPS

- If you don't have an immersion blender, you can use a blender or food processor. In batches, transfer the mixture into a blender or food processor, and blend until creamy, adding more broth if necessary for a thinner consistency. Return all blended batches to pot, and stir.
- For a homemade vegetable broth, *see* page 42; For homemade Italian seasoning blends, *see* page 9.

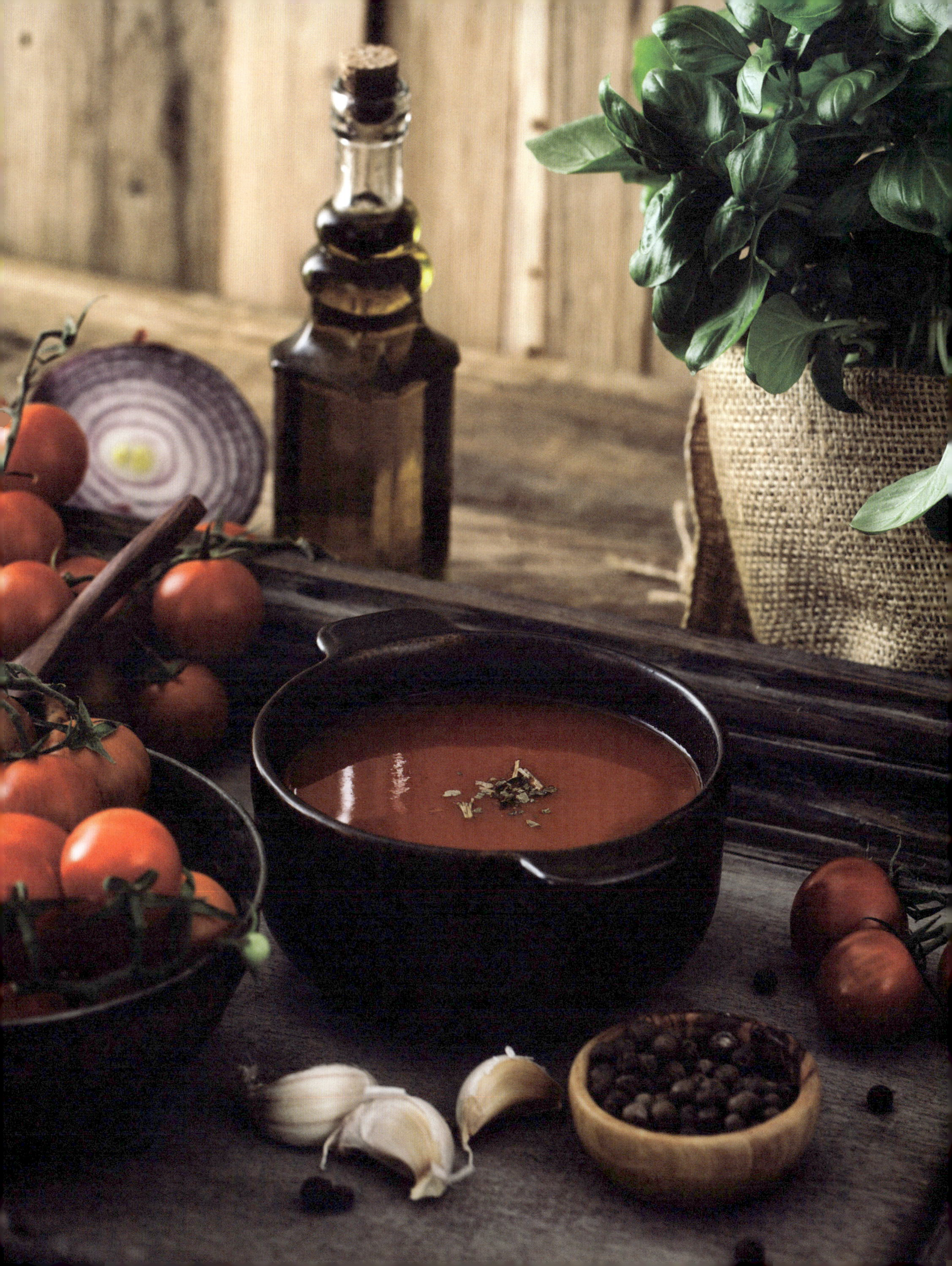

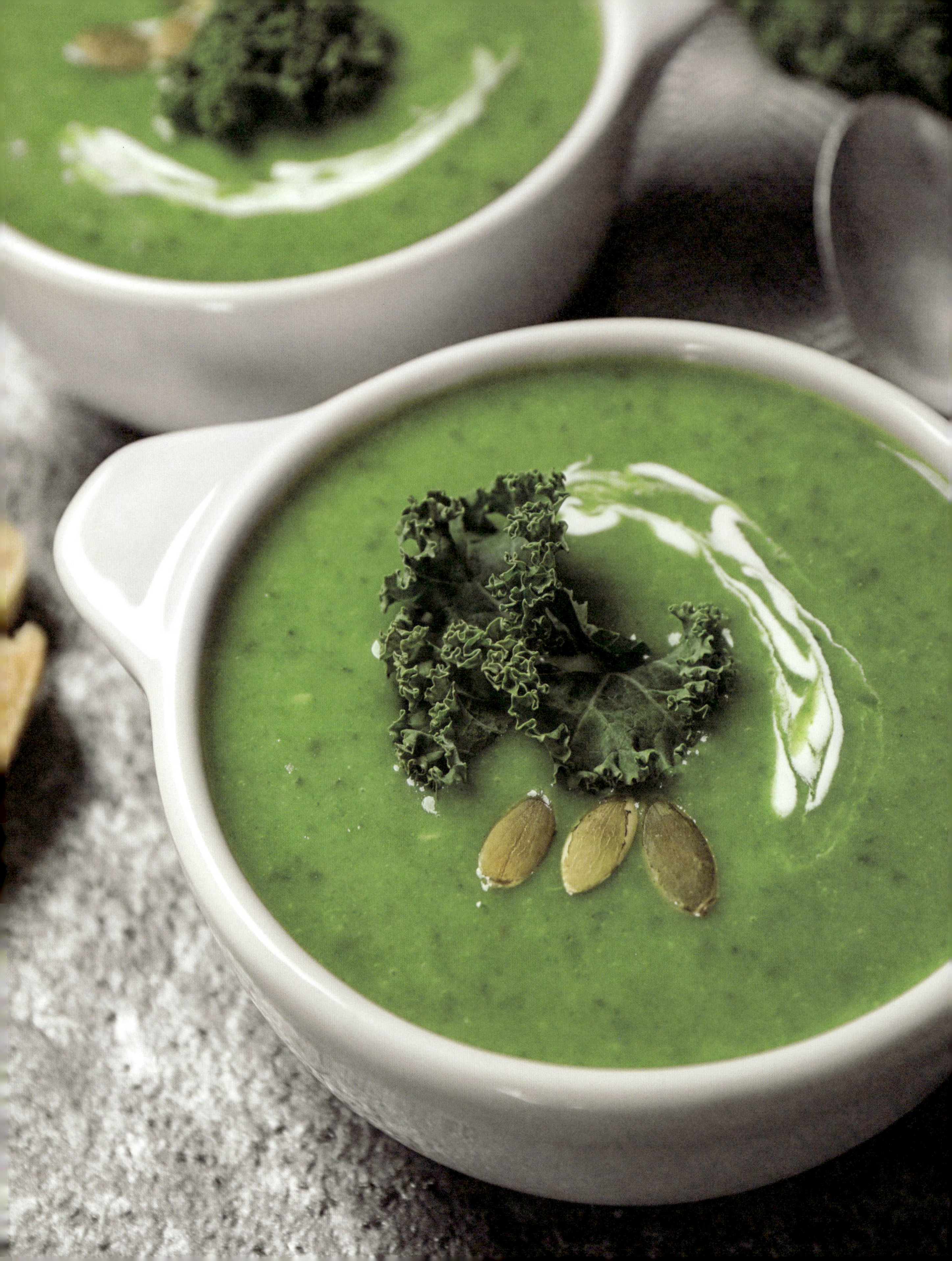

KALE POTATO SOUP

The vibrant color of this nutrient-rich vegan soup makes it perfect as a summer starter or main course.

SERVES: 4 · PREP TIME: 10 MINUTES · COOK TIME: 20 MINUTES

INGREDIENTS

- 1 tablespoon olive oil
- 1 small onion, chopped
- 1 cloves of garlic, minced
- 2–3 potatoes, cut into small cubes
- 2 medium carrots, chopped into small pieces
- ½ cup (65g) celery root, cleaned, peeled, and chopped into small pieces
- 3–4 large leeks, cut into rings
- 3½ cups (840mL) vegetable broth
- 2–3 handfuls of kale, cut into strips, saving the tops for garnish.
- ½ teaspoon salt (or to taste)
- ¼ teaspoon black pepper (or to taste)
- 1 tablespoon roasted pumpkin seeds
- 1–2 tablespoons soy cream (or oat cream)

CONTAINS
- SOY

FREE FROM
- GLUTEN
- NUTS
- SUGAR

METHOD
ASSEMBLY

DIRECTIONS

- In a soup pot, heat the oil over medium-high heat, and then sauté the onion for about 2 minutes. Add the garlic and sauté for another minute.
- Stir in the potatoes, carrots, celery root, and leeks. Cook for 3 minutes.
- Add the vegetable broth, and simmer for 15 minutes.
- Add the kale, and cook for another 2 minutes.
- Season the mixture with salt and pepper to taste, and then, in batches, transfer the mixture into a blender or food processor, and blend until creamy, adding more broth if necessary for a thinner consistency. Return all blended batches to pot, and stir.
- Pour the soup onto bowls, and swirl in a bit of the soy cream, sprinkle with the roasted pumpkin seeds, and garnish with kale florets.

CHEF'S TIPS

- For a soy-free version, use oat cream instead of the soy cream, or omit it entirely.
- For a homemade vegetable broth, *see* page 42.

FRENCH ONION SOUP

A traditional continental soup, this rich onion broth is flavored with red wine—be sure it's vegan—and herbs.

SERVES: 6 · PREP TIME: 10 MINUTES · COOK TIME: 1 HOUR 45 MINUTES

INGREDIENTS

- 2 tablespoons virgin olive oil
- 3 large yellow onions, sliced into thin half-moons
- 3 fresh sprigs of thyme sprigs, leaves stripped
- ¼ cup (60mL) dry red wine
- 4 cup (960 mL) vegetable broth
- 2 cups (480mL) water
- 1 bay leaf
- 3 teaspoons sea salt
- ½ teaspoon freshly ground black pepper

DIRECTIONS

- In a large soup pot, heat 1 tablespoon of the olive oil over medium-high heat. When the oil is hot, add the onions, thyme and 1 teaspoon of the salt, and drizzle another tablespoon of oil over the onions. Lower the heat to medium low.
- Cook uncovered, stirring occasionally, until the onions caramelize and turn light golden brown, about 50 to 60 minutes. Add the wine, and cook another 15 minutes.
- Add the stock, water, bay leaf, remaining salt and pepper, and bring to a boil. Turn the heat to low and simmer for 30 minutes.
- Remove the bay leaf, and serve hot.

CHEF'S TIPS

- Replace the wine with 2 tablespoons of balsamic vinegar for an alcohol-free version.

CONTAINS

- ALCOHOL

FREE FROM

- GLUTEN
- NUTS
- SUGAR

METHOD

STOVETOP

POTATO & CORN CHOWDER

This creamy, comforting soup is a great starter for a hearty winter supper or makes a light meal on its own.

SERVES: 4 · PREP TIME: 15 MINUTES · COOK TIME: 20 MINUTES

INGREDIENTS

- 1 tablespoon vegan butter or light oil
- 2 medium carrots, peeled and chopped
- 2 celery stalks, chopped
- 1 yellow onion, chopped
- 3 cloves garlic, minced
- ¼ cup (30g) all-purpose flour
- 1 teaspoon dried thyme leaves
- 3 large potatoes
- 2 cups (480mL) vegetable broth
- 2 cups (480mL) almond milk (or the nondairy milk of your choice)
- 3 tablespoons nutritional yeast
- 1 cup (150g) fresh or frozen corn kernels
- 1 teaspoon salt (or to taste)
- ¼ teaspoon pepper (or to taste)

CONTAINS
- GLUTEN
- NUTS

FREE FROM
- SUGAR

METHOD
- STOVETOP

DIRECTIONS

- In a large soup pot, heat the oil over medium-high heat. When the oil is hot, add the carrots, celery, onion, and garlic. Sauté about 5 minutes, just until the vegetables start to soften and the onion turns translucent and begins to brown.
- Sprinkle the flour and thyme over the vegetables, and stir to coat. Continue to stir for about 1 minute, until the flour starts to brown.
- Stir in the potatoes, and then add the vegetable broth, milk, and nutritional yeast, continuing to stir until the mixture is smooth.
- Bring the soup to a simmer, and continue to simmer until the potatoes are fork tender and the broth has thickened (about 7 to 10 minutes).
- Add in the corn and season with salt and pepper to taste.
- Serve hot with your choice of bread or other accompaniment.

CHEF'S TIPS

- For a gluten-free version, use gluten-free flour, such as rice. For a nut-free version, use nondairy milk, such as soy or oat.
- For a homemade vegetable broth, see page 42.

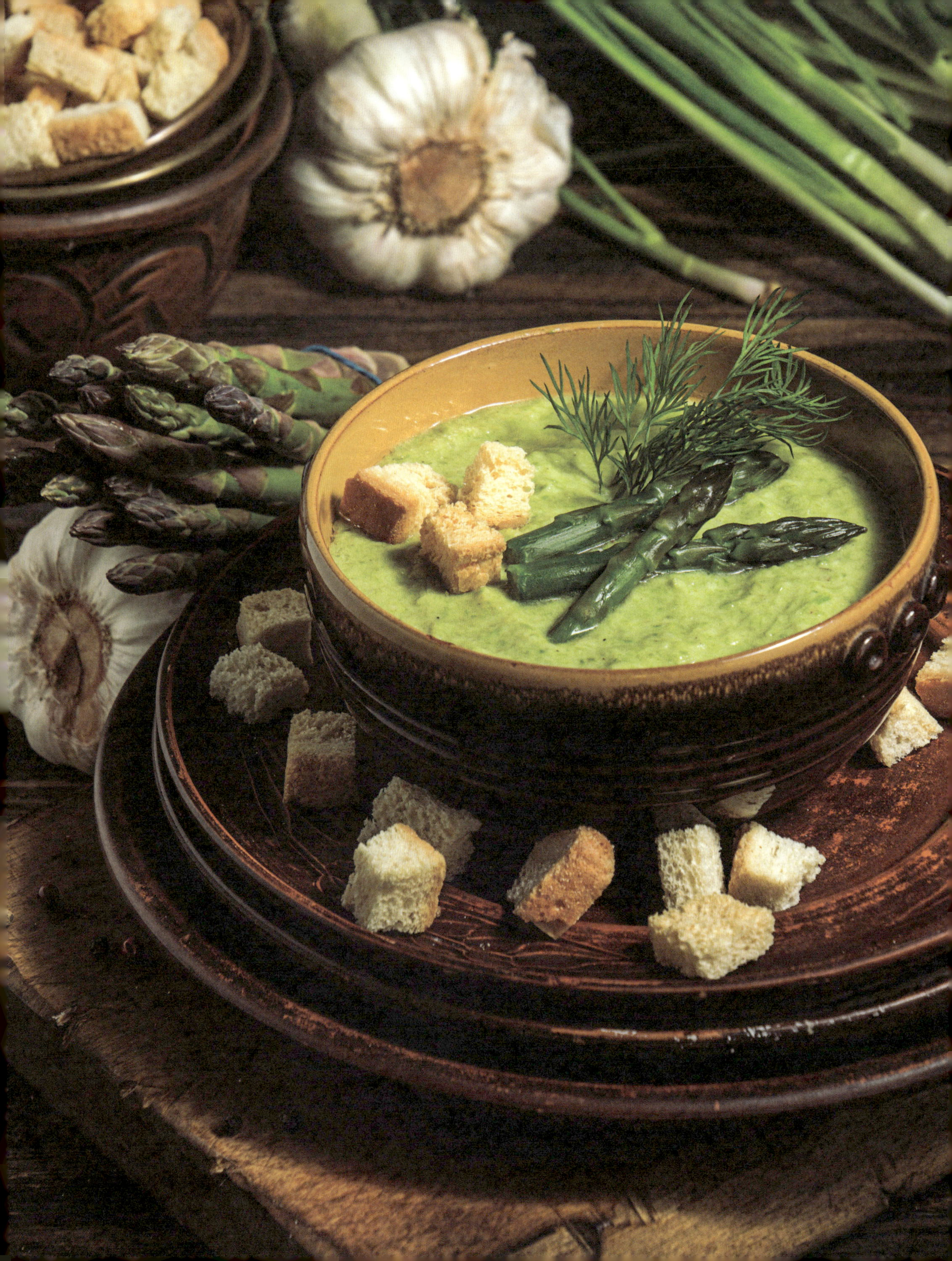

ROASTED ASPARAGUS SOUP

Roasting the asparagus adds a depth of flavor to this easy, silky springtime soup.

SERVES: 6 · PREP TIME: 10 MINUTES · COOK TIME: 45 MINUTES

INGREDIENTS

- 2 tablespoon olive oil, divided
- 1 onion, coarsely chopped
- 2 cloves garlic, minced
- 2 pounds (about 1kg) asparagus, ends trimmed and chopped, saving a 6 to 18 tops for garnish
- 2 medium russet potatoes
- Kosher salt, to taste
- black pepper, to taste
- 4 cups (960 mL) vegetable broth
- 1–2 cups (240–480mL) unsweetened almond milk
- 1 lemon, juiced
- croutons, for serving

FREE FROM
- GLUTEN
- NUTS
- SUGAR

METHOD
- OVEN ROAST
- STOVETOP
- BLENDER

DIRECTIONS

- Preheat oven to 400°F (200°C). Spread asparagus on a baking sheet. Drizzle with 1 tablespoon of the olive oil, and season with salt and pepper to taste. Toss to coat, and then and roast for 10 to 15 minutes until the asparagus slightly softens.
- In a soup pot, heat the rest of the oil over medium-high heat. When the oil is hot, add the onions and garlic. Sauté about 5 minutes, just until the onion turns translucent.
- Add the potatoes, season with salt and pepper to taste, and then cook with the onions and garlic for about 5 minutes.
- Pour in the broth and milk, bring mixture to a boil, and then reduce heat. Simmer until the potatoes are tender, about 20 minutes. Add the roasted asparagus to the pot.
- In batches, transfer the mixture into a blender or food processor, and blend until creamy, adding more broth if necessary for a thinner consistency. Return all blended batches to the pot. Stir in the lemon juice.
- Pour the soup onto bowls, garnish with asparagus tops, and serve with croutons.

CHEF'S TIPS

- If you have an immersion blender, skip the food processor or blender, and blend the soup right in the pot.
- For a homemade vegetable broth, *see* page 42.

LEMON & ROSEMARY BARLEY SOUP

This easy-to-make recipe blends Italian spices with lemon and rosemary for a fragrant and tasty soup.

SERVES: 6 · PREP TIME: 15–20 MINUTES · COOK TIME: 40–70 MINUTES

INGREDIENTS

- 1 cup dry barley
- 3 cups (720 mL) vegetable broth
- 1 14.5-ounce (411g) can crushed tomatoes
- 1 14-ounce (400g) can chickpeas, drained and rinsed
- 3 medium carrots, peeled and diced
- 3 stalks celery
- 1 large white onion, diced
- 3 cloves garlic, minced
- 1 cup (75g) cremini mushrooms
- 3 sprigs rosemary
- juice of 1 lemon
- 1 tablespoon Italian seasoning
- sea salt, to taste
- black pepper, to taste

FREE FROM

- GLUTEN
- NUTS
- SUGAR

METHOD

STOVETOP

DIRECTIONS

- Heat a large soup pot on medium-high heat. Once heated, add 1 tablespoon of vegetable broth and the onions. Cook the onions until they become translucent, about 7 minutes.
- Add the carrots, celery, mushrooms, and garlic with another tablespoon of vegetable broth. Stir, and cook until they begin to soften, about 7 to 10 minutes.
- Continue adding broth in tablespoon increments while cooking the vegetables so that they don't stick to the pot.
- Add the chickpeas, barley, rosemary, Italian seasoning, crushed tomatoes, and the rest of the vegetable broth to the soup pot. Bring to a boil, and then quickly reduce to a simmer.
- Simmer for approximately 40 minutes, or until the barley is firm and chewy, but not mushy.
- Add the salt, pepper, and lemon juice, and stir to combine. Remove the rosemary from the pot.
- Serve with a side salad and Italian bread.

CHEF'S TIPS

- For homemade Italian seasoning blends, *see* page 9.

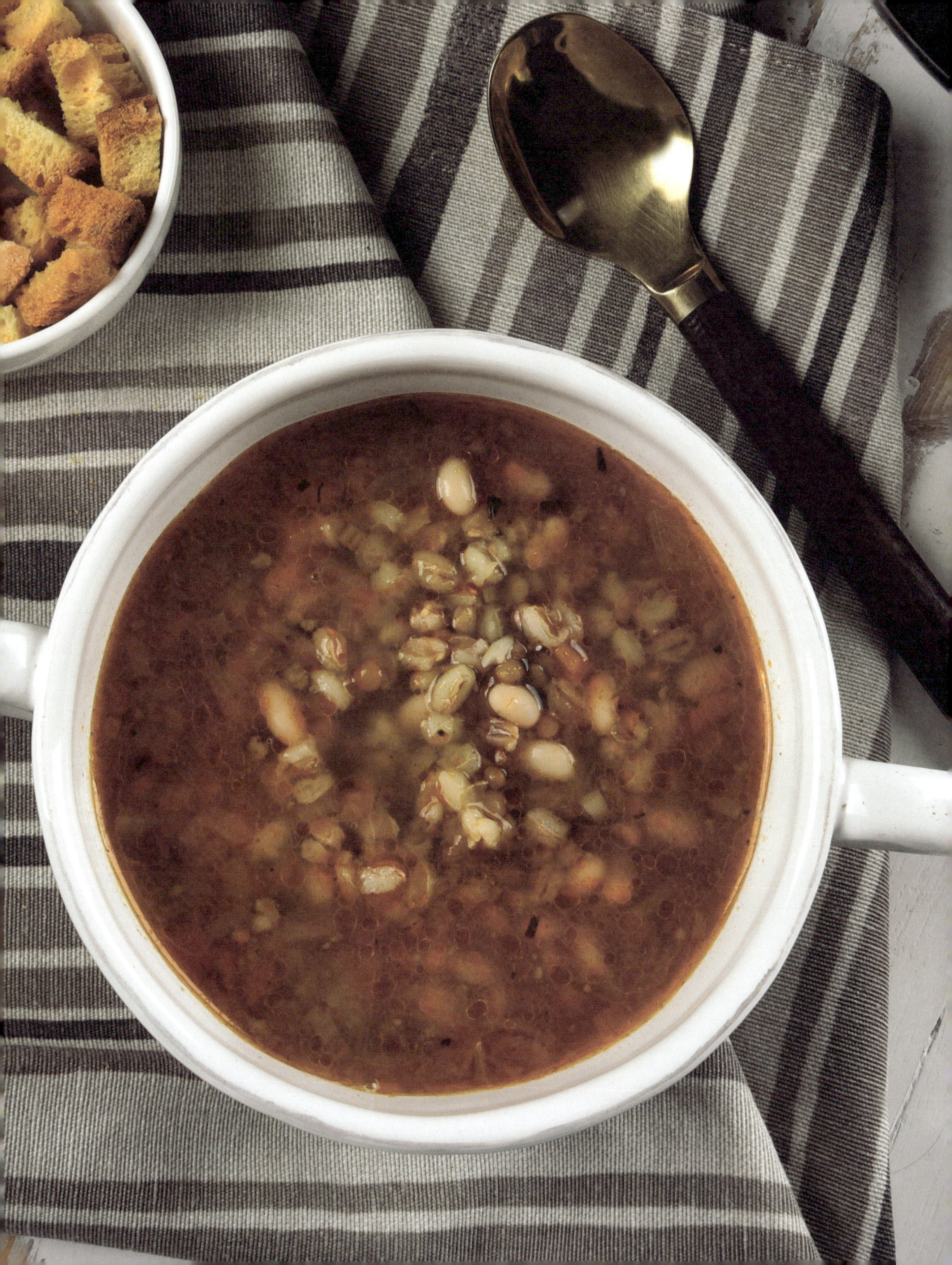

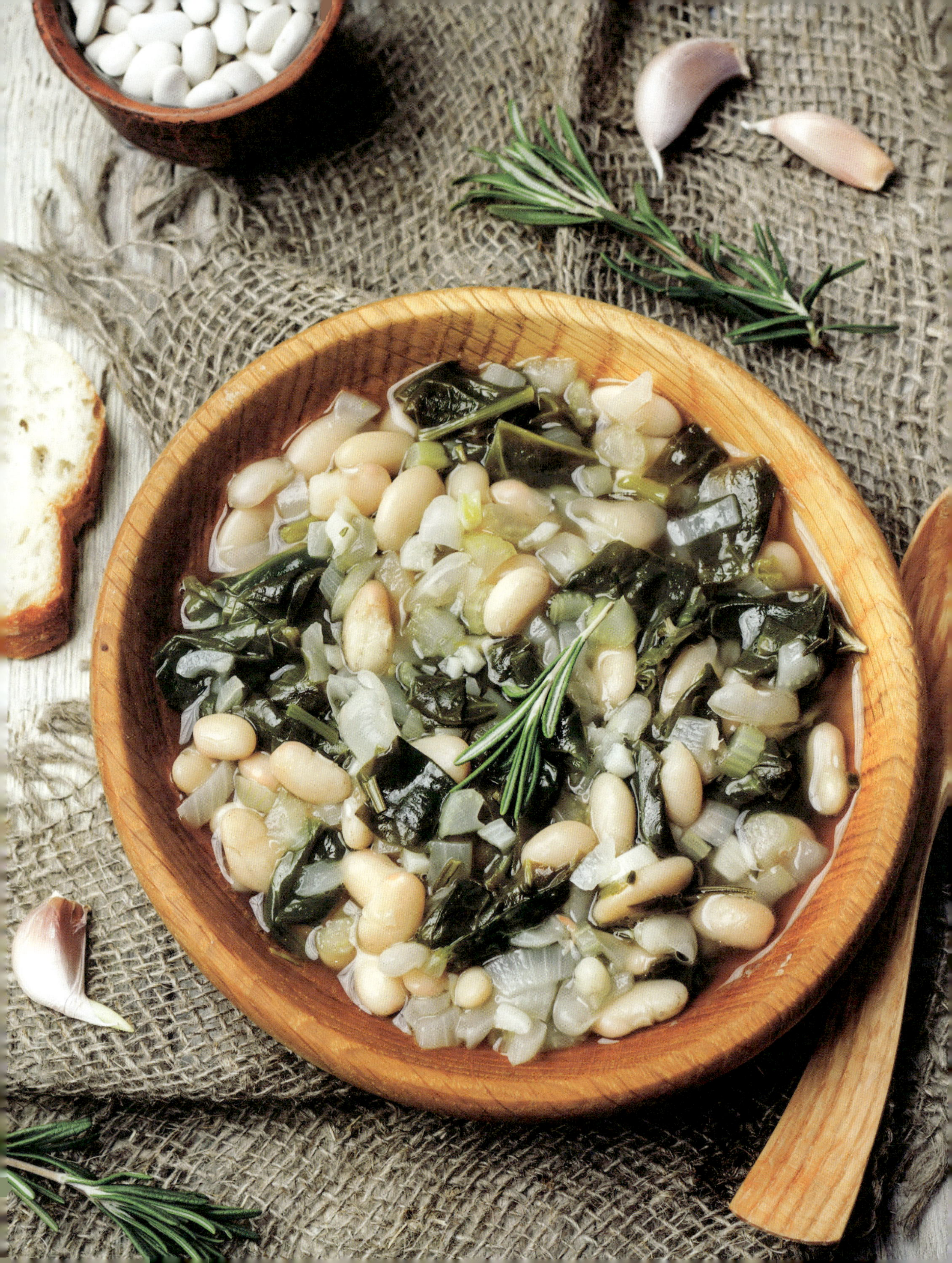

SPINACH & CANNELINI SOUP

This healthy, hearty soup is warm and comforting for a winter's lunch or dinner.

SERVES: 6 · PREP TIME: 10 MINUTES · COOK TIME: 20 MINUTES

INGREDIENTS

- 1 tablespoon olive oil
- 3 cloves garlic, minced
- 1 onion, diced
- ½ teaspoon dried thyme
- ½ teaspoon dried basil
- 4 cups (960 mL) vegetable broth
- 2 bay leaves
- 2 cups (60g) baby spinach
- 1 15-ounce (425g) can cannellini beans, drained and rinsed
- juice of 1 lemon
- 2 tablespoons fresh parsley leaves, chopped
- salt, to taste
- ground black pepper, to taste

FREE FROM
- GLUTEN
- NUTS
- SUGAR

METHOD
STOVETOP

DIRECTIONS

- In a large soup pot, heat the olive oil over medium-high heat. When the oil is hot, add the onions and garlic. Sauté about 3 to 5 minutes, stirring frequently, just until the onion turns translucent. Stir in thyme and basil until fragrant, about 1 minute.
- Whisk in vegetable broth and bay leaves, bring to a boil. Reduce heat, and simmer for about 10 minutes.
- Stir in spinach and cannellini beans until the spinach has wilted, about 2 minutes. Stir in lemon juice and parsley, and then season with salt and pepper, to taste.
- Serve immediately with the bread of your choice.

CHEF'S TIPS

- For any even more filling soup, add 1 cup (210g) uncooked orzo pasta when you add in the vegetable broth, being sure to simmer until orzo is tender.
- Substitute escarole for the spinach for a more traditional Italian-style soup.
- For a homemade vegetable broth, see page 42.

GAZPACHO

This refreshing soup is perfect for a light lunch or dinnertime starter on a hot summer day.

SERVES: 8–12 · PREP TIME: 10 MINUTES · TOTAL TIME: 4 HOURS

INGREDIENTS

- 2 cups (500 mL) vegetable juice cocktail
- 1½ pounds (0.6 kg) tomatoes, cored and roughly chopped
- 1 medium red pepper, seeded and roughly chopped
- 1 large English cucumber, peeled and roughly chopped
- ¼ cup (30 g) sweet onion, chopped
- 2 tablespoons red wine vinegar
- 1 medium garlic clove
- 1 tablespoon fresh lime juice
- ½ teaspoon red pepper flakes, or to taste
- ½ teaspoon freshly ground black pepper, or to taste
- sea salt, to taste
- celery stalks, for garnish

CONTAINS
- CHILIS

FREE FROM
- GLUTEN
- NUTS
- SUGAR

METHOD
BLENDER

DIRECTIONS

- Reserve some of the chopped pepper, cucumber, and tomatoes for garnish, and then place the vegetable cocktail, tomatoes, red pepper, cucumber, onion, garlic, lime juice in a blender, and blend until smooth.
- Add in the rest of the vinegar, red pepper flakes, pepper, and salt, and blend again.
- Pour into a 8-cup (2-litre) lidded glass jar, and place in the refrigerator. Chill for 3 to 4 hours, or overnight.
- When chilled, shake the jar to thoroughly combine.
- Pour into bowls for a meal-sized portion or into dessert cups for an appetizer, and garnish with chopped peppers, cucumbers, and tomatoes, and a celery stalk.

CHEF'S TIPS

- You can store leftovers gazpacho in the refrigerator for up to 3 days

CHILLED CUCUMBER & MINT SOUP

As its name suggests, this luscious and minty cream soup is as cool as a cucumber.

SERVES: 4 · PREP TIME: 15 MINUTES · TOTAL TIME: 4 HOURS

INGREDIENTS

- 2 English cucumbers, peeled, seeded, and chopped
- 1 cup unsweetened oat milk
- 2 garlic cloves
- 1/4 cup fresh mint
- 4 fresh basil leaves
- 2 green onions
- 1 apple, peeled and cored
- juice of ½ lime
- ½ teaspoon Himalayan pink salt (or to taste)

FREE FROM
- GLUTEN
- NUTS
- SUGAR

METHOD
BLENDER

DIRECTIONS

- Reserve 4 to 8 slices of cucumber for garnish, and place the cucumbers, milk, garlic, basil, onion, apples, lime juice, and salt in a blender, and puree until smooth. Add water to thin, if needed.
- Transfer to an airtight container, and refrigerate for 2 to 4 hours.
- Once chilled, garnish with cucumber and mint, and serve.

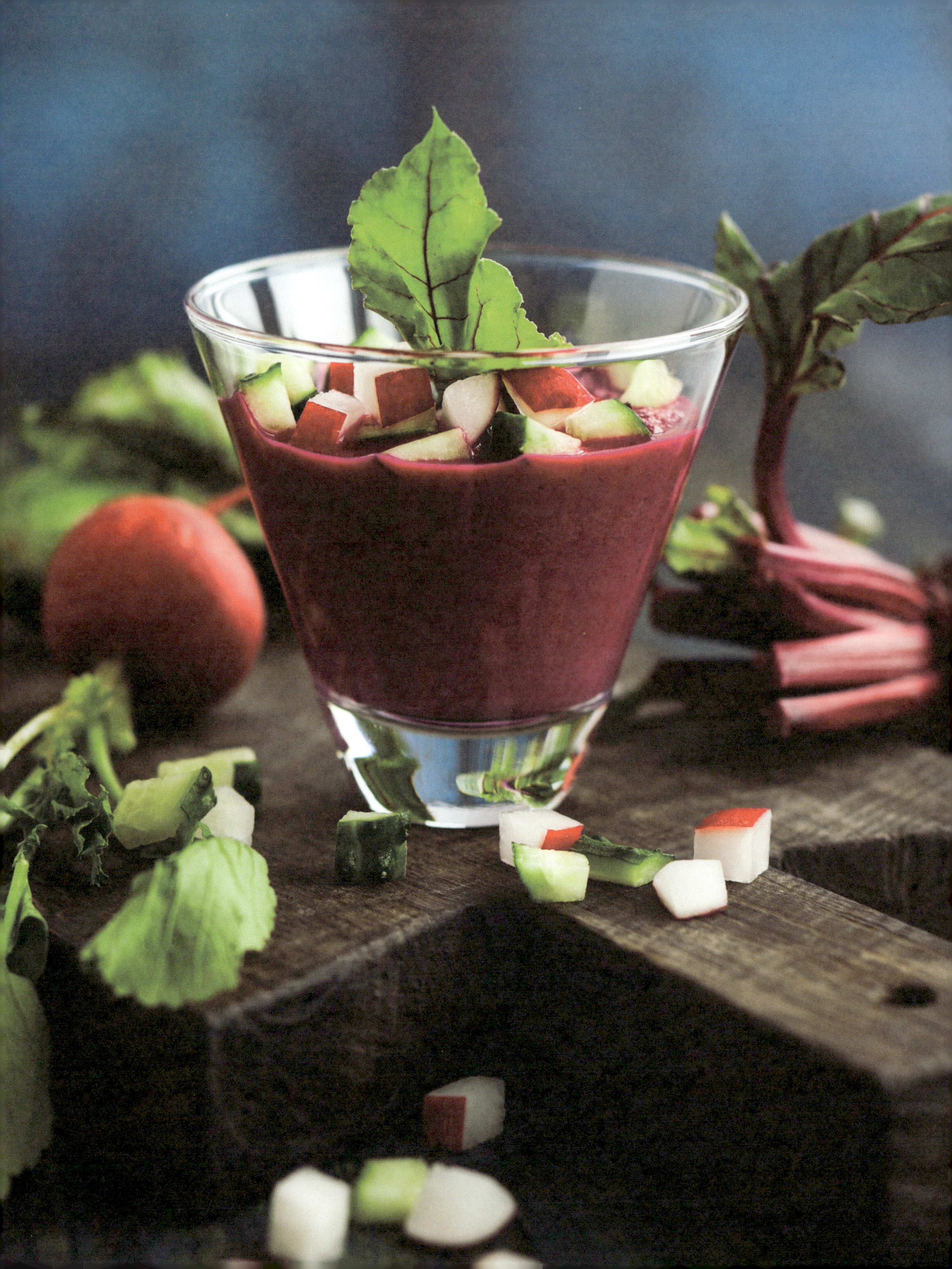

RED BEET GAZPACHO

Serve this bright-colored cold soup in small glasses for a stunning starter for a summertime dinner.

SERVES: 4–8 · PREP TIME: 20 MINUTES · TOTAL TIME: 50 MINUTES

INGREDIENTS

- 4 medium red beets, tops cut off and set aside
- ½ cucumber, seeded, diced, and divided
- 1 small ripe avocado
- ½ red onion, diced
- 2 garlic cloves, minced
- ½ cup (5g) fresh dill
- 2 cups (480mL) vegetable broth
- 2 tablespoons red wine vinegar
- ½ teaspoon salt
- ¼ teaspoon freshly ground black pepper
- 3 radishes, diced

FREE FROM
- GLUTEN
- NUTS
- SUGAR

METHOD

BLENDER

DIRECTIONS

- Place beets in a medium soup pot, and cover with water. Simmer over medium heat until tender, about 40 to 50 minutes. Remove them from the pot, and place on a plate to cool.
- When cool, remove the skin from the beets, using your fingers, and then cut the peeled beets into quarters.
- Dice one of the beets, and set aside.
- Place the remaining quartered beets in a blender, and add ½ of the cucumber, ½ of the avocado, ½ of the red onion, the garlic, ⅔ of the dill, vegetable broth, vinegar, salt, and pepper, and blend until very smooth. Pour into a container, and place in the refrigerator to chill.
- In a small bowl, mix together the diced beet and radishes, along with the rest of the avocado, cucumber, and dill.
- When the beet mixture has chilled, pour soup into bowls or small glasses, and top with diced veggies. Garnish with a beet leaf.

ROASTED BEETROOT HUMMUS

This brilliantly colored hummus works as an appetizer or snack, or you can use it in toasted sandwiches.

SERVES: 6 · PREP TIME: 5 MINUTES · TOTAL TIME: 1 HOUR 5 MINUTES

INGREDIENTS

- 2 medium beetroots, skin on
- 1 14-ounce (400g) can chickpeas, drained and rinsed
- 2½ tablespoons tahini
- 2 cloves garlic
- 1 tablespoon lemon juice
- ½ teaspoon salt
- ¼ teaspoon cumin
- water to thin

DIRECTIONS

- Preheat the oven to 400°F (200°C).
- Wrap each beetroot in aluminum foil, and roast them for 1 to 2 hours (depending on the size of your beets), until they are tender.
- Remove them from the oven, and let them cool.
- Peel the skins, and chop the beetroots into chunks.
- Place the beetroots, chickpeas, and garlic into a food processor, and blend for 1 minute.
- Add tahini, lemon juice, salt, cumin, 1 teaspoon of water, and blend until smooth and creamy, adding more water until the proper consistency.
- Serve with pita bread or chips.

FREE FROM

- GLUTEN
- NUTS
- SUGAR

METHOD

OVEN ROAST

BLENDER

CHEF'S TIPS

- This hummus will last in the refrigerator for up to a week stored in an airtight container.

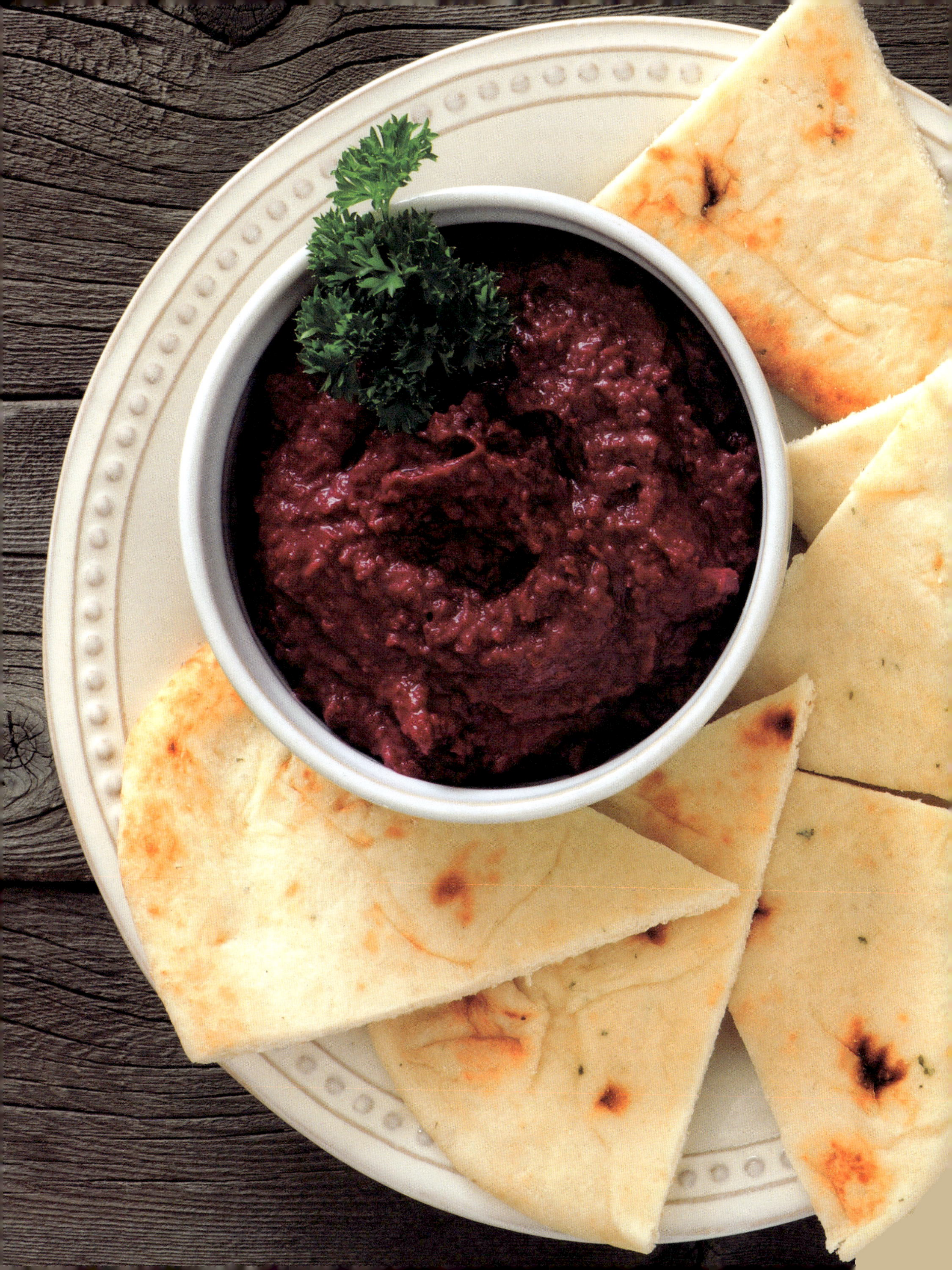

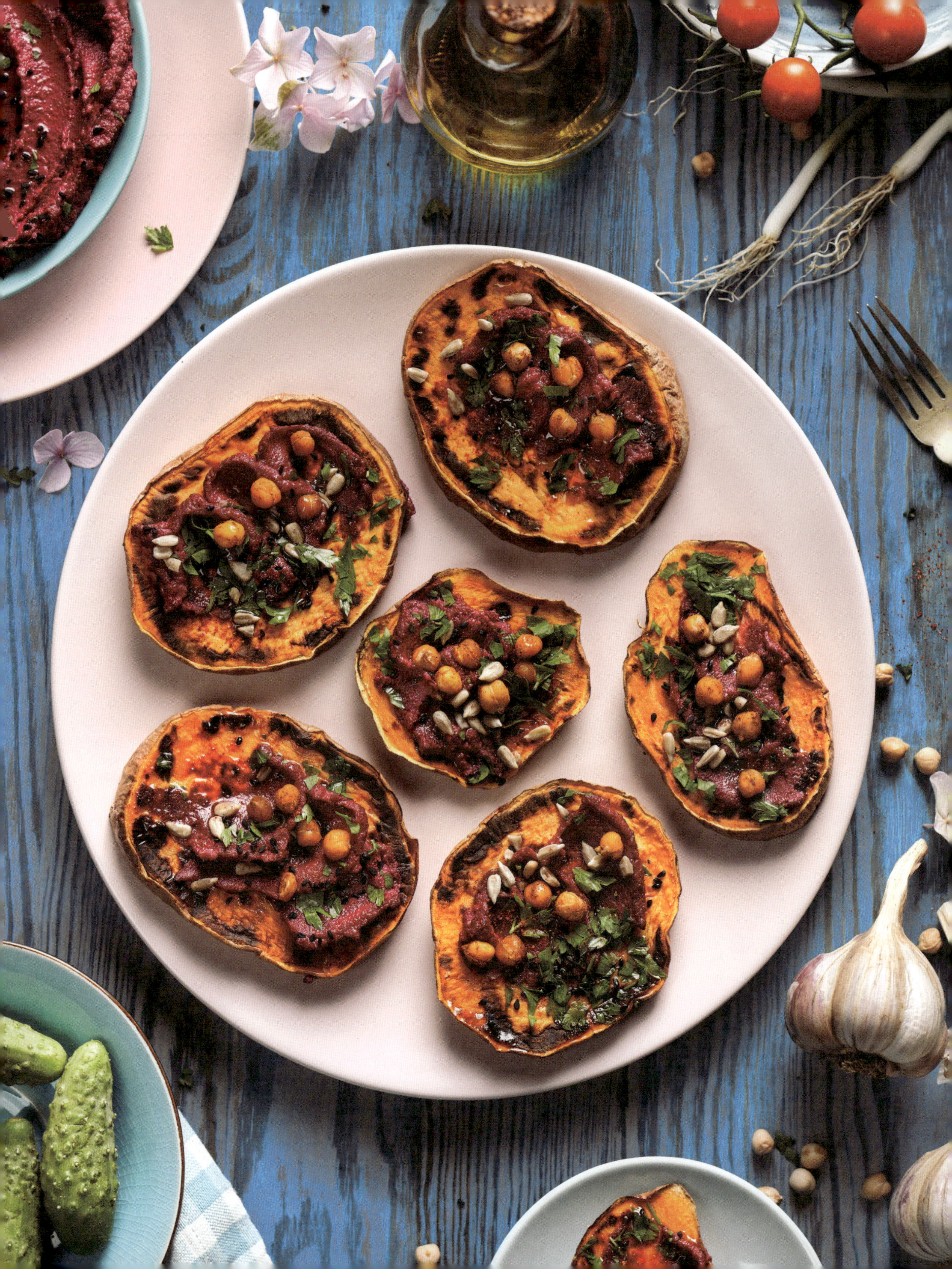

SWEET POTATO TOAST WITH BEETROOT HUMMUS & ROASTED CHICKPEAS

Curried roasted chickpeas add an aromatic crunch to these tasty sweet potato appetizers.

SERVES: 6 · PREP TIME: 10 MINUTES · COOK TIME: 65 MINUTES

INGREDIENTS

- 1 large sweet potato
- 1 14-ounce (400g) can chickpeas, drained and rinsed
- ¾ cup (180g) beetroot hummus
- olive oil spray
- ⅛ teaspoon kosher salt
- ¼ teaspoon ground cumin
- ¼ teaspoon paprika
- ¼ teaspoon ground coriander
- ¼ teaspoon curry powder
- ¼ teaspoon garlic powder
- 1–2 tablespoons nigella seeds
- parsley, for garnish

DIRECTIONS

- Preheat oven to 375°F (190°C).
- Drain chickpeas in a colander, and dry completely, patting them with paper towels if needed. Arrange them in a single layer on a baking sheet, and roast or about 35 to 45 minutes, shaking the pan every 10 minutes, until they are golden brown.
- In a medium bowl, combine all the spices. When the chickpeas are roasted, remove from oven, and spray them with olive oil. While hot, toss with spices.
- Lower the oven temperature to 350°F (180°C), and place a wire rack on a large rimmed baking sheet.
- Trim both ends from the sweet potato using a knife, and then slice them into ¼-inch (6-mm) slabs. Arrange the slabs in a single layer on the wire rack.
- Bake for 15 to 20 minutes or until potatoes are tender. Remove pan from oven, and cool completely on wire rack.
- When potatoes are cool, spread each with beetroot hummus, and sprinkle chickpeas and nigella seeds on top.
- Garnish with parsley, and serve immediately.

CONTAINS
- SEEDS

FREE FROM
- GLUTEN
- NUTS
- SUGAR

METHOD
OVEN ROAST

ASSEMBLY

CHEF'S TIPS

- Be sure to save the liquid from the chickpeas to use as aquafaba in dessert recipes.
- For a homemade beetroot hummus, see page 116.
- Save any leftover roasted chickpeas to enjoy as a snack.

BABA GANOUSH

This spicy Levantine dip is a typical meze served with pita bread in Eastern Mediterranean restaurants.

SERVES: 2 · PREP TIME: 5 MINUTES · TOTAL TIME: 10 MINUTES

INGREDIENTS

- 1 eggplant
- 1½ tablespoons olive oil
- 2 cloves garlic
- 2 tablespoons tahini
- juice of 1 lemon
- ½ teaspoon salt
- ½ teaspoon smoked paprika

DIRECTIONS

- Preheat oven to broil.
- Slice the eggplant into ½-inch (1.25-cm) pieces. Arrange eggplant in one layer on a baking sheet. Sprinkle with salt, and brush both sides with olive oil. Broil for 5 minutes. Flip, and cook another 5 minutes. When cool, remove the skin.
- In a food processor, Place eggplant, garlic, tahini, lemon juice, and salt in a blender or food processor, and blend until smooth, adding more oil, if needed.
- Top with paprika, drizzle with olive oil, and serve with pita.

FREE FROM
- GLUTEN
- NUTS
- SUGAR

METHOD

OVEN BROIL

BLENDER

GUACAMOLE

Enjoy this traditional Mexican dip as a snack with chips, or spread it on toast for yummy sandwiches.

SERVES: 8–8 · PREP TIME: 5 MINUTES · TOTAL TIME: 5 MINUTES

INGREDIENTS

- 3 ripe avocados
- 1 jalapeño pepper, cored and finely diced
- ½ cup (75g) finely diced red onion
- 1 tablespoon fresh lime juice
- ⅓ (17g) cup fresh cilantro leaves, finely chopped
- ½ teaspoon fine sea salt
- ¼ teaspoon ground cumin

DIRECTIONS

- Slice the avocados in half, remove the pits and skin, and place in a medium mixing bowl.
- Mash the avocado with a fork until it is chunky.
- Stir in the jalapeño, onion, lime juice, cilantro, salt, and cumin until the mixture is well combined. Taste and season with extra salt, lime juice, jalapeños, and/or cilantro, if needed.
- Serve immediately with tortilla chips.

CONTAINS
- CHILIS

FREE FROM
- GLUTEN
- NUTS
- SUGAR

METHOD
ASSEMBLY

CHEF'S TIPS

- To store guacamole and prevent browning, cover the bowl with plastic wrap so that the plastic touches the entire top layer of guacamole, and refrigerate for up to 2 days.

ROASTED EGGPLANT ROLLS WITH SPINACH HUMMUS

A vegan take on sushi rolls, these eggplant appetizers are slathered in bright green spinach hummus.

SERVES: 4–8 · PREP TIME: 30 MINUTES · COOK TIME: 15 MINUTES

INGREDIENTS

- 1 large eggplant
- 2 tablespoons olive oil
- ½ teaspoon sea salt

For hummus:
- ¼ cup (65g) tahini
- 3 tablespoons lemon juice, freshly squeezed
- 3 ounces (85g) baby spinach
- 1 tablespoons fresh parsley, chopped
- 1 garlic clove, minced
- 2 tablespoons olive oil
- ½ teaspoon sea salt
- 1 14-ounce (400g) can chickpeas, drained and rinsed
- sesame seeds, for garnish

CONTAINS
- SEEDS

FREE FROM
- GLUTEN
- NUTS
- SUGAR

METHOD
OVEN ROAST

BLENDER

DIRECTIONS

- Preheat oven to 400°F (200°C).
- Cut ends off eggplants, and slice them lengthwise into roughly 8 slices total. Arrange them in a single layer on a baking sheet, and sprinkle both sides with salt. Let stand for 15 minutes, and then rinse off salt under cold running water, and pat slices dry.
- Brush both sides of eggplant slices with olive oil, and again arrange them in single layers on baking sheet. Roast for 15 minutes, until tender, turning eggplant slices over halfway through. Set baking sheet on a wire rack, and let cool.
- To prepare the hummus, place tahini and lemon juice in a blender or food processor, and blend until smooth and creamy. Add the spinach, parsley, garlic, olive oil, and salt, blend for 1 minute, scraping down the sides as needed. Add the chickpeas, in batches if needed, and process for about 3 minutes.
- Spread the hummus on each of the eggplant strips, and then tightly roll up.
- Serve with a sprinkling of sesame seeds.

CHEF'S TIPS

- Be sure to save the liquid from the chickpeas to use as aquafaba in dessert recipes.

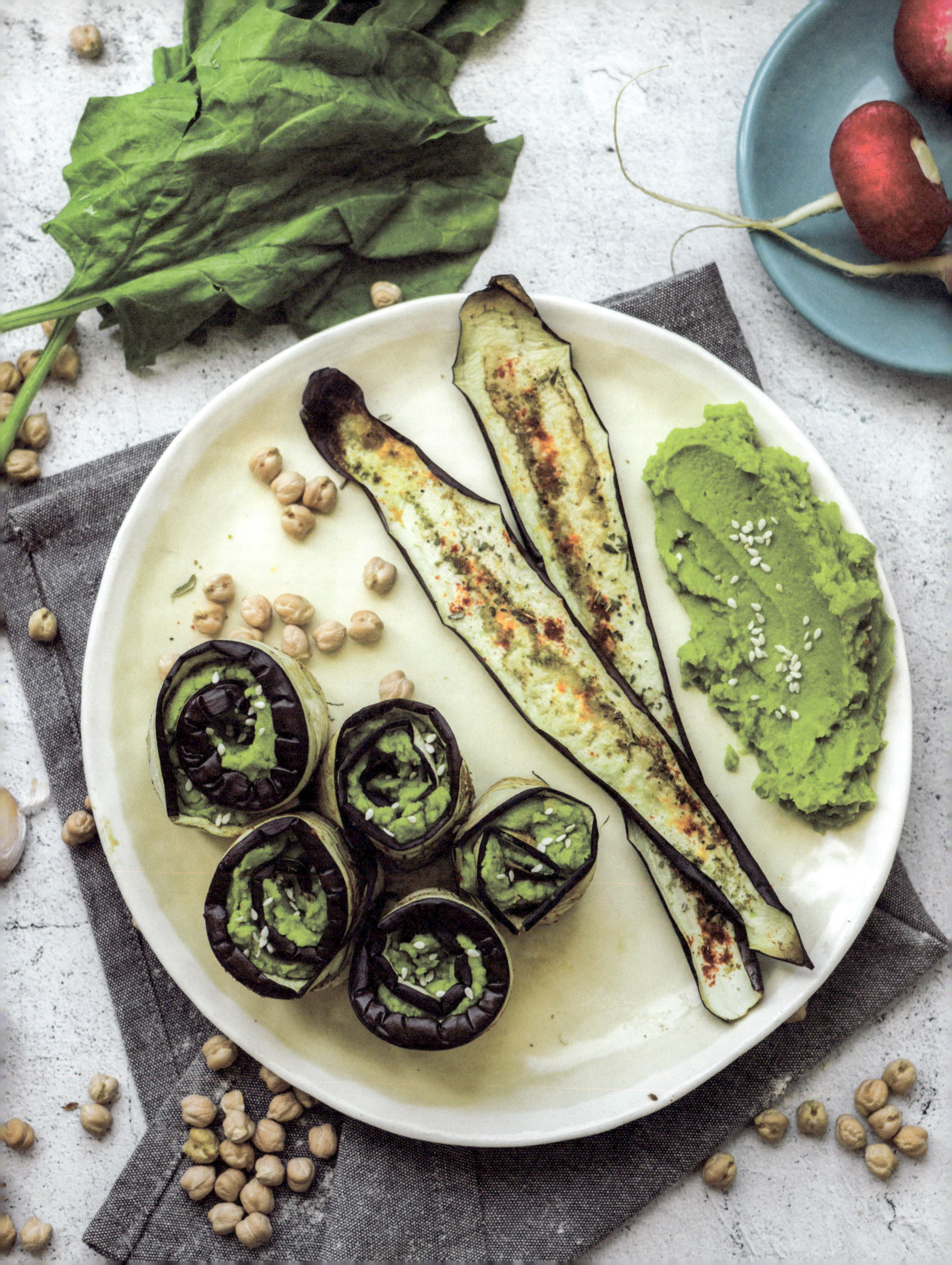

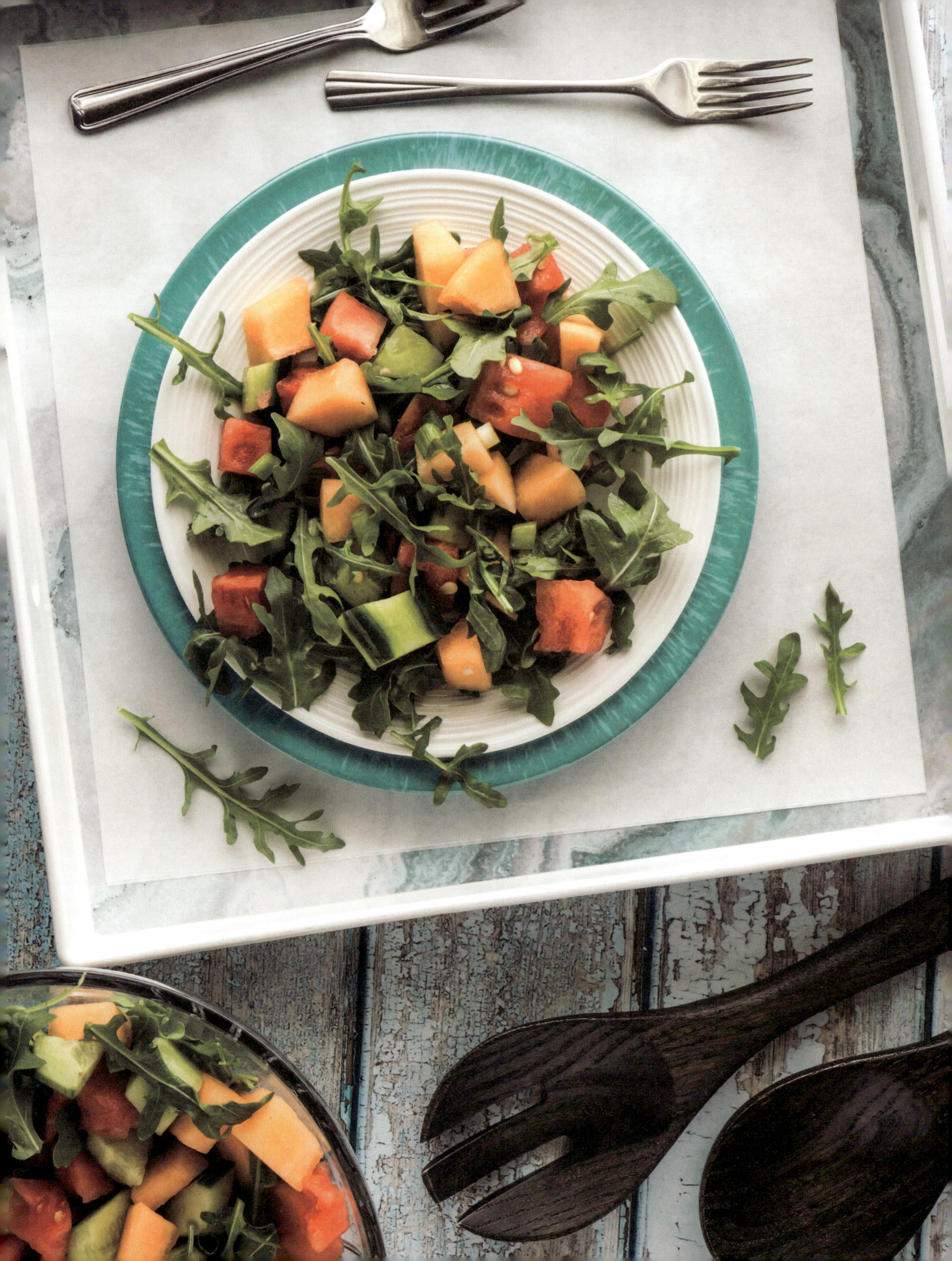

MELON & ARUGULA SALAD WITH WATERMELON VINAIGRETTE

Spicy arugula gives an edge to this sweet salad that brings together summer melons and crisp cucumber.

SERVES: 4 · PREP TIME: 15 MINUTES · TOTAL TIME: 15 MINUTES

INGREDIENTS

For the vinaigrette:

4 cups (600g) seedless watermelon

1½ cups (360 mL) cups extra-virgin olive oil

4 tablespoons apple cider vinegar

4 tablespoons maple syrup

3 Medjool dates

sea salt, to taste

For the salad:

5 cups (100g) arugula

1 cup (150g) seedless watermelon

1 cup (160g) cantaloupe, cubed and rind removed

1 cucumber peeled and cubed

CONTAINS

SUGAR

FREE FROM

GLUTEN

NUTS

METHOD

BLENDER

ASSEMBLY

DIRECTIONS

- Cut the watermelon into cubes, removing the rind. Reserve a cup of them for the salad and 4 cups for the vinaigrette.
- Cut the cantaloupe into cubes, remove the rind.
- Peel the cucumber, and cut into cubes.
- Place all the vinaigrette ingredients in a blender, and blend until well combined.
- In a large serving bowl, toss the arugula with the cubed watermelon, cantaloupe, and cucumber. Add enough vinaigrette to coat, and toss again.
- Serve with the dressing on the side.

CHEF'S TIPS

- You can store any extra vinaigrette in an airtight glass container in the refrigerator. Stir before using, because it will separate.

BABY SPINACH, PLUM & WALNUT SALAD WITH HONEY MUSTARD DRESSING

This refreshing fruity salad will work as a starter to just about any late-summer main dish.

SERVES: 8 · PREP TIME: 15 MINUTES · TOTAL TIME: 15 MINUTES

INGREDIENTS

4 cups baby spinach leaves

3 large plums, cut into segments

½ cup (32g) walnut halves

1 cup (130g) dried cranberries

½ cup (32g) pumpkin seeds

½ cup (250g) Dijon mustard

½ cup (120mL) maple syrup

½ teaspoon garlic powder

DIRECTIONS

- Toss the spinach, plums, and walnuts in a large salad bowl
- In a separate bowl, add the Dijon mustard, maple syrup, and garlic, and then stir until thoroughly combined.
- Toss the salad with the dressing, and then serve, or distribute salad to plates, and serve the dressing on the side.

CONTAINS

- NUTS
- SEEDS
- SUGAR

FREE FROM

- GLUTEN

METHOD

ASSEMBLY

CHEF'S TIPS

- This is a versatile salad; feel free to add other fruits, or substitute the plums for peaches or pears. You can replace the cranberries with other dried fruits, such as raisins, and the walnuts, with pecans or your favorite nuts.

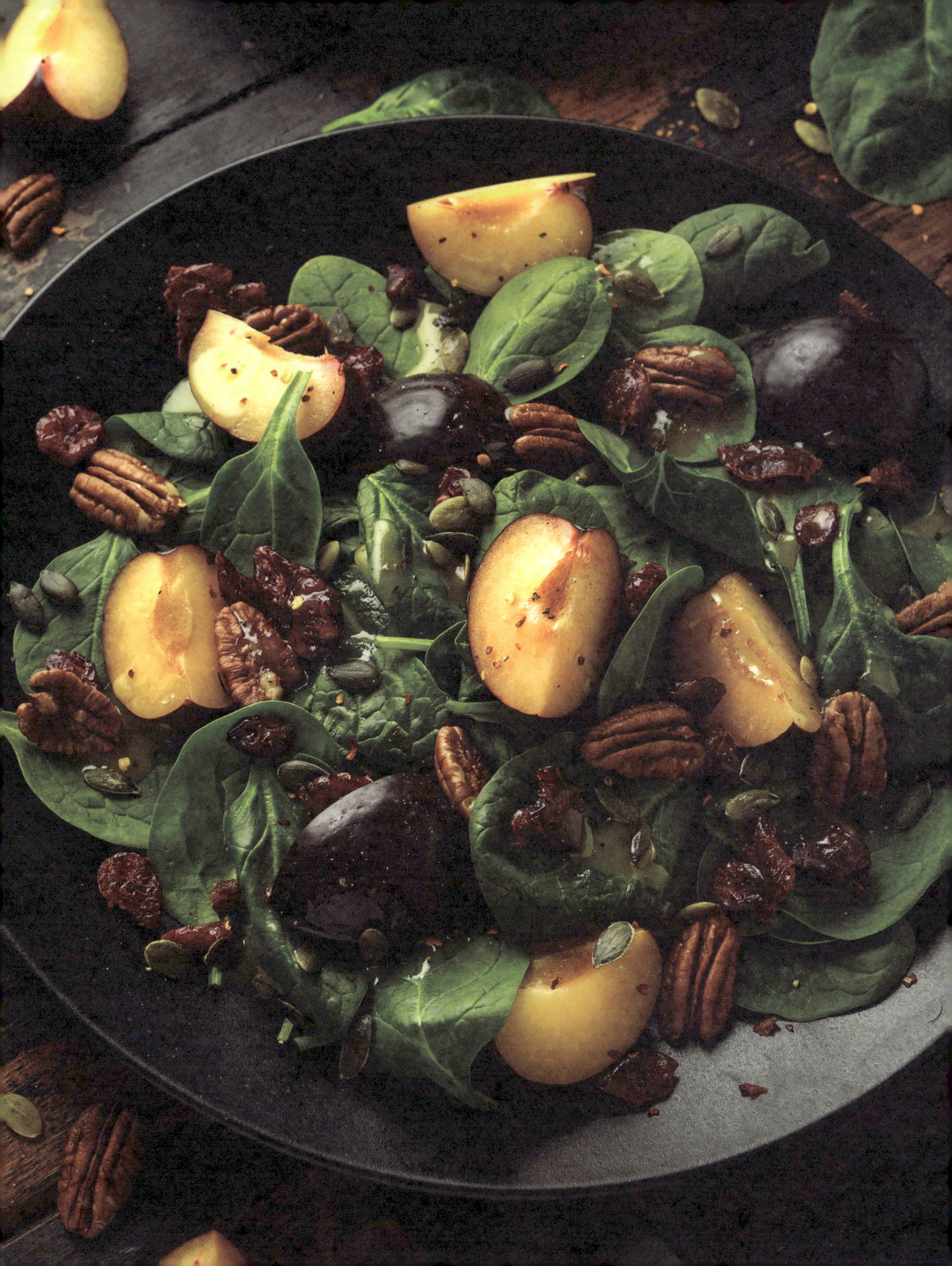

CURRIED ROASTED CAULIFLOWER DIP

Slather this rich curried cauliflower mixture on pita bread, or use it as a dip with chips and crackers.

SERVES: 3–4 · PREP TIME: 15 MINUTES · COOK TIME: 20 MINUTES

INGREDIENTS

- 1 small head of cauliflower, cut into florets
- 2 teaspoons curry powder
- ⅓ cup + 2 tablespoons (95 mL) extra-virgin olive oil
- 1 tablespoon fresh lemon juice
- 2 cloves garlic
- ½ teaspoon dried cilantro
- ½ teaspoon sea salt
- ¼ teaspoon black pepper
- green onions, for garnish

FREE FROM

- GLUTEN
- NUTS
- SUGAR

METHOD

OVEN ROAST

BLENDER

DIRECTIONS

- Preheat oven to 400°F (200°C).
- In a zipper bag, toss the cauliflower florets and 2 tablespoons of the olive oil. Add curry powder, and toss again.
- Arrange the cauliflower in a single layer on a baking sheet, and roast until tender, about 20 minutes.
- Pour the ⅓ cup of oil into a blender, add roasted cauliflower, lemon juice, garlic, cilantro, salt, and pepper, and puree until smooth, pausing to scrape down the sides as needed.
- Transfer to a serving container, and garnish with green onions and a drizzle of olive oil. Serve with chips or bread.

HOT & SWEET CAULIFLOWER BITES

Serve these lively cauliflower snacks when friends gather to watch sports.

SERVES: 2–3 · PREP TIME: 5 MINUTES · COOK TIME: 25 MINUTES

INGREDIENTS

- 1 medium head cauliflower, chopped into 1½-inch (4-cm) florets
- 2–3 tablespoons hot sauce
- 1½ teaspoons maple syrup
- 2 teaspoons avocado oil
- 2–3 tablespoons nutritional yeast
- ¼ teaspoon sea salt
- 1 tablespoon cornstarch or arrowroot starch

DIRECTIONS

- Set air fryer temperature to 360°F (180°C).
- Add all ingredients, except cauliflower, to a large mixing bowl. Whisk to combine thoroughly.
- Add cauliflower, and toss florets to coat evenly.
- Add half of the coated cauliflower to air fryer. Cook for 12 to 14 minutes, shaking halfway, or until they reach desired consistency. Repeat with remaining cauliflower, cook for 9 to 10 minutes.
- Serve as desired.

CONTAINS
- CHILIS
- SUGAR

FREE FROM
- GLUTEN
- NUTS

METHOD
AIR FRY

CHEF'S TIPS

- These will keep tightly sealed in the refrigerator up to 4 days. To reheat, place leftover florets in air fryer for 1 to 2 minutes, until they are warmed through and slightly crispy.

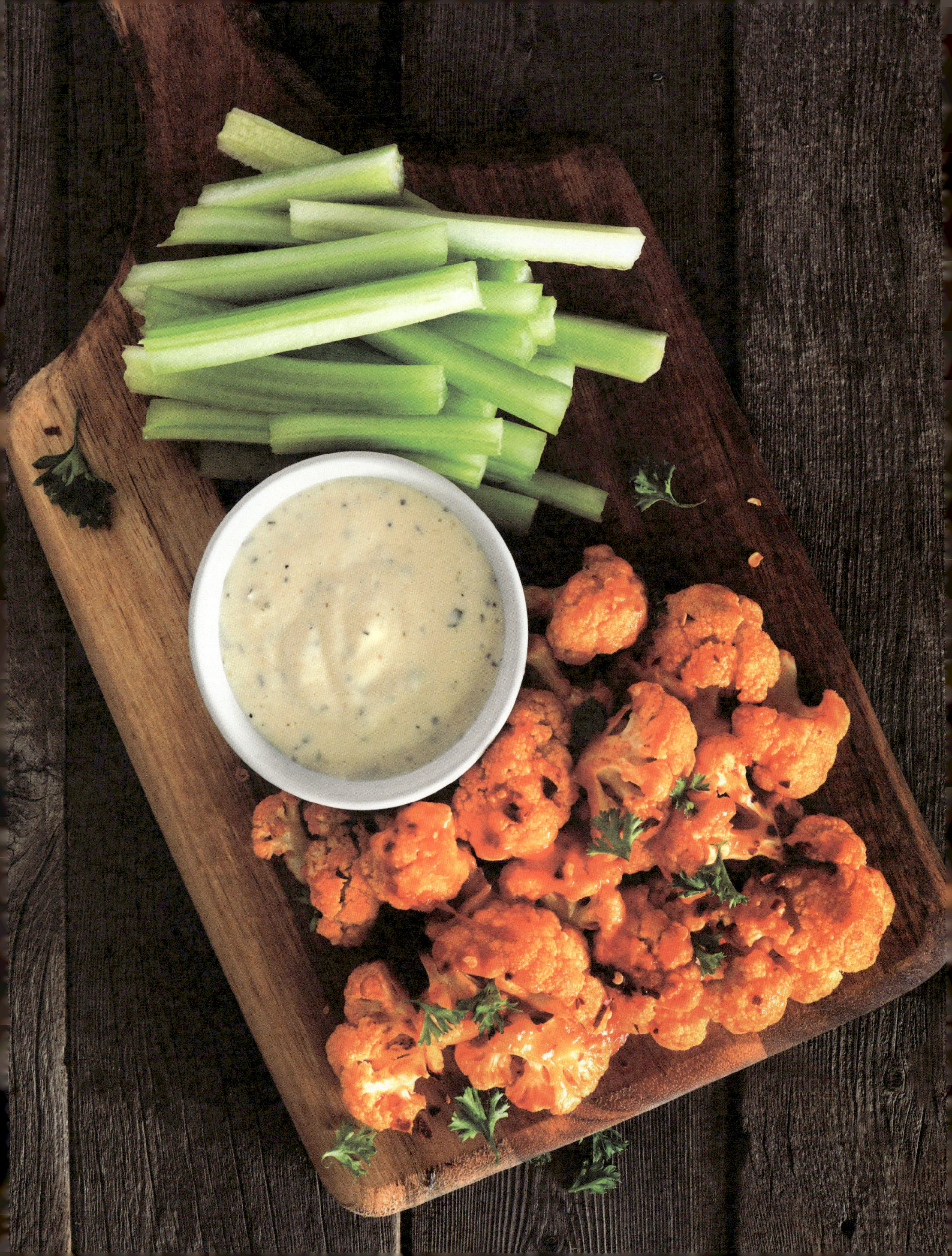

CAULIFLOWER HOT WINGS

A bite into these spicy crisp nibbles reveals a wonderfully soft center.

SERVES: 4 · PREP TIME: 10 MINUTES · COOK TIME: 30 MINUTES

INGREDIENTS

- 1 head of cauliflower
- ½ cup (120mL) water
- ½ cup (120mL) soy milk
- ¾ cup (90g) all-purpose flour
- 2 teaspoons garlic powder
- 1 teaspoon cumin
- 1 teaspoon paprika
- ¼ teaspoon salt
- ¼ teaspoon ground pepper
- 1 cup (240mL) vegan hot sauce
- 1 tablespoon buttery spread

DIRECTIONS

- Preheat oven to 425°F (220°C), and line a baking sheet with parchment paper or grease very well with vegetable oil.
- Wash cauliflower, and cut into bite-sized florets.
- Stir together the water and milk in a medium mixing bowl, and then add flour and spices. Mix until the batter is thick and able to coat the cauliflower without dripping.
- Dip the florets in the batter, shaking off any excess before placing on baking sheet. Spread in a single layer on the baking sheet.
- Bake for 10 minutes until golden brown, and then flip the florets, and bake another 10 minutes so that both sides are golden brown and crispy.
- While the cauliflower is baking, melt buttery spread in a small saucepan over low heat, and mix in hot sauce. Remove from the heat just as it starts to melt. Stir together, and set aside.
- When the cauliflower florets complete the first bake in the batter, remove them from the oven, and place into a mixing bowl. Add the buttery hot sauce mixture, and toss to coat evenly.
- Return cauliflower to the baking sheet, and bake for another 10 to 15 minutes, until they reach desired level of crispness.
- Serve with a vegan ranch dressing and celery sticks.

CONTAINS

- CHILIS
- GLUTEN

FREE FROM

- NUTS
- SUGAR

METHOD

OVEN BAKE

VEGAN RECIPES: SOUPS, STARTERS & SNACKS

RED LENTIL DAL (see page 99)

MAIN COURSES & SIDE DISHES

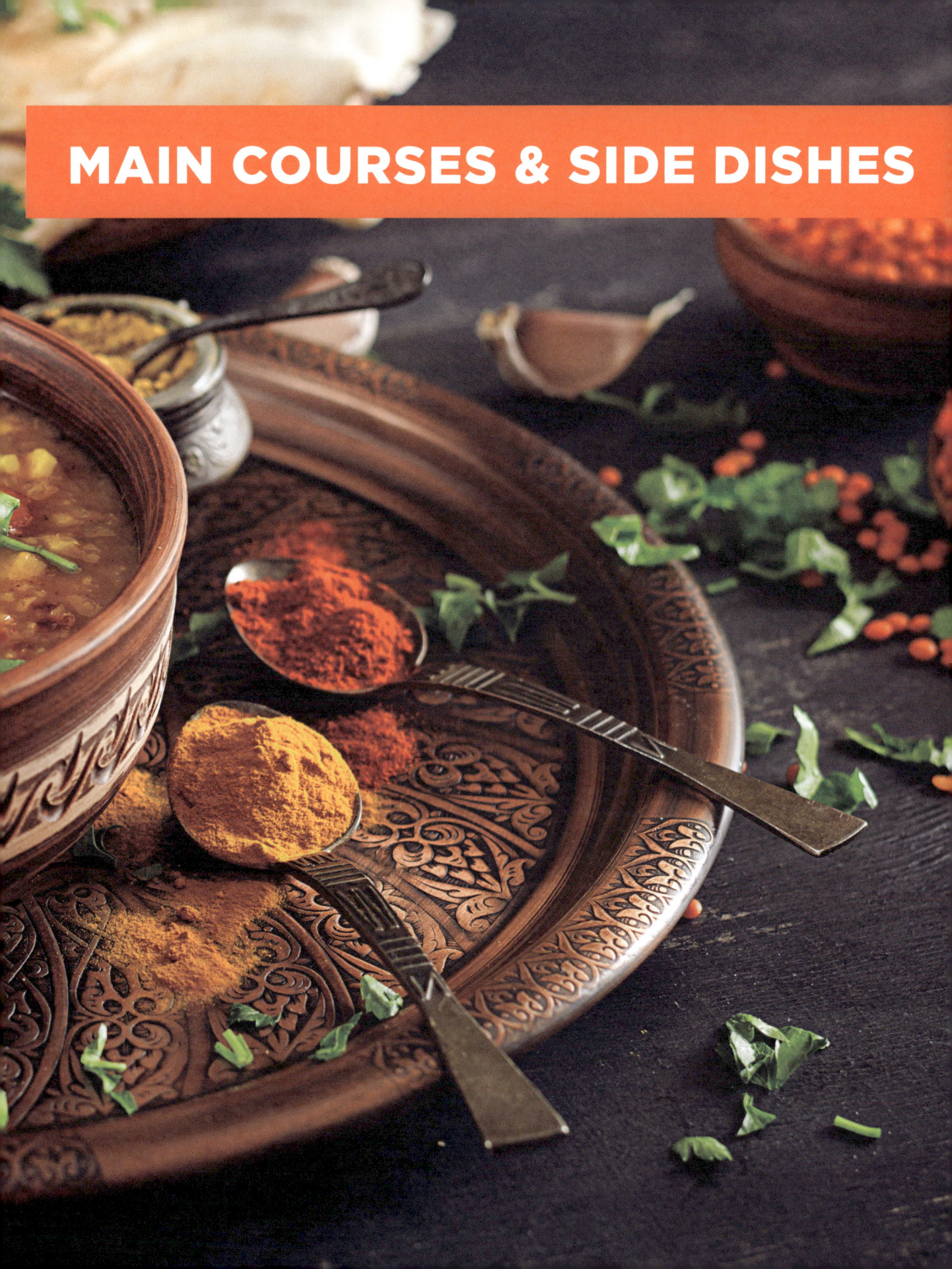

TOFU BREAKFAST SCRAMBLE WITH SPINACH & TOMATOES

Start your day with this healthy breakfast that supplies you with both protein and green veggie.

SERVES: 2 · PREP TIME: 15 MINUTES · COOK TIME: 10 MINUTES

INGREDIENTS

- 1 14-ounce (397g) package firm or extra-firm tofu
- 2 tablespoons extra-virgin olive oil
- 3 scallions, thinly sliced, green and white parts separated
- 5 cups (150g) fresh spinach, roughly chopped
- 1–2 teaspoons freshly squeezed lemon juice
- 1 cup grape tomatoes, halved
- ½ cup (10g) fresh basil, roughly chopped
- ½ teaspoon ground turmeric
- ¼ teaspoon salt
- ½ teaspoon black pepper

CONTAINS
- SOY

FREE FROM
- GLUTEN
- NUTS
- SUGAR

METHOD
OVEN ROAST

DIRECTIONS

- Drain the tofu, and cut it into small pieces. Chop the spinach and basil, and halve the tomatoes.
- In a medium bowl, combine the tofu, turmeric, salt, and black pepper. Toss well to combine, and set aside.
- In a large skillet, heat the oil over medium-high heat. When the oil is hot, add the scallion whites and sauté, stirring often, until soft, about 1 minute. Add the tofu mixture and cook, stirring occasionally with a fork, until the tofu is lightly browned and crumbly, resembling scrambled eggs, about 5 minutes.
- Add the spinach and lemon juice, and stir until the spinach is beginning to wilt, about 1 minute. Add the tomatoes and scallion greens, and stir until the tomatoes are just heated through and beginning to soften, about 1 minute. Remove from heat, add the basil, and stir to combine well.
- Serve on bread or with toast on the side.

CHEF'S TIPS

- This is a versatile recipe: feel free change up the ingredients, using mushrooms, carrots, red onions, or any of your favorite vegetables.

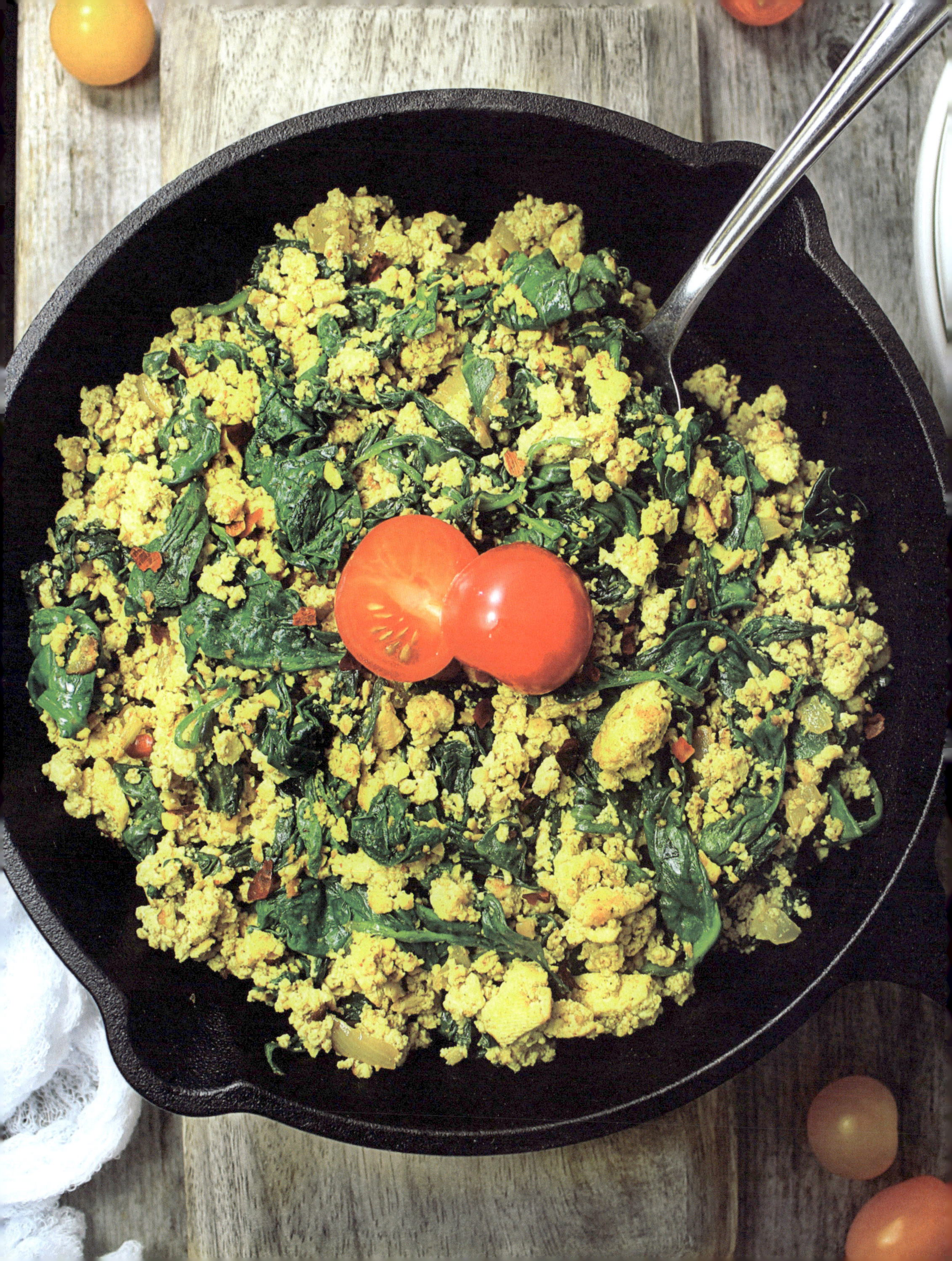

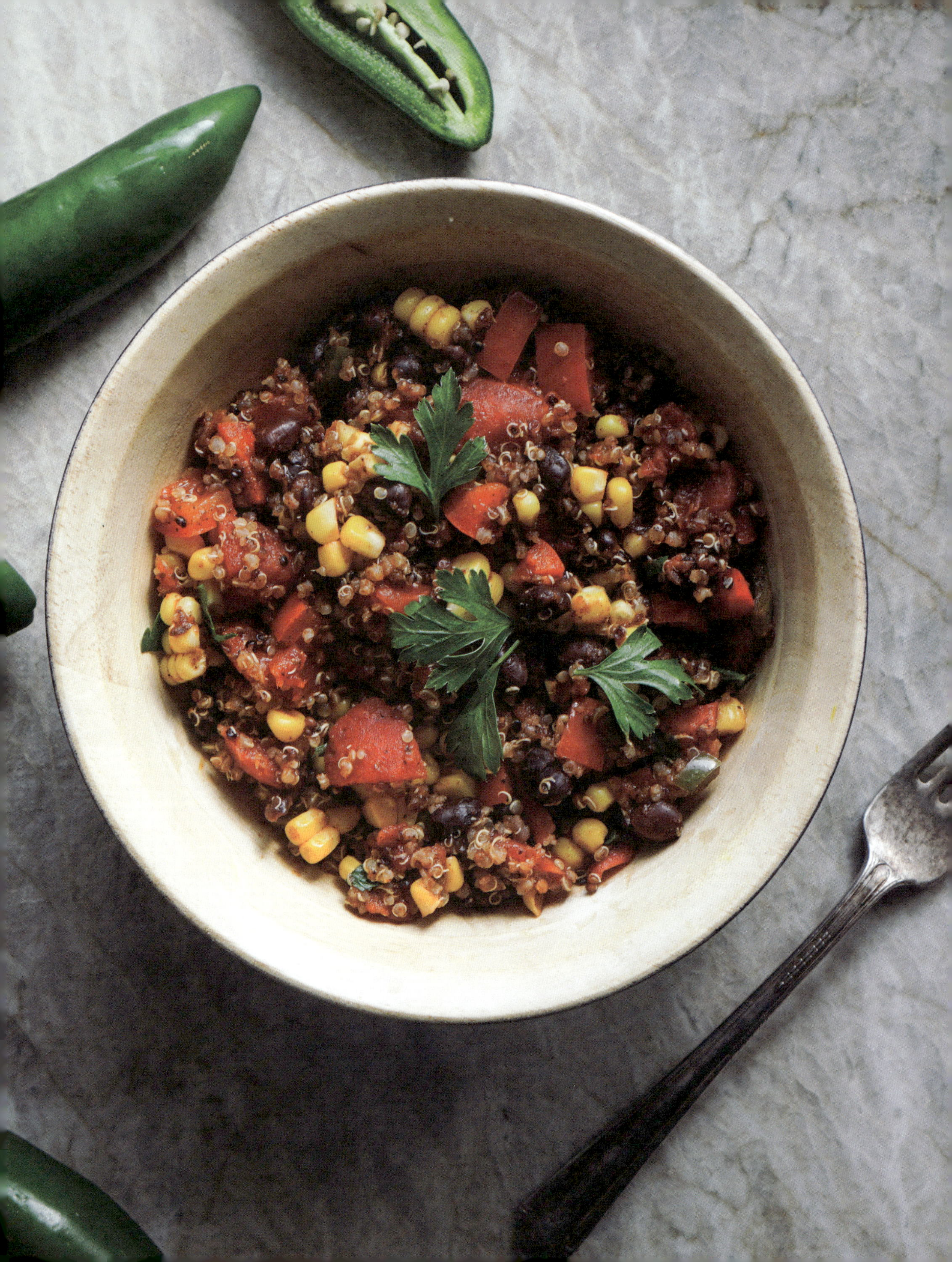

MEXICAN QUINOA SALAD WITH CHILI LIME DRESSING

This healthy quinoa bowl is packed with bright citrusy flavor. Serve it for a summer or spring supper party.

SERVES: 8 · PREP TIME: 15 MINUTES · TOTAL TIME: 2 HOURS

INGREDIENTS

- 1½ cups (265g) quinoa, rinsed and drained
- 2¼ (540mL) cups water
- 1–2 red bell peppers
- 2 cups (600g) black beans
- 2 large ripe tomatoes
- 1 cup (154g) corn
- ¾ cup (112g) onion, finely chopped
- ¼ cup (15g) fresh cilantro, chopped

For the dressing:
- ⅓ cup (80 mL) avocado oil
- 2 tablespoons white wine vinegar
- 1 tablespoon lime juice, plus extra to taste
- 1 clove garlic (peeled and minced)
- 1 teaspoon chili powder
- ½ teaspoon cumin
- ¼ teaspoon salt, or to taste
- ¼ teaspoon black pepper

CONTAINS
- CHILIS

FREE FROM
- GLUTEN
- NUTS
- SUGAR

METHOD
STOVETOP

DIRECTIONS

- Bring medium saucepan to medium heat to lightly toast the quinoa and remove any excess water, stirring constantly.
- Add water, set burner on high, and bring to a boil. Reduce heat to low, cover, and simmer with the lid slightly ajar for 12 to 15 minutes, or until quinoa is fluffy and all the liquid has been absorbed.
- While the quinoa cooks, chop the peppers, tomatoes, onion, and cilantro. If using canned bean, drain and rinse them.
- In a small bowl, whisk together all the dressing ingredients.
- Using a fork, fluff the quinoa, and transfer to a serving bowl. Add peppers, tomatoes, onion, and cilantro and combine well. Add the dressing, and mix well so that all the ingredients are covered,
- Refrigerate for 1 to hours (or more), and then serve.

CHEF'S TIPS

- This is a versatile salad; feel free to add your favorite veggies, such as jalapeño peppers, olives, or avocados.

AVOCADO & ROASTED SWEET POTATO SALAD WITH SPINACH & CHICKPEAS

Served warm or at room temperature, this hearty salad is filling enough to serve as a main course.

SERVES: 6 · PREP TIME: 10 MINUTES · COOK TIME: 30 MINUTES

INGREDIENTS

- 3 large sweet potatoes, chopped into bite-size chunks
- 1 avocado, chopped in chunks
- 1 tablespoon olive oil
- 1 teaspoon sea salt
- 4 ounces (114g) baby spinach leaves
- 2 tablespoons apple cider vinegar
- 2 tablespoons lemon juice, fresh-squeezed
- ½ teaspoon sea salt
- ground black pepper, to taste
- 1–2 tablespoons sesame seeds

DIRECTIONS

- Preheat oven to 400°F (200°C).
- Place sweet potato chunks into a large bowl, and toss with oil and sea salt.
- Arrange the chunks in a single layer on a baking sheet, and roast until tender, about 20 minutes, flipping once. Remove from oven and let the potato chunks cool.
- While the potatoes are roasting, add the chopped spinach, apple cider vinegar, and lemon juice in a large bowl. When the sweet potato chunks are cooled, add them to the bowl, and stir to combine. Gently stir in avocado and sea salt. Add ground pepper to taste.
- Distribute salad to plates, sprinkle sesame seeds over top, and serve immediately.

CONTAINS
- SEEDS

FREE FROM
- GLUTEN
- NUTS
- SUGAR

METHOD
OVEN ROAST

CHEF'S TIPS

- This is a versatile salad; feel free to add fruit such as cranberries.

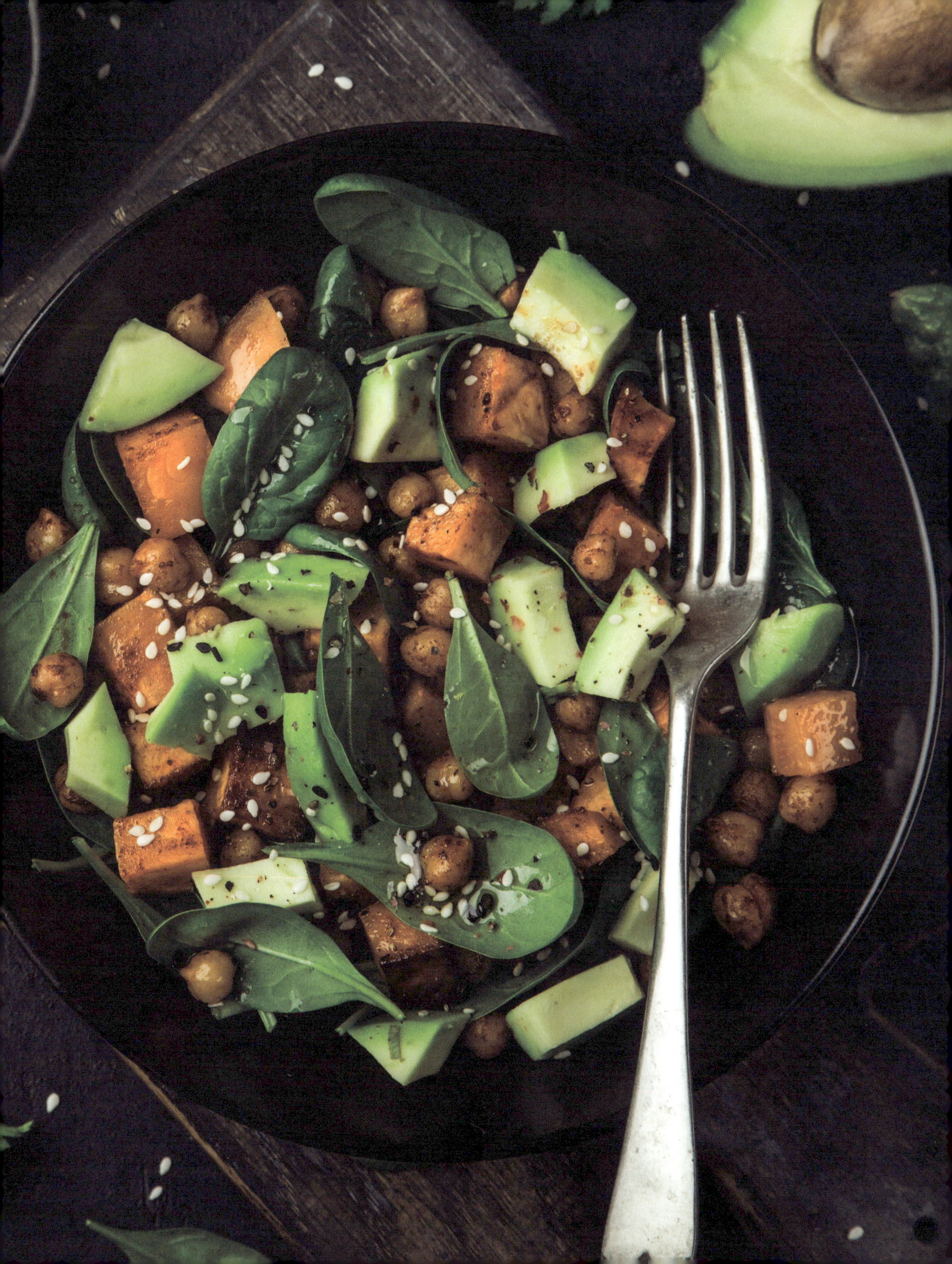

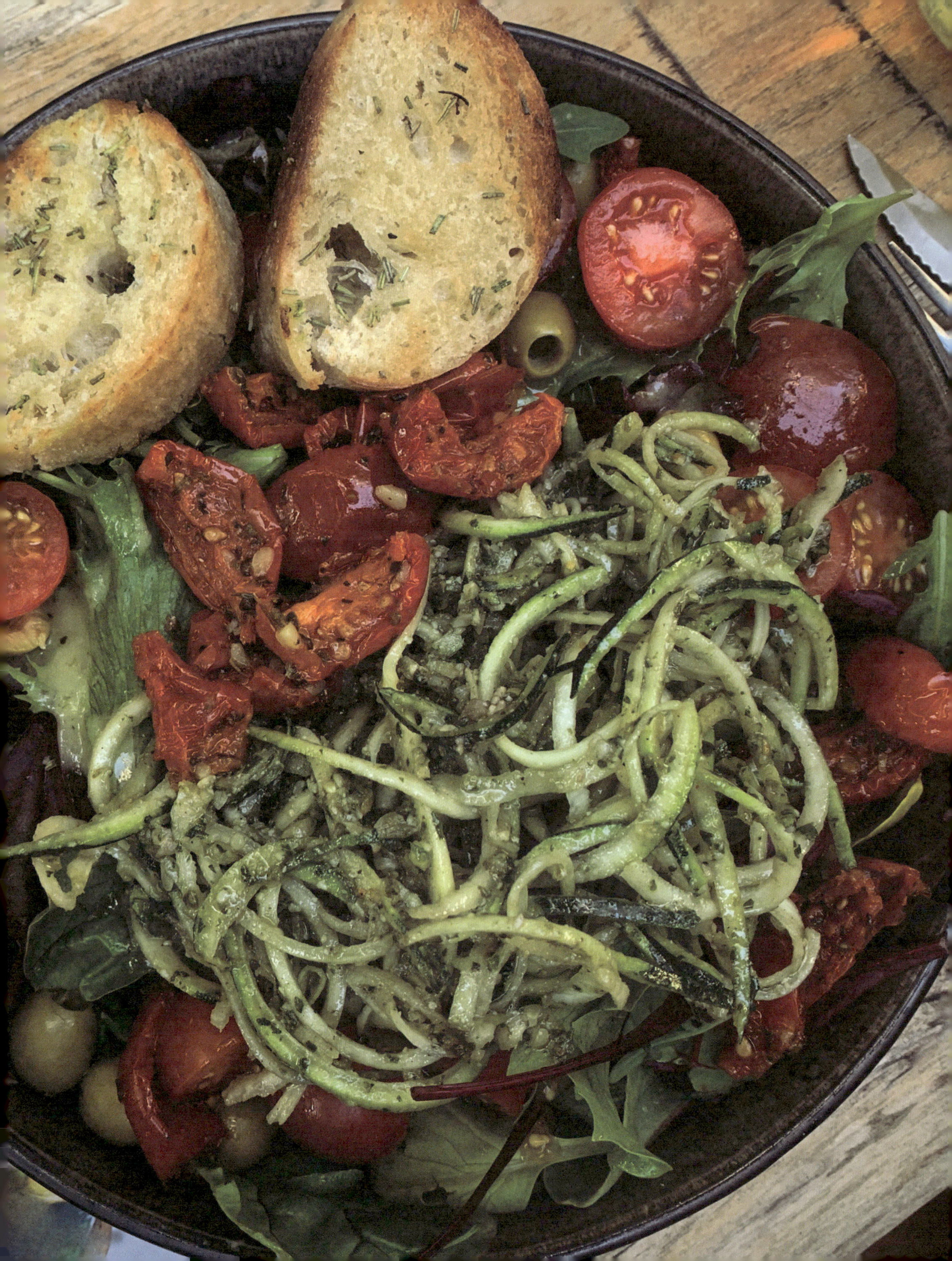

ZUCCHINI SPIRAL NOODLES WITH BASIL PESTO SALAD BOWL

Fresh and vibrant spiralized zucchini forms the base of this lively salad bowl.

SERVES: 2–4 · PREP TIME: 5 MINUTES · TOTAL TIME: 10 MINUTES

INGREDIENTS

- 12 ounces (340g) basil pesto
- 3 large green zucchini
- 1 5-ounce (142g) bag of organic spring mix lettuce
- 1 cup (180g) green olives
- 1 pint (10 ounces/275g) cherry tomatoes
- salt, to taste
- pepper, to taste

DIRECTIONS

- To prepare the noodles, spiralize the zucchini with a spiralizer. You can also turn the zucchini into noodles with a julienne peeler, or grate the zucchini the long way on a large cheese grater.
- Toss the zucchini with pesto until well coated, and season with salt and pepper to taste.
- Place the lettuce mix in a large bowl, and toss with the tomatoes and green olives.
- Transfer the pesto noodles to the bowl, and serve with a crusty Italian bread.

FREE FROM

- GLUTEN
- NUTS
- SUGAR

METHOD

ASSEMBLY

CHEF'S TIPS

- For a homemade basil pesto *see* page 132.
- You can make this recipe with any long summer squash, such as yellow zucchini, Costata Romanesco zucchini, yellow squash, zephyr squash, or cousa squash.

AIR-FRIED FALAFEL

This easy recipe yields falafel balls packed with flavorful fresh herbs.

YIELD: 30 BALLS · PREP TIME: 10 MINUTES · COOK TIME: 20 MINUTES

INGREDIENTS

6 ounces (170g) dried chickpeas/garbanzo beans, soaked*

1 small yellow onion, sliced

2 cloves of garlic

½ bunch fresh parsley, chopped

¼ bunch fresh cilantro, chopped

⅛ tablespoon cumin

¼ teaspoon cayenne pepper

black pepper, to taste

1½ teaspoon salt

juice of ½ lemon

¼ cup (30g) chickpea flour

2 tablespoons tahini

olive oil cooking spray

FREE FROM

GLUTEN

NUTS

SUGAR

METHOD

AIR FRY

DIRECTIONS

- Place the chickpeas, onion, and garlic into a large food processor. Process until the mixture is finely chopped, but not mushy.
- Add in herbs, spices, and lemon juice. Process again until well incorporated—the mixture should turn a bright green color.
- Add the chickpea flour and tahini, and pulse until well combined.
- Transfer the falafel mixture to a large bowl. Form into balls, using about 2 tablespoons of the mixture per ball.
- Spray the basket for your air fryer with olive oil cooking spray. Add as many falafel balls into the basket as can fit without them touching each other, and spray very lightly with olive oil.
- Air fry the falafel at 350°F (180°C) for 8 minutes. Flip and fry for another 6 minutes on the second side.
- Repeat until you use up all the falafel mixture, and then drain on paper towels.
- Serve with tahini sauce.

CHEF'S TIPS

- If you do not have an air fryer, you can bake the falafel balls in the oven at 350°F (180°C) for 20 minutes. For extra crispy falafel, spray the balls with some oil or a nonstick cooking spray before baking.

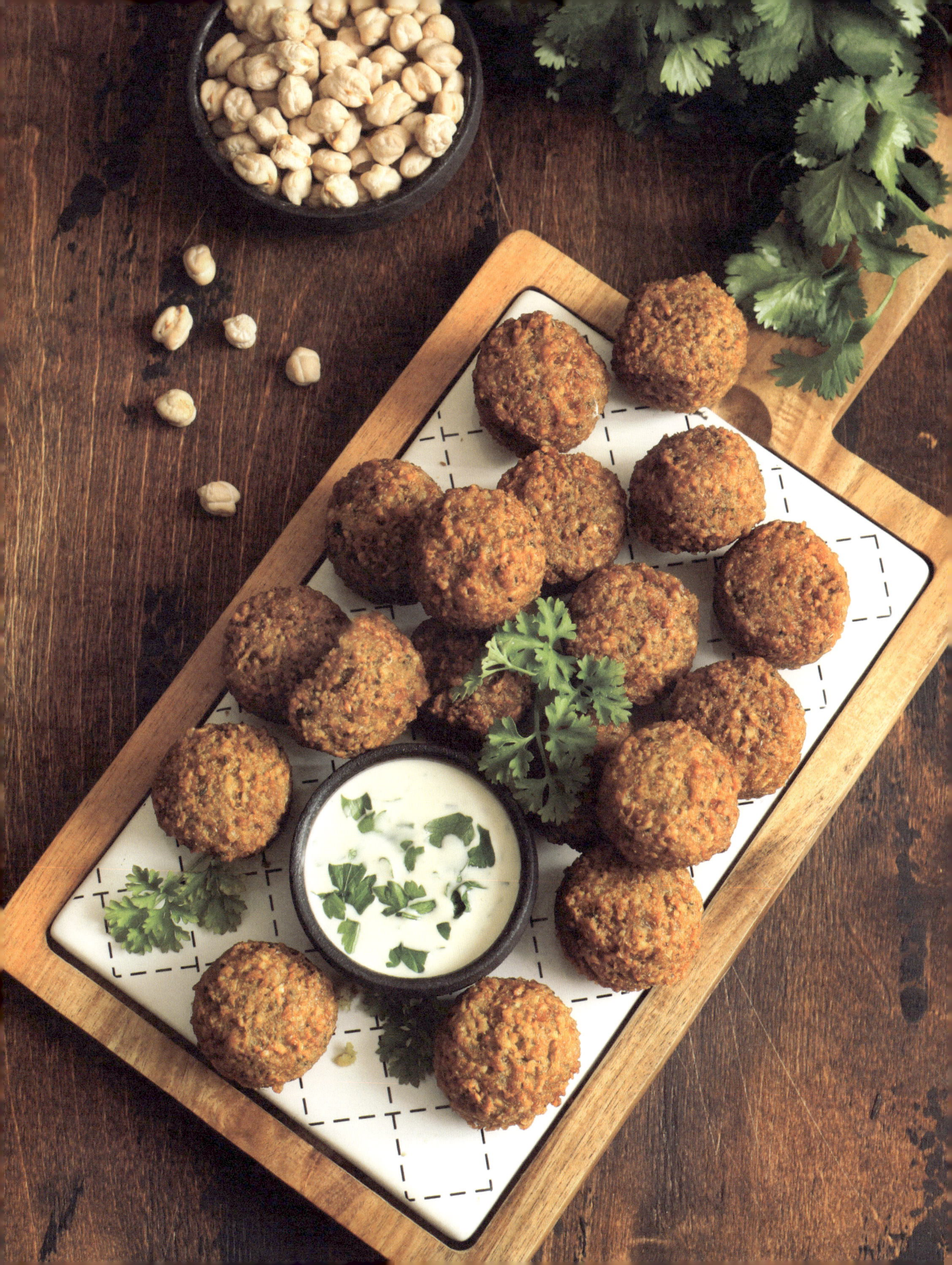

FALAFEL, TOMATO & CUCUMBER SALAD

This bright Mediterranean-style salad makes a light and nutritious summertime meal.

SERVES: 2-5 · PREP TIME: 10 MINUTES · TOTAL TIME: 10 MINUTES

FREE FROM

- GLUTEN
- NUTS
- SUGAR

METHOD

ASSEMBLY

INGREDIENTS

- ¼ cup (60 mL) extra-virgin olive oil
- 2 tablespoons red wine vinegar
- ½ teaspoon kosher salt
- ½ teaspoon black pepper
- 12 cherry tomatoes, sliced
- 4 cups (85g) arugula
- 2 small cucumbers, sliced
- 1 small red onion, thinly sliced
- 12 cooked falafel balls
- sprigs of fresh mint

DIRECTIONS

- Place oil, vinegar, salt, and pepper in a large bowl, and stir with a whisk to combine into a vinaigrette. Add tomatoes, and toss gently to coat. Let stand 2 minutes.
- Arrange arugula on a platter so that leaves overlap slightly. Arrange falafel cucumber, onion, and mint, over the arugula.
- To serve, drizzle remaining vinaigrette over salad.

CHEF'S TIPS

- For homemade falafel balls, *see page* 92.

LENTIL LOAF WITH BARBEQUE GLAZE

Craving comfort food? Serve this "meatloaf" with mashed potatoes and a veggie for a soothing supper.

SERVES: 8 · PREP TIME: 15 MINUTES · COOK TIME: 45 MINUTES

INGREDIENTS

- 2 cups (400g) green or brown lentils
- 1 tablespoon olive oil
- ½ yellow onion, diced
- 2 carrots, diced
- 2 celery stalks, diced
- ½ cup red bell pepper, diced
- 1¼ cup (94g) mushrooms, diced
- 2 cloves garlic, minced
- 2 tablespoons tomato paste
- 2 tablespoons flax meal
- 1 tablespoon dried parsley
- ¼ teaspoon salt
- ¼ teaspoon pepper
- ½ cup (45g) quick oats
- ½ cup (60g) breadcrumbs

For the barbeque sauce:
- 3½ tablespoons organic ketchup
- 1½ tablespoon balsamic vinegar
- 1½ tablespoon maple syrup

CONTAINS
- CHILIS
- SUGAR

FREE FROM
- GLUTEN

METHOD
STOVETOP
BLENDER

DIRECTIONS

- In a small bowl, mix ketchup, balsamic vinegar, and maple syrup. Stir well, and set aside.
- Preheat oven to 350°F (180°C), and line a baking sheet with parchment paper.
- In a large skillet, heat the oil over medium-high heat. When the oil is hot, add the onion, carrots, celery, pepper, and mushrooms, and sauté and until softened. Add the garlic and sauté 1 minute.
- Add the lentils, vegetables, tomato paste, 1 tablespoon barbeque sauce, flax meal, parsley, salt, pepper, oats, and breadcrumbs to a blender or food processor, and pulse the mixture until it forms a lumpy dough, with plenty of veggie bits for texture.
- Form the dough into a ball, and place on the baking sheet. Pat it into a loaf shape. Bake for 35 minutes, and spread the barbeque sauce over the top, and then bake for another 10 minutes.
- Remove from oven, and let the loaf set for about 10 minutes, and then serve with your favorite vegetables or salad.

PUMPKIN LENTIL CURRY

Mild pumpkin gets a bit of oomph from the addition of fragrant Indian spices in this warming curry.

SERVES: 2 · PREP TIME: 10 MINUTES · COOK TIME: 20 MINUTES

INGREDIENTS

- 1 tablespoon extra-virgin olive oil
- 2 cloves garlic, crushed
- 1 tablespoon fresh ginger, grated
- 1 tablespoons ground cumin
- 1 teaspoon ground turmeric
- 1 teaspoon ground coriander
- 2–3 dried red chili peppers, to taste
- 1 cup (200g) brown lentils
- 3 cups (350g) pumpkin, cut into bite-sized cubes
- 2 cups (480mL) vegetable broth or water
- 2 14-ounce (400g) cans diced tomatoes
- 4 tablespoons fresh cilantro, chopped
- 1 lime, cut into wedges
- salt, to taste
- ground pepper, to taste

CONTAINS
- CHILIS

FREE FROM
- GLUTEN
- NUTS
- SUGAR

METHOD
STOVETOP

DIRECTIONS

- In a soup pot or large skillet, heat the olive oil over medium-high heat, and sauté the garlic with the ginger, cumin, turmeric, coriander, and dried chili peppers for about 1 minute, until fragrant.
- Add the pumpkin cubes, lentils, diced tomatoes, and broth (or water), and stir until combined well. Bring to a boil, and then lower heat. Cover and simmer for 20 minutes, until the pumpkin has softened. Stir in coriander, and add salt and pepper to taste.
- Serve over rice with a squeeze of lime.

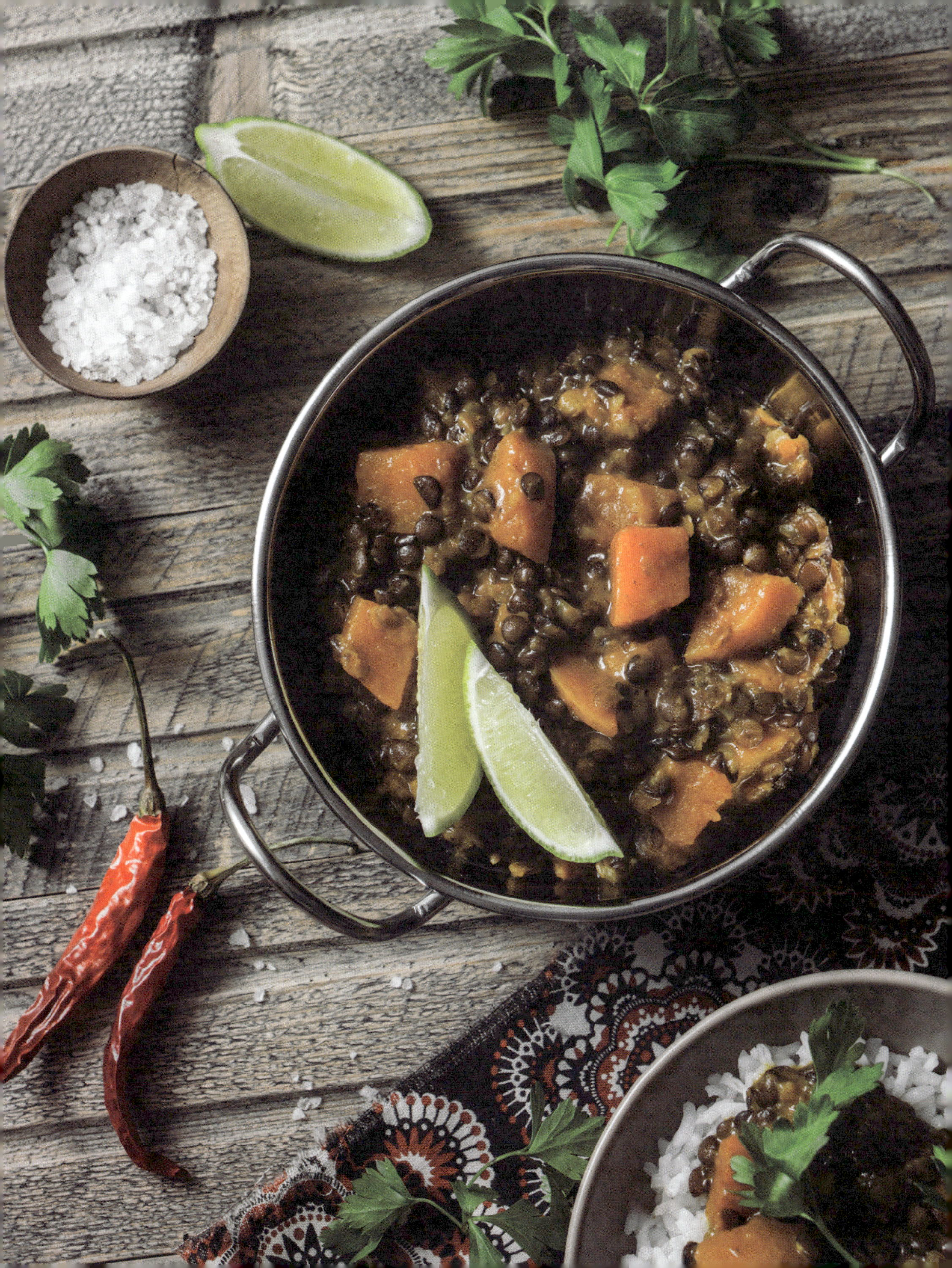

RED LENTIL & BULGUR WHEAT PATTIES

Feature these healthy Turkish patties as a main course with salad and pita, or enjoy them as a tasty snack.

SERVES 4 · PREP TIME: 15 MINUTES · COOK TIME: 45 MINUTES

INGREDIENTS

- 1 cup (200g) red lentils
- 2½ (600mL) cups water
- 1½ cups (275g) bulgur wheat
- 1 onion, finely chopped
- 1 tablespoon chili paste
- 3–5 tablespoons olive oil
- 2 teaspoon ground cumin
- salt and pepper, to taste

DIRECTIONS

- Place the lentils in a saucepan with 2 cups (480mL) of the water, bring to a boil, and then simmer for 10 minutes.
- Remove from the heat, and add the bulgur wheat, chili paste, cumin, salt and pepper, 1 tablespoon of the olive oil, and ½ cup boiling water. Mix until well combined, and then let the mixture sit for 15 minutes, or until the water has been fully absorbed.
- In a large skillet, heat 1 tablespoon oil over medium heat. When the oil is hot, add the onions, and sauté them for 5 minutes, until soft and translucent. Allow them to cool for a few minutes, and then add them to the lentil mixture, stirring until they are well combined. Form the mixture into small patties
- In the same skillet, add another tablespoon of oil, add the patties (in batches if necessary), and fry for 3 to 5 minutes on each side, adding more oil as necessary. Remove from skillet, and drain the patties on paper towels.

CONTAINS
- CHILIS
- GLUTEN

FREE FROM
- SUGAR

METHOD
STOVETOP

RED LENTIL DAL

Indian cuisine offers a wealth a vegan meal options, such as this hearty curry featuring red lentils.

SERVES: 6 · PREP TIME: 10 MINUTES · COOK TIME: 20 MINUTES

INGREDIENTS

- 1½ cups (300g) dry red lentils, rinsed
- 1 large carrot, finely diced
- 1 small red bell pepper
- 1 large white onion, chopped
- 4 cloves garlic, minced
- 1 tablespoon fresh ginger, minced
- ½ tablespoon vegetable oil
- 3 cups (720 mL) vegetable broth
- 1 cup (240 mL) canned coconut milk
- 1½ teaspoons ground cumin
- 1 tablespoon curry powder
- ½ tablespoon coconut sugar
- 1 teaspoon ground turmeric
- 1 teaspoon paprika
- sea salt, to taste
- black pepper, to taste

CONTAINS
- CHILIS

FREE FROM
- GLUTEN
- NUTS
- SUGAR

METHOD
STOVETOP

DIRECTIONS

- In a large pot, heat the oil over medium heat. When the oil is hot, add the onion, and sauté for 3 to 4 minutes.
- Add ginger, garlic, carrot, and bell pepper, stir to combine, and then add all spices, sugar, the lentils, and vegetable broth. Bring to a boil, sand then simmer for about 10 minutes.
- Pour in coconut milk, and simmer for another 5 minutes, or until the mixture reaches the desired thickness.
- Season with black pepper and salt, and then taste, adjusting the seasonings as needed.
- Garnish with fresh cilantro, and serve with basmati rice and/or any vegan Indian bread.

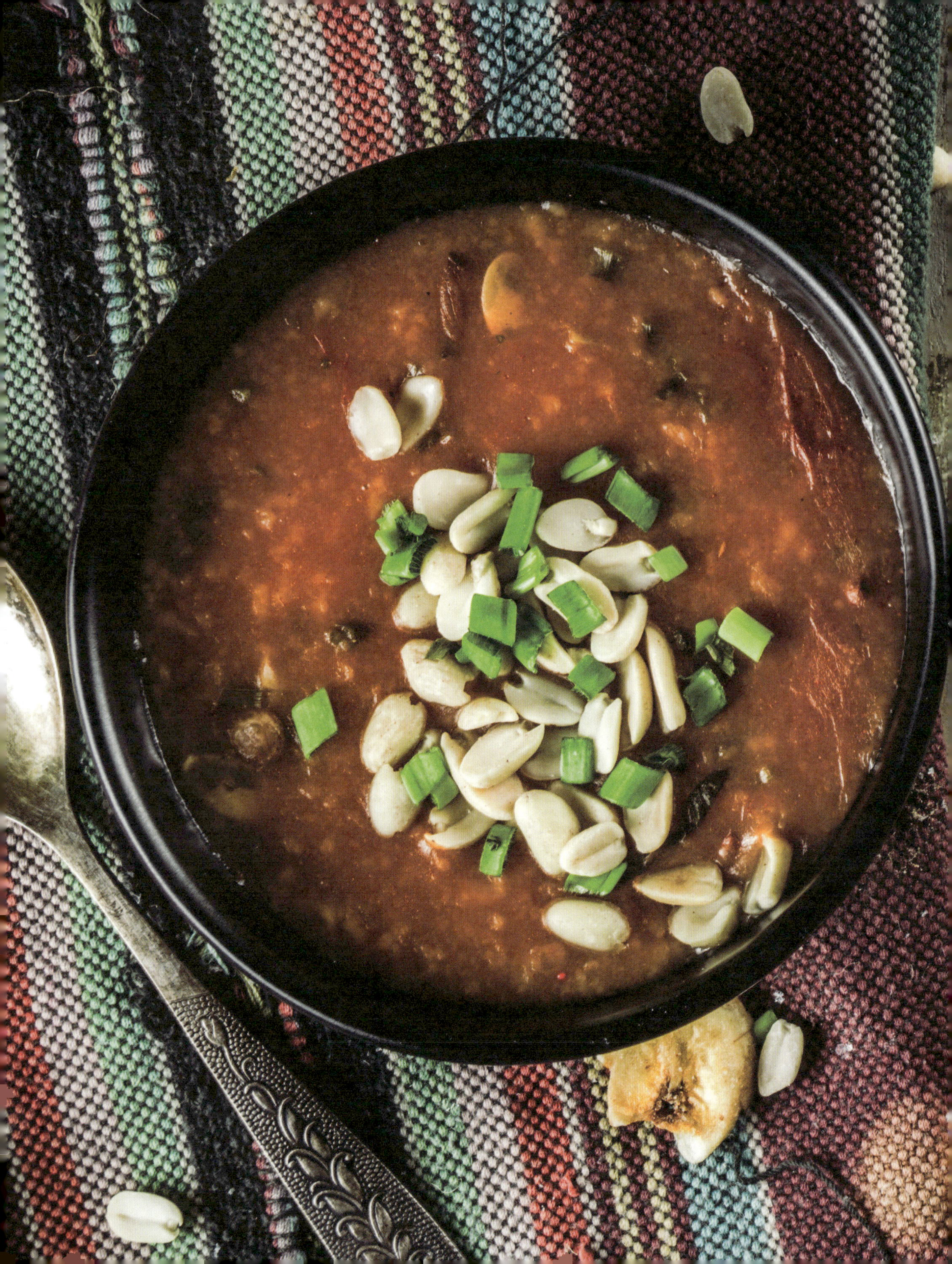

PEANUT STEW

This nourishing soup features sweet potatoes and collard greens in a creamy peanut and tomato sauce.

SERVES: 4 · PREP TIME: 10 MINUTES · COOK TIME: 45 MINUTES

INGREDIENTS

- 1 tablespoon olive oil
- 4 cloves garlic, minced
- 2 tablespoons fresh ginger, peeled and grated
- 1 sweet potato
- 1 medium red onion, diced
- 1 tablespoon cumin
- ¼ teaspoon crushed red pepper
- 6-ounce (170g) can tomato paste
- ¾ cup unsalted peanut butter
- 4 cups (960 mL) vegetable broth
- 2 cups (480mL) water
- ½ bunch collard greens
- ⅓ cup peanut, roughly chopped, for garnish
- hot sauce, to taste

DIRECTIONS

- In a large soup pot, heat the oil over medium-high heat. When the oil is hot, add the ginger, garlic, and onion, and sauté until the onion turns translucent. While the ginger, garlic, and onions are sautéing, peel and dice the sweet potato into bite-sized cubes. Add the cubes, cumin, and red pepper to the pot, and continue to sauté for about 5 minutes.
- Add the tomato paste, peanut butter, vegetable broth, and water, and stir until well combined. Cover the pot, and turn heat up to high to bring the stew to a boil, and then reduce the heat. Simmer for 15 to 20 minutes.
- While the soup is simmering, prepare the collard greens. Using a sharp knife, remove each stem. Stack the leaves, and cut them into thin strips. Place the chopped greens in a colander, and rinse very well
- Once the sweet potatoes are very soft, stir in the collard greens, and let the stew simmer for about 5 minutes, mashing the sweet potatoes against the side of the pot to help thicken the stew.
- Pour the soup onto bowls, garnish with chopped peanuts and a sprinkle of hot sauce if desired, and serve with cooked rice.

CONTAINS

- CHILIS
- NUTS

FREE FROM

- GLUTEN
- SUGAR

METHOD

STOVETOP

CHEF'S TIPS

- For a homemade vegetable broth, *see* page 42.
- You can substitute the collard greens with kale.

STUFFED SWEET POTATO WITH ARUGULA, OLIVES & GUACAMOLE

Packed with creamy avocado, peppery arugula, and meaty olives, these make a hearty lunch or light dinner.

SERVES: 4 · PREP TIME: 10 MINUTES · COOK TIME: 50–60 MINUTES

INGREDIENTS

- 2 medium sweet potatoes
- 2 ripe avocados, pitted and peeled
- juice of 1 lime
- a large handful of arugula
- a handful of bean sprouts
- 4 tablespoons sun-dried tomatoes
- 4 tablespoons green olives
- salt, to taste
- pepper, to taste

FREE FROM

- GLUTEN
- NUTS
- SUGAR

METHOD

OVEN BAKE
ASSEMBLY

DIRECTIONS

- Preheat oven to 400°F (200°C), and line a baking tray with parchment paper.
- Wash the sweet potatoes, and then prick each one a few times with a fork or a knife to allow steam to escape.
- Place potatoes on the baking tray, and bake for 50 to 60 minutes or until very tender. Remove from oven and cut in half lengthwise.
- While the sweet potatoes bake, slice the avocados in half, remove the pits and skin, and place in a medium mixing bowl. Mash with the back of a fork until it is chunky. Mix in salt and lime juice, and gently mash again to incorporate.
- Slice the olives into small pieces.
- Fill each half with a quarter each of the mashed avocado, arugula, sliced olives, and bean sprouts.
- Sprinkle with salt and pepper to taste, and serve immediately.

VEGAN RECIPES: MAIN COURSES & SIDE DISHES

HASSELBACK POTATOES

These gorgeous potato accordions make a tasty side dish flavored with rosemary and garlic.

SERVES: 4 · PREP TIME: 20 MINUTES · COOK TIME: 60 MINUTES

FREE FROM
- GLUTEN
- NUTS
- SUGAR

METHOD

OVEN BAKE

INGREDIENTS

- 4 large baking potatoes
- 4 tablespoons olive oil
- 1 tablespoon fresh rosemary
- 4 cloves garlic, minced
- 1 teaspoon pink Himalayan salt
- fresh black pepper, to taste
- pinch of red pepper flakes
- parsley, for garnish

DIRECTIONS

- Preheat oven 425°F (220°C), and lightly oil a baking dish.
- Wash the potatoes, and pat them dry, and then cut thin (about ⅛ inch, or 3mm) vertical slits into them, stopping about ¼ inch (6mm) from the bottom.
- Place the potatoes in the baking dish, and slip a bit of garlic in every other slit, and tuck a rosemary leaf or two into the others. Brush with 2 tablespoons of the oil. Sprinkle with a pinch of salt.
- Bake for 30 minutes, and then remove from oven. Brush on the rest of the olive oil, and sprinkle with black pepper, red pepper flakes and the rest of the salt. Bake for another 30 minutes, until the potatoes are well browned with crispy edges.
- Garnish with parsley, and serve immediately.

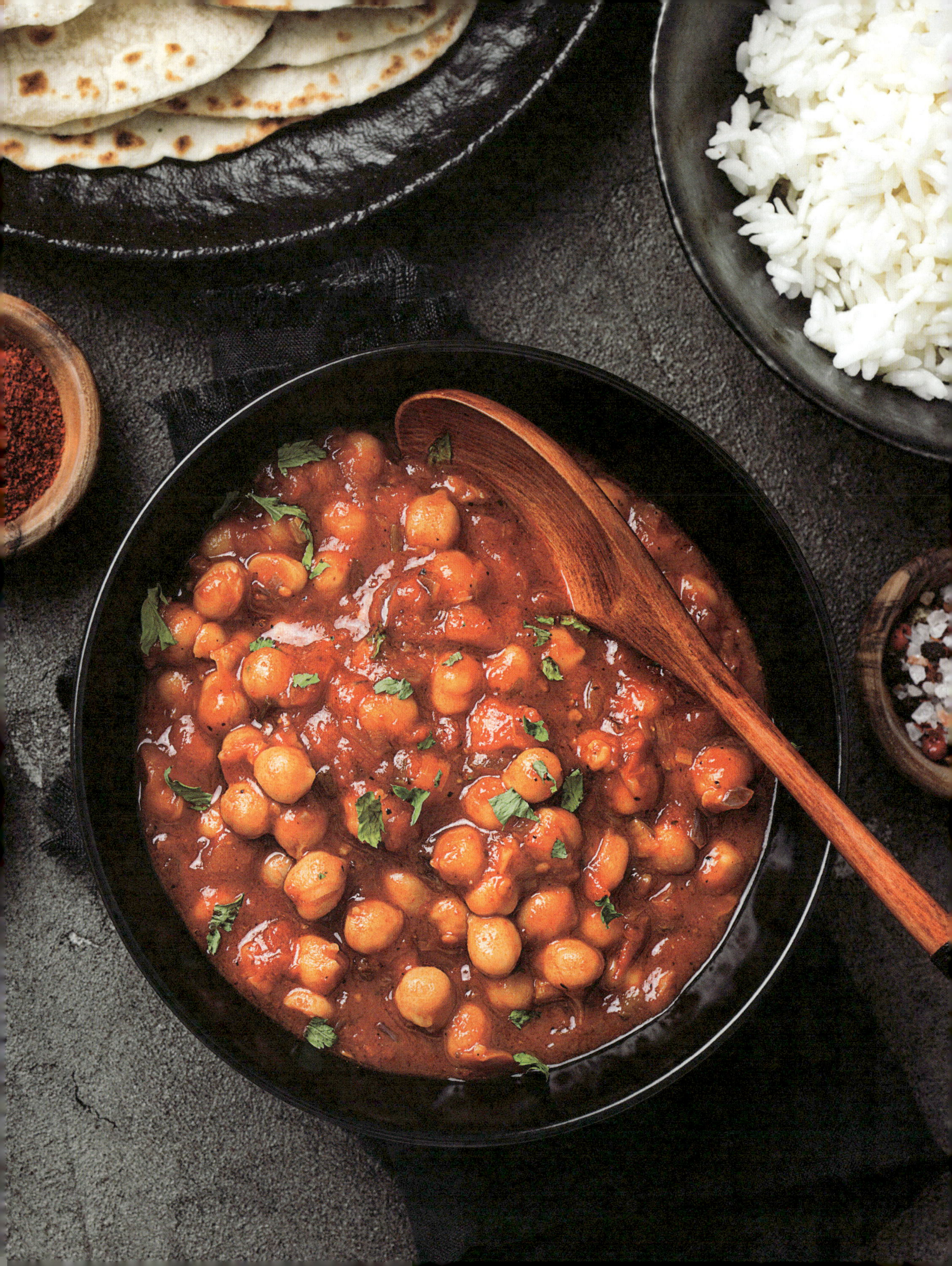

CHANA MASALA

This highly flavorful dish that originated in northern India makes a healthy and filling main dish.

SERVES: 6 · PREP TIME: 5 MINUTES · COOK TIME: 25 MINUTES

INGREDIENTS

- 1 medium white or yellow onion, finely diced
- 1 tablespoon ground cumin
- ¾ teaspoon sea salt, divided
- 6 cloves garlic, minced
- 2 tablespoon fresh ginger, minced
- ½ cup (25g) fresh cilantro, chopped
- 2–3 fresh green chilies, sliced with seeds
- 1 tablespoon ground coriander
- 1 teaspoon chili powder
- 1 teaspoon ground turmeric
- 1 28-ounce (440g) can tomato puree
- 2 15-ounce (400g) cans chickpeas, slightly drained
- 1 teaspoon garam masala
- 2–3 teaspoon coconut sugar
- 2 tablespoons lemon juice

CONTAINS
- CHILIS
- SUGAR

FREE FROM
- GLUTEN
- NUTS

METHOD
STOVETOP

DIRECTIONS

- In a large pot, heat the oil over medium heat. When the oil is hot, add the onion, cumin, and ¼ teaspoon of the salt.
- Place garlic, ginger, cilantro, and chilies in a mortar and pestle and grind into a rough paste, and then add to the pot.
- Add ground coriander, chili powder, and turmeric, and stir to coat. If the pan is dry, add a little more oil.
- Add pureed tomatoes and chickpeas and remaining salt. If the mixture is too thick, add up to 1 cup (240 ml) water.
- Raise heat to medium-high until the mixture reaches a rolling simmer, and then reduce heat to low. Simmer uncovered for 15 to 20 minutes, until the mixture thickens to a stew-like consistency, stirring occasionally.
- When the mixture is thickened and is bubbling, taste and adjust seasonings as needed, adding as much of the coconut sugar as needed. Remove from heat, and add lemon juice and garam masala.
- Serve with basmati rice and/or any vegan Indian bread.

ALOO GOBI

This Indian classic features potatoes and cauliflower flavored with onion, tomatoes, and aromatic spices.

SERVES: 2 · PREP TIME: 10 MINUTES · COOK TIME: 30 MINUTES

CONTAINS
- CHILIS

FREE FROM
- GLUTEN
- NUTS
- SUGAR

METHOD

STOVETOP

INGREDIENTS

- 2 medium potatoes, cubed
- 1 medium cauliflower, cut into small florets
- 1 medium onion, chopped
- 2 medium tomatoes, chopped
- ½ teaspoon cumin seeds
- 1½ teaspoons ginger-garlic paste
- ½ teaspoon turmeric powder
- ½ teaspoon amchur
- ¼ teaspoon red chili powder
- ¼ teaspoon garam masala
- 1 teaspoon coriander powder
- 3–4 teaspoons olive oil
- 2 tablespoons chopped cilantro
- salt, to taste

DIRECTIONS

- In a large skillet, heat the oil over medium heat. When the oil is hot, add the cauliflower florets and sauté for 2 to 3 minutes, and then add the sliced potatoes. On a medium-low flame continue to sauté for 7 to 8 minutes, until the potatoes and cauliflower have begun brown. Drain on paper towels, and set aside.
- In the same pan, heat 1½ teaspoon of oil the oil over medium heat, add the cumin seeds, and let them crackle. Add the onions, and cook for 2 minutes, until they turn translucent.
- Add the ginger-garlic paste, and cook for another 2 minutes.
- Add the chopped tomatoes, and cook for 2 minutes.
- Add turmeric powder, red chili powder, coriander powder, and amchur. Cover the skillet, and simmer for 2 to 3 minutes, and then add the potatoes and cauliflower, and mix well.
- Add chopped coriander leaves, and stir well, and then add garam masala, and simmer on medium-low heat for 5 to 6 minutes.
- Add salt, cover, and simmer on a low flame for an additional 6 to 7 minutes, or until the potatoes and cauliflower are tender.
- Garnish with coriander leaves, and serve.

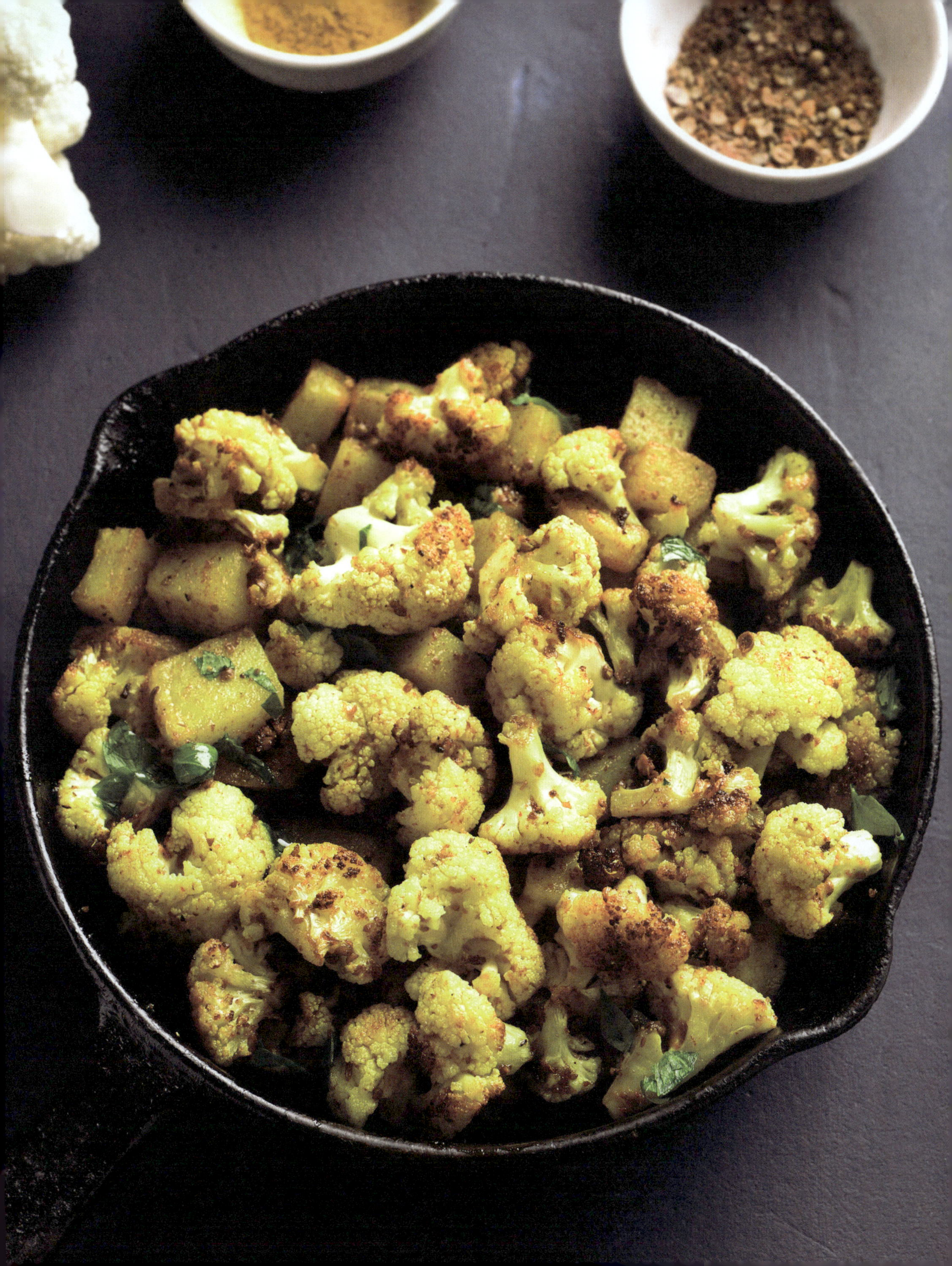

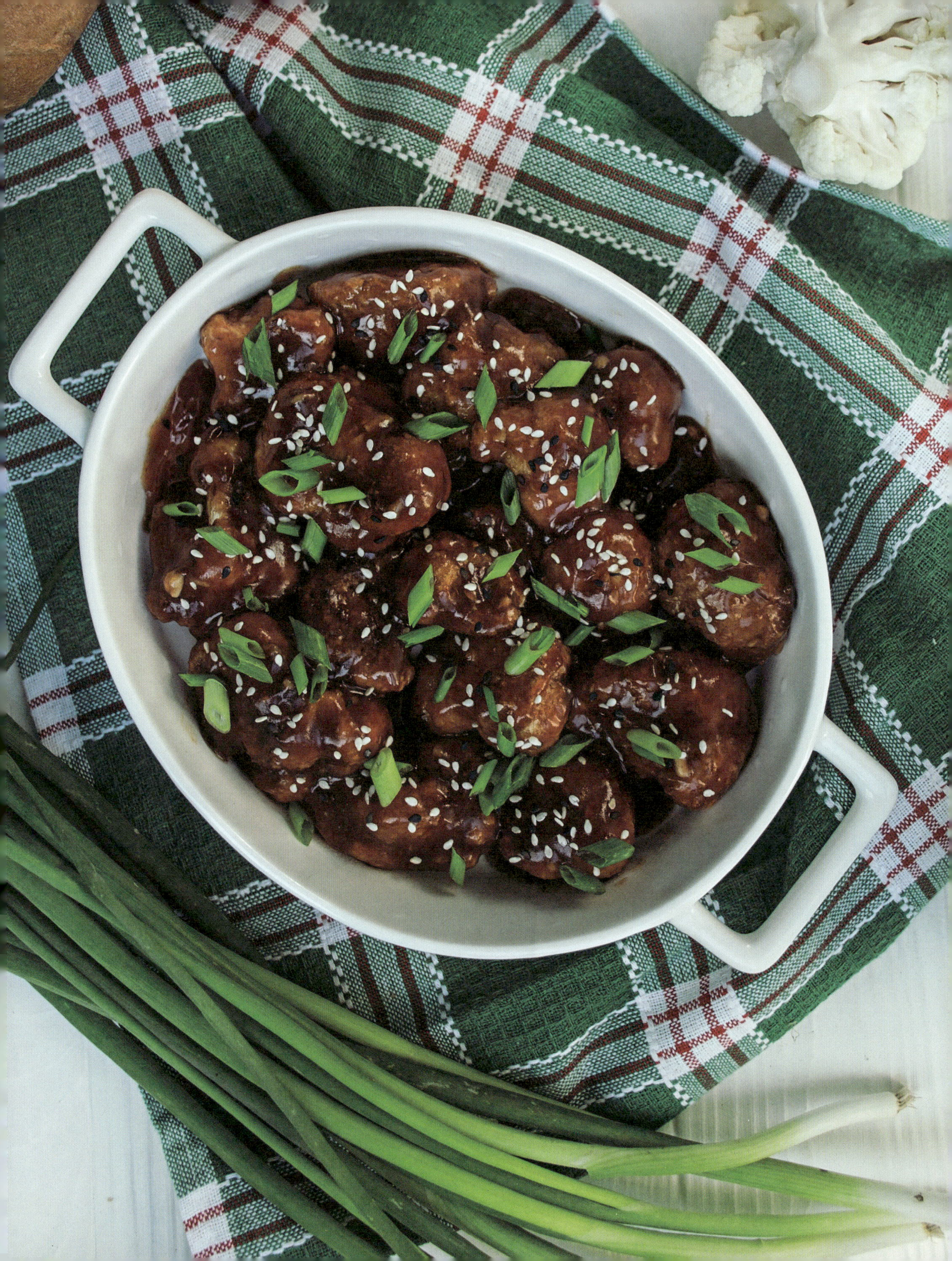

SESAME CAULIFLOWER

Sweet and sticky, this vegan cauliflower recipe evokes Chinese takeout—but is far healthier for you.

SERVES: 3–4 · PREP TIME: 5 MINUTES · COOK TIME: 25 MINUTES

INGREDIENTS

- 1 small head cauliflower
- ⅓ cup (80mL) low-sodium soy sauce
- ¼ cup (60mL) pure maple syrup, honey, or agave syrup
- ¼ cup (60mL) rice vinegar
- 1 tablespoon minced garlic
- ½ teaspoon toasted sesame oil
- ½ teaspoon powdered ginger
- 1½ tablespoon cornstarch or arrowroot
- ¼ cup (60mL) water
- sesame seeds, for garnish
- spring onion, chopped, for garnish

CONTAINS
- SOY
- SUGAR

FREE FROM
- GLUTEN
- NUTS

METHOD
- STOVETOP
- OVEN BAKE

DIRECTIONS

- Preheat oven to 450°F (230°C), and grease a baking pan.
- Wash cauliflower, and cut into bite-sized florets. Arrange florets in a single layer on the greased pan. Bake 10 minutes on the center rack.
- While the cauliflower is baking, whisk together the soy sauce, sweetener, vinegar, garlic, sesame oil, and ginger in a saucepan. Bring to a boil.
- While the sauce mixture heats, stir together the cornstarch and water until cornstarch fully dissolves, and then slowly whisk into the saucepan as soon as reaches a boil.
- Lower heat to medium, and cook 2 minutes, stirring more frequently once it returns to a boil. Cook until thick.
- Flip cauliflower florets, and bake 10 additional minutes. For crispier florets, move the pan to the top rack and broil for the final 1 to 2 minutes.
- Remove from oven, place in serving bowl, and pour sauce over florets, tossing to coat evenly.
- Sprinkle sesame seeds and spring onion on top, and serve with rice or in lettuce cups.

PAD THAI

This Thai classic combines crispy tofu with rice noodles, fresh vegetables, and fragrant herbs.

FIVE INGREDIENTS

SERVES: 2 · PREP TIME: 10 MINUTES · COOK TIME: 10–15 MINUTES

INGREDIENTS

- 7 ounces (200g) pack rice noodles
- ½ cup (124g) extra-firm tofu, cubed
- 2 tablespoons sesame oil
- ¼ cup–½ cup (60–120mL) water
- 1 clove garlic, finely minced
- 1 large handful chives
- 2 tablespoons soy sauce
- 1 tablespoon coconut sugar
- juice of ½ lime
- 1 cup (33g) bean sprouts
- 1 green onion, chopped
- crushed peanuts, for garnish
- lime wedges, for garnish
- cilantro, for garnish

CONTAINS
- NUTS
- SOY
- SUGAR

FREE FROM
- GLUTEN

METHOD
STOVETOP

DIRECTIONS

- Fill a large bowl with just-boiling water. Carefully submerge the rice noodles in the water, stir, and let soak for about 5 to 6 minutes, or until *al dente*). Drain noodles, toss with a little sesame oil to prevent sticking, and then set aside.
- In a large skillet, heat the sesame oil over medium-high heat. When the oil is hot, add the tofu and sauté for 2 to 3 minutes, turning the cubes until each side is golden brown.
- Push the tofu to the side of the skillet, lower the heat to medium, and add the garlic, soy sauce, coconut sugar, and lime juice.
- Slowly add water to the skillet, 1 to 2 tablespoons at a time, to prevent the noodles from sticking.
- Turn the heat to low, and add the bean sprouts and chives, and mix together.
- To serve, divide the mixture between two plate, and then garnish with crushed peanuts, cilantro, and lime wedges.

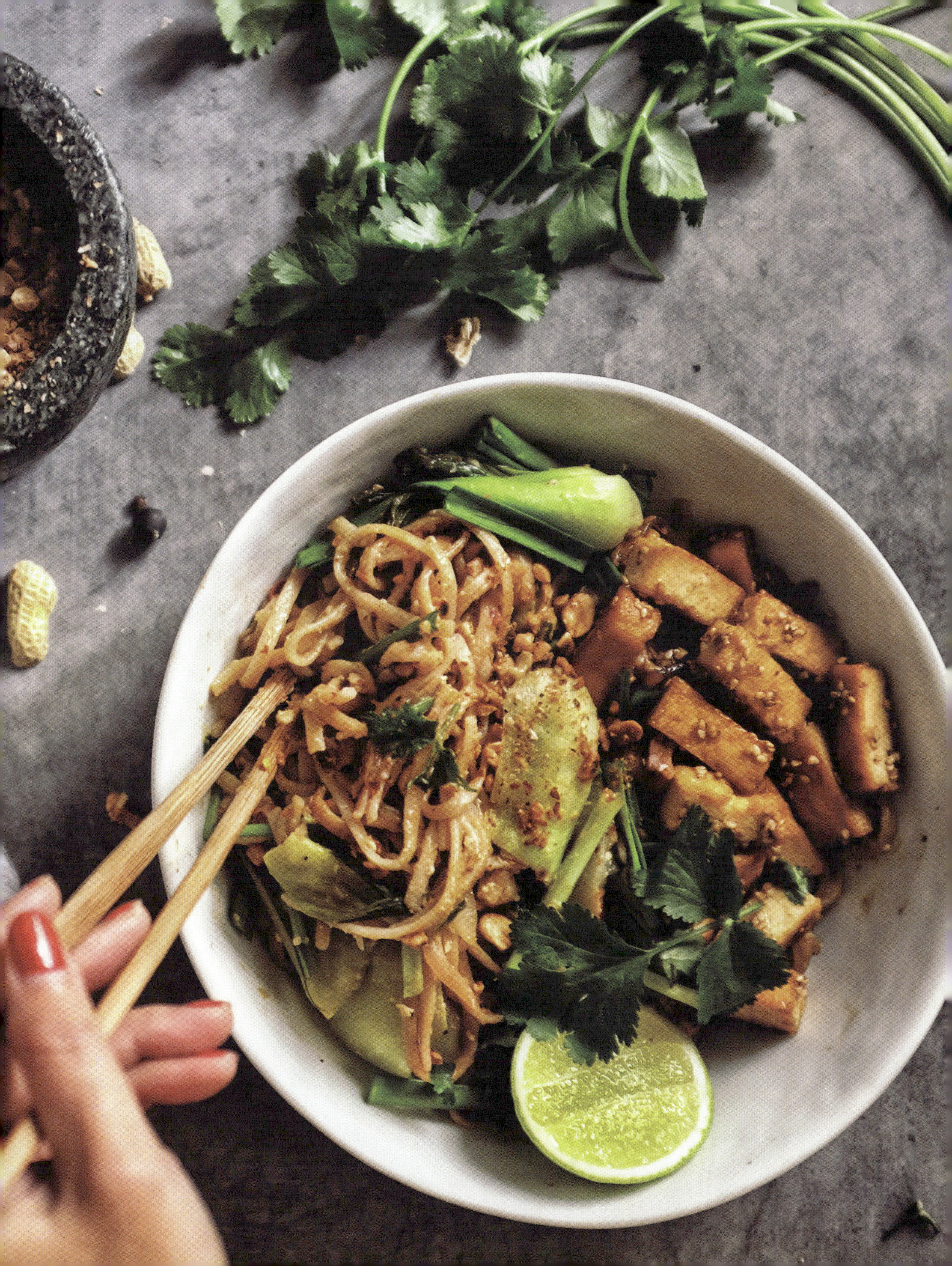

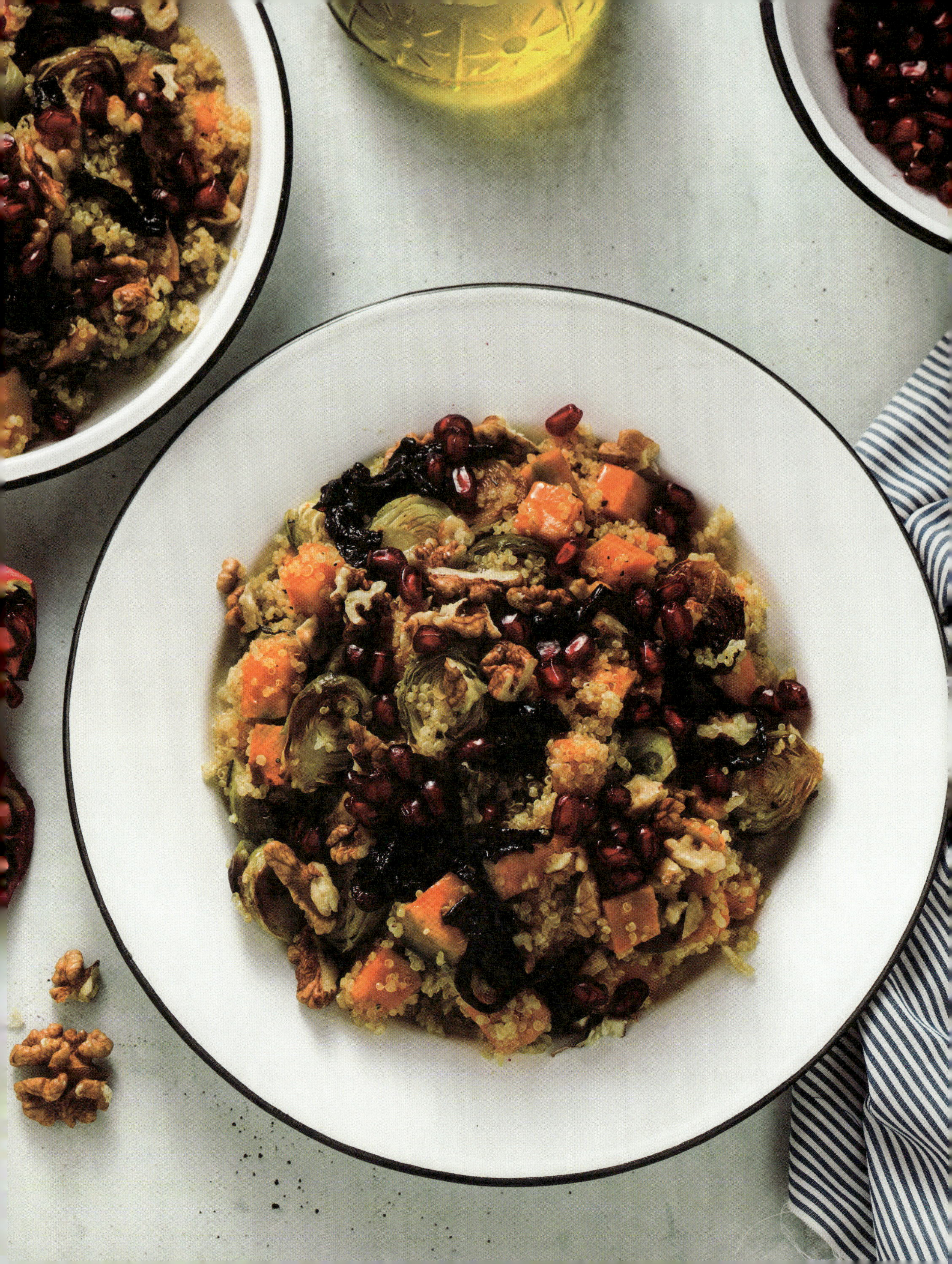

BRUSSELS SPROUTS & KABOCHA SQUASH QUINOA SALAD

This festive autumn salad gets its depth of flavor from roasted vegetables and caramelized onions.

SERVES: 4–6 · PREP TIME: 20–30 MINUTES · COOK TIME: 35 MINUTES

INGREDIENTS

- 2½ cups (250g) brussels sprouts, halved
- 1 kabocha or acorn squash, skin removed and cut into bite-sized pieces
- 1 onion, thinly sliced
- ¼ cup + 1 tablespoons (75mL) olive oil
- 1 cup (175g) quinoa
- 1¾ cups (420mL) water
- ¾ cup (130g) pomegranate seeds
- ½ cup (56g) walnuts, chopped
- sea salt, to taste
- ground pepper, to taste

DIRECTIONS

- Preheat oven to 400°F (200°C).
- Place the halved brussels sprouts and squash cubes in a large bowl. Add ¼ cup (60mL) olive oil and a pinch of salt, and toss to coat.
- Arrange the brussels sprouts and squash in a single layer on a baking sheet, season with salt and pepper to taste, and then roast for 25 to 35 minutes, or until browned.
- While the brussels sprouts and squash roast, heat 1 tablespoon olive oil in a frying pan over medium-high, add the onions and a pinch of salt, and sauté, stirring frequently until the onion is soft and brown, about 20 minutes. Set aside when caramelized.
- While vegetable roast and onions cook, bring a medium saucepan to medium heat to lightly toast the quinoa and remove any excess water, stirring constantly. Add water, set burner on high, and bring to a boil. Reduce heat to low, cover, and simmer with the lid slightly ajar for 12 to 15 minutes, or until quinoa is fluffy.
- Transfer quinoa to a serving bowl, add the brussels sprouts, squash, and chopped walnuts, and toss to combine.
- To serve, sprinkle with the pomegranate seeds.

CONTAINS

- NUTS
- SEEDS

FREE FROM

- GLUTEN
- SUGAR

METHOD

OVEN ROAST
STOVETOP

OPEN-FACED BEETROOT HUMMUS SANDWICH WITH POMEGRANATE & CORN SALSA

Vibrant beetroot hummus forms an earthy base for this fresh blend of crunchy veggies and piquant salsa.

SERVES: 2 · PREP TIME: 10 MINUTES · TOTAL TIME: 10 MINUTES

INGREDIENTS

- 2 large slices of hearty multigrain bread
- ¾ cup (180g) beetroot hummus
- 1 small English cucumber, sliced
- ½ tomato, chopped
- 2 large lettuce leaves
- 1 tablespoon fresh dill, chopped
- 1–2 radishes, sliced

For salsa:
- ½ cup (75g) fresh corn kernels
- ¾ cup (130g) pomegranate seeds
- ½ tablespoon cilantro, chopped
- 1 tablespoon black sesame seeds
- juice of ½ fresh lime
- salt, to taste

CONTAINS
- GLUTEN
- SEEDS

FREE FROM
- NUTS
- SUGAR

METHOD
ASSEMBLY

DIRECTIONS

- To make the salsa, place the corn kernels, pomegranate seeds, sesame, seeds, and cilantro in a small bowl.
- Squeeze the lime juice over all the ingredients, add salt to taste, and toss to completely coat all ingredients. Add the salt, and then toss to coat. Set aside.
- Evenly spread the beetroot hummus on each slice of bread.
- Layer a lettuce leave over the hummus, and then spoon some of the chopped tomatoes over the lettuce.
- Arrange cucumber and radish slices over the tomatoes, and then spoon the pomegranate and corn salsa over each.
- Sprinkle with fresh dill, and serve.

CHEF'S TIPS

- For a homemade beetroot hummus, *see* page 116.

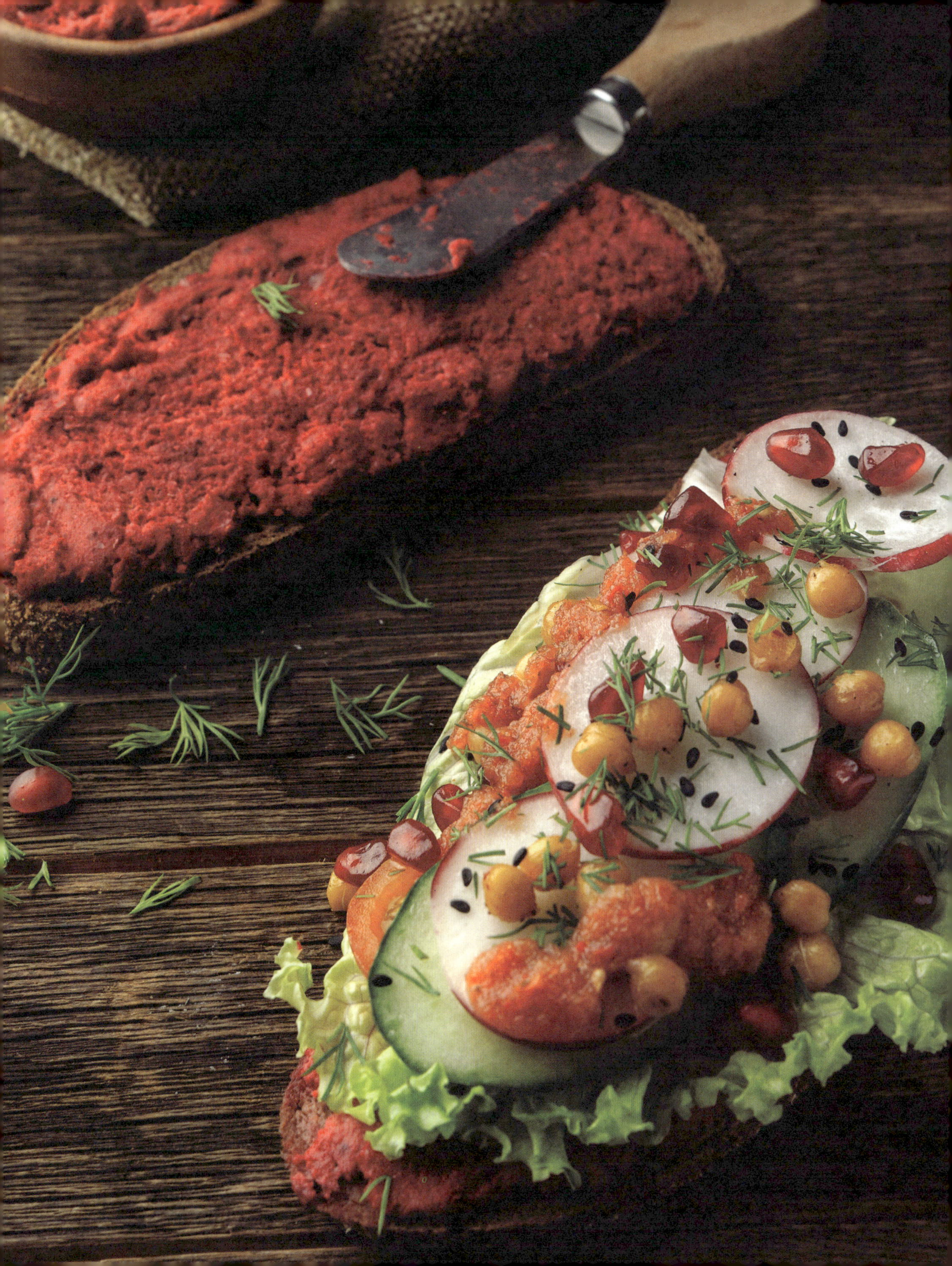

BRUSCHETTA WITH BEETROOT HUMMUS, CHOPPED NUTS & MICROGREENS

A fast and easy open-faced sandwich makes a delicious and nutritious lunch.

SERVES: 2 · PREP TIME: 5-10 MINUTES · TOTAL TIME: 5-10 MINUTES

INGREDIENTS

- 2 large slices of crusty Italian or French bead
- ½ cup (120g) beetroot hummus
- 2-3 tablespoons walnuts, finely chopped
- a large handful of microgreens
- salt, to taste

DIRECTIONS

- Toast the bread, and then evenly spread the beetroot hummus on each slice of toast.
- Sprinkle each with nuts and microgreens.
- Add salt to taste and serve.

CHEF'S TIPS

- For a homemade beetroot hummus, *see* page 66.

FIVE INGREDIENTS

CONTAINS
- GLUTEN
- NUTS

FREE FROM
- SUGAR

METHOD
- TOASTER
- ASSEMBLY

AVOCADO-POMEGRANATE SWEET POTATO TOAST

Serve these easy open-face sandwiches for a quick and nourishing vegan breakfast, lunch, or snack.

SERVES: 2–4 · PREP TIME: 10 MINUTES · COOK TIME: 25 MINUTES

INGREDIENTS

- 1 medium sweet potato
- 1 ripe avocado, pitted and peeled
- juice of ½ to 1 lime, to taste
- ⅓ cup (58g) pomegranate seeds
- ¼ cup (30g) crushed toasted hazelnuts

DIRECTIONS

- Preheat oven to 375°F (190°C), and line a baking tray with parchment paper.
- Wash the sweet potato, and then slice it lengthwise into 4 slices
- Spread the sweet potato slices in a single layer on the baking tray, and bake for 20 to 25 minutes, or until tender.
- While the sweet potatoes bake, slice the avocados in half, remove the pits and skin, and place in a medium mixing bowl. Mash with the back of a fork until it is chunky. Mix in salt and lime juice, and gently mash again to incorporate.
- Generously spread mashed avocado on each sweet potato toast, and then top with the pomegranate seeds and hazelnuts. Season with a pinch of sea salt, if desired, and serve immediately.

CONTAINS

- NUTS
- SEEDS

FREE FROM

- GLUTEN
- SUGAR

METHOD

OVEN BAKE
ASSEMBLY

TOMATO & AVOCADO TOAST

Combine two kinds of tomatoes—fresh cherry and sun-dried—to brighten tasty avocado toast.

SERVES: 2 · PREP TIME: 5–10 MINUTES · TOTAL TIME: 5–10 MINUTES

INGREDIENTS

- 2 slices thick-sliced whole-grain bread
- 1 ripe avocado
- 4 tablespoons sun-dried tomatoes
- 2 cherry tomatoes
- 2–4 lettuce leaves, such as baby spinach or arugula
- ⅛ teaspoon salt, or to taste
- freshly ground black pepper, to taste
- dried basil, to taste

DIRECTIONS

- Toast the bread until golden and firm.
- Slice the cherry tomatoes.
- Slice the avocado in half, remove the pit and skin, and place in a medium mixing bowl. Mash with a fork until it is chunky. Mix in salt.
- Spread avocado on top of the toast. Layer with lettuce, sun-dried tomatoes, and sliced cherry tomatoes.
- Garnish with basil and pepper to taste, and serve immediately.

FREE FROM

- GLUTEN
- NUTS
- SUGAR

METHOD

OVEN BAKE

ASSEMBLY

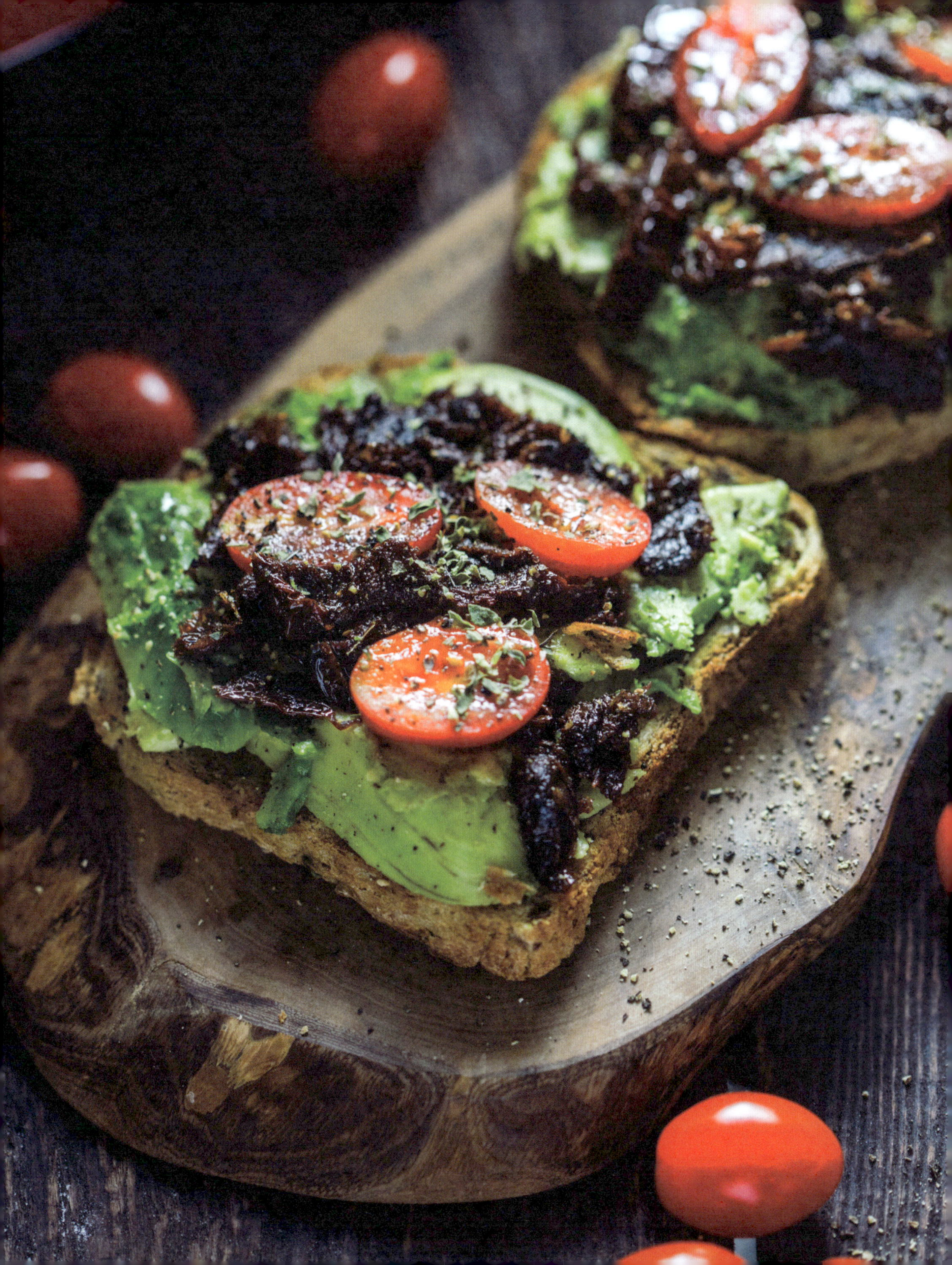

ROASTED BRUSSELS SPROUTS, PECAN & CRANBERRY QUINOA SALAD

Roasted brussels sprouts get a lift from nutty pecans and tart cranberries in this main dish salad.

SERVES: 4–6 · PREP TIME: 10 MINUTES · COOK TIME: 35 MINUTES

INGREDIENTS

- 2½ cups (250g) brussels sprouts, halved
- 3 tablespoons olive oil
- 1 cup (175g) quinoa
- 1¾ cups (420mL) water
- 1 head romaine lettuce
- ½ head radicchio, broken into individual leaves
- ½ cup (50g) pecans, halved
- ¼ cup (25g) dried cranberries
- sea salt, to taste
- ground pepper, to taste

DIRECTIONS

- Preheat oven to 400°F (200°C).
- Place the halved brussels sprouts in a large bowl, and with 2 tablespoons of the olive oil and a sprinkle of salt. Toss to coat.
- Arrange the brussels sprouts in a single layer on a baking sheet, season with salt and pepper to taste, and then roast for 25 to 35 minutes, or until browned.
- While the brussels sprouts roast, bring a medium saucepan to medium heat to lightly toast the quinoa and remove any excess water, stirring constantly. Add water, set burner on high, and bring to a boil. Reduce heat to low, cover, and simmer with the lid slightly ajar for 12 to 15 minutes, or until quinoa is fluffy.
- Transfer quinoa to a serving bowl, add the brussels sprouts, radicchio, romaine, lettuce. pecan halves, and cranberries, and toss to combine well.
- To serve, sprinkle with salt and freshly ground pepper to taste.

CONTAINS

NUTS

FREE FROM

GLUTEN

SUGAR

METHOD

STOVETOP

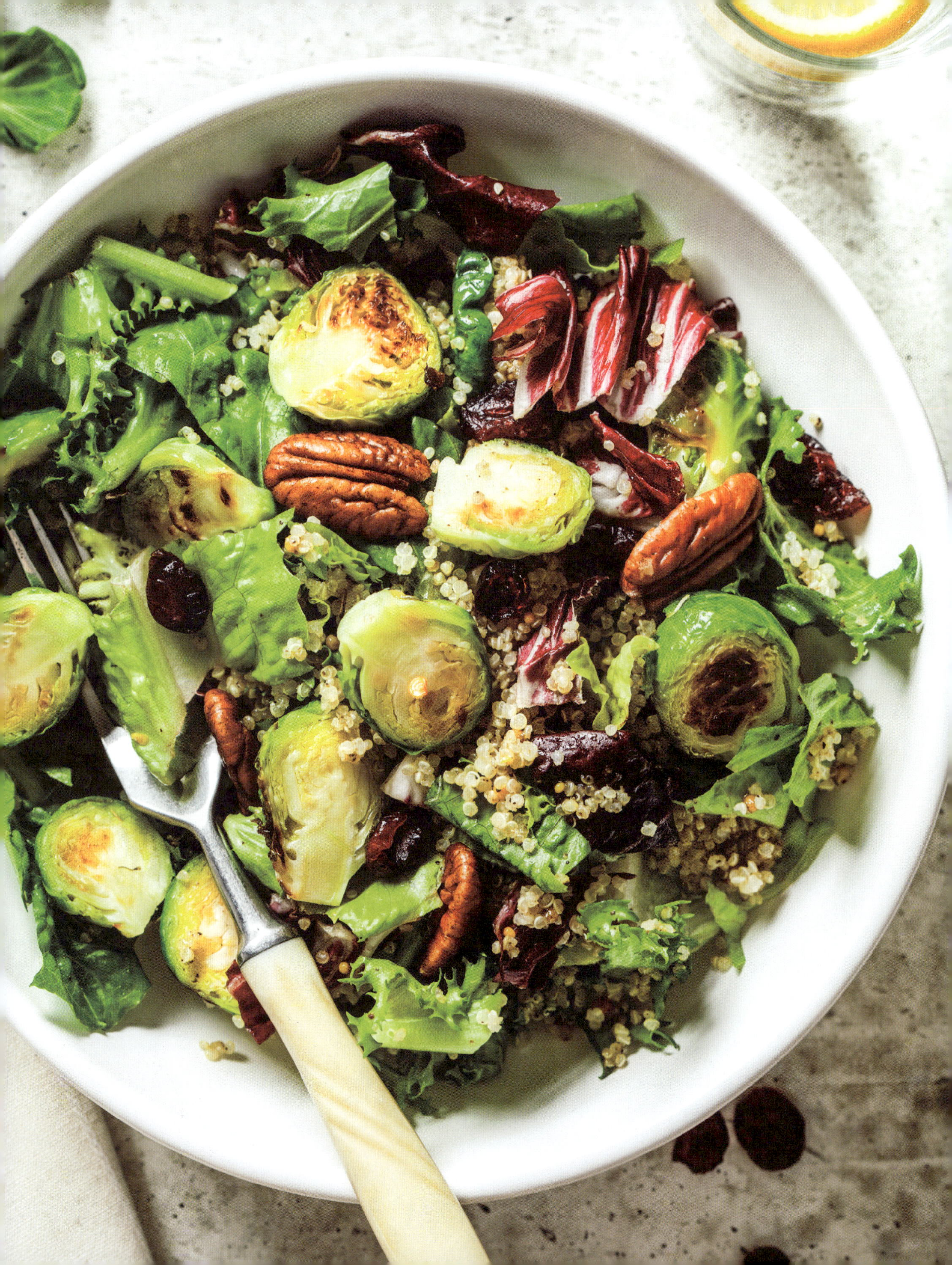

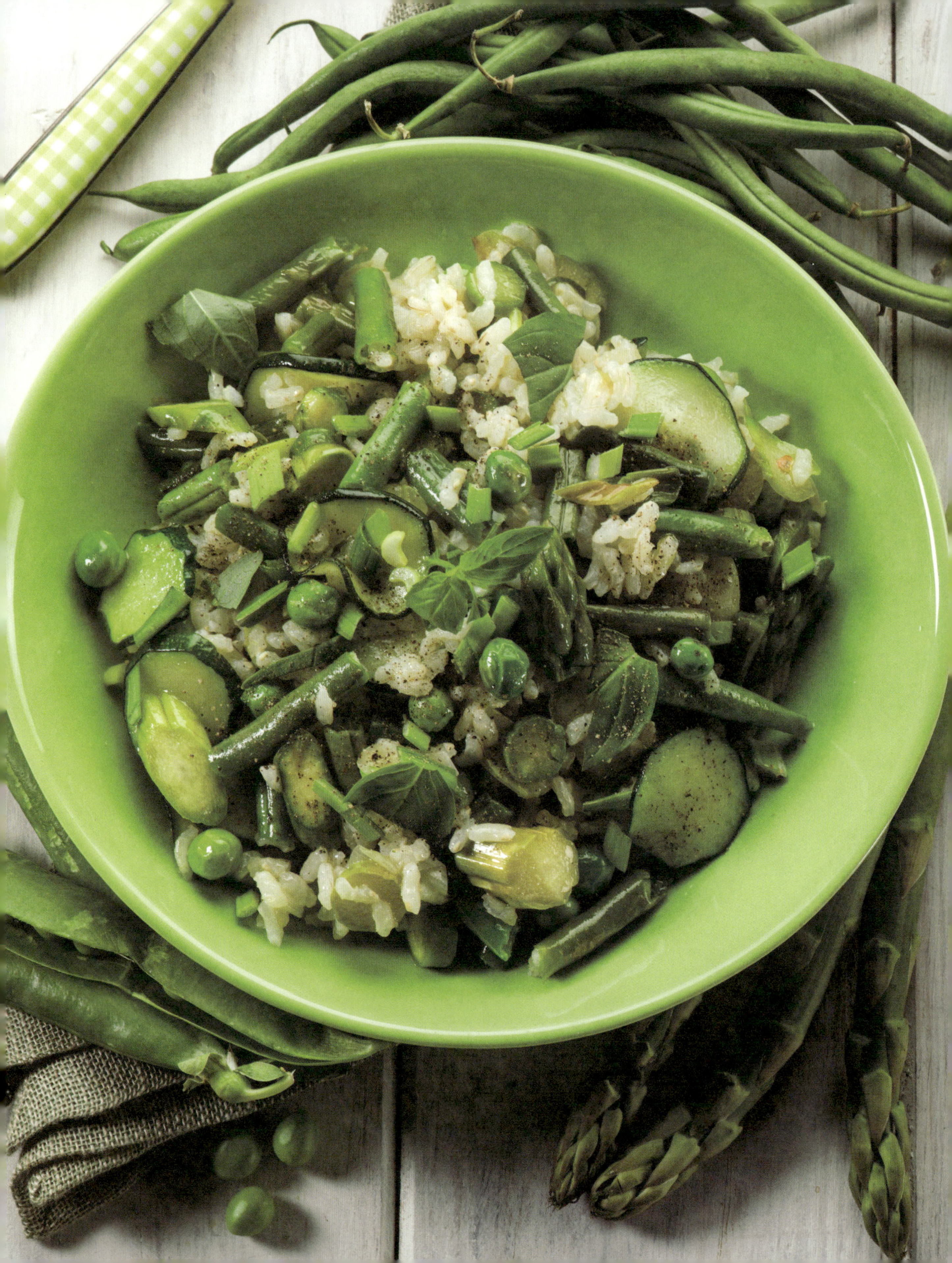

SPRING VEGGIE RISOTTO

Serve this creamy vegan risotto as a light springtime lunch or as a side dish for a heartier meal.

SERVES: 4–6 · PREP TIME: 10 MINUTES · COOK TIME: 1 HOUR 15 MINUTES

INGREDIENTS

5 tablespoons olive oil
1 onion, diced
3 garlic cloves, minced
1½ cups (300g) short-grain rice
⅓ cup (80 mL) white wine
4 cups (960 mL) vegetable broth
1 cup (150g) frozen peas, thawed
1 bunch asparagus
½ pound (226g) green beans
1 large zucchini
salt to taste
black pepper to taste

FREE FROM

- GLUTEN
- NUTS
- SUGAR

METHOD

STOVETOP

DIRECTIONS

- Cut the asparagus, green beans, and zucchini into bite-size pieces.

- In a saucepan, bring ¼ cup of the vegetable broth and the green beans to a boil, and then cook until the beans are tender, about 10 minutes. With a slotted spoon, remove the green beans, and set them aside. Add the remaining broth, cover, and keep warm.

- In a soup pot, heat 2 tablespoons of the oil over medium-high heat, and then sauté the onion for about 2 minutes. Add the garlic and sauté for another minute. Add the rice and toast for 1 to 2 minutes, stirring constantly. Add the white wine to deglaze the pan, and bring to a simmer, cooking until all liquid is absorbed.

- Add one cup of the vegetable broth. Stirring often, cook the rice until the broth is nearly absorbed. Adding broth one cup at time, repeat the process until the rice is tender, about 30 minutes.

- While the rice cooks, heat 3 tablespoons of the oil in a skillet. Add the asparagus and sauté for 4 minutes. Add in the zucchini, and continue to cook until the zucchini is golden and the asparagus is tender, about 4 to 5 minutes.

- When the rice is almost done cooking, add in the peas. Add in the green beans, asparagus, and zucchini. Serve warm, seasoning with salt and pepper to taste.

CHEF'S TIPS

- For a homemade vegetable broth, *see* page 42.

- For a creamier risotto, stir in ⅓ cup (65g) nutritional yeast flakes after you add the peas.

RATATOUILLE

This French classic features layered veggies flavored with tomato sauce and aromatic Provençal herbs.

SERVES: 4–6 · PREP TIME: 15 MINUTES · COOK TIME: 1 HOUR

INGREDIENTS

- 2 tablespoons olive oil
- 2 cloves garlic, minced
- 1 white onion, finely diced
- 1 15-ounce (424g) can crushed tomatoes
- 3 medium zucchinis
- 1 medium eggplant
- 5 medium Roma tomatoes
- ¼ teaspoon dried rosemary, crushed in a spice grinder
- ¼ teaspoon dried oregano
- ¼ teaspoon dried marjoram
- ½ teaspoon dried thyme
- ¼ teaspoon dried tarragon
- 1 tablespoon fresh basil, chopped
- ½ teaspoon salt
- ¼ teaspoon red pepper flakes
- ¼ teaspoon black pepper

CONTAINS
- CHILIS

FREE FROM
- GLUTEN
- NUTS
- SUGAR

METHOD
- STOVETOP
- OVEN BAKE

DIRECTIONS

- Preheat oven to 350°F (176°C).
- In a skillet, heat 1 tablespoon of the oil over medium heat, and then sauté the onion and garlic until onion softens, about 5 minutes. Add crushed tomatoes, and gently simmer uncovered until tomatoes have the texture of a thick paste, about 10 minutes.
- While tomatoes simmer, thinly slice unpeeled zucchini, eggplant, and tomatoes into ⅛-inch (3mm) thick slices
- Remove tomato mixture from heat, and stir in herbs.
- To assemble, spread tomato mixture in the bottom of a large casserole dish. Working from the outer edge, layer veggie slices on top of the sauce in an alternating pattern.
- Brush veggies with remaining olive oil, and bake for 1 hour, or until veggies are tender.
- Serve warm with French bread.

CHEF'S TIPS

- You can substitute the individual herbs with 1 to 2 tablespoons of a prepared herbes de Provence.

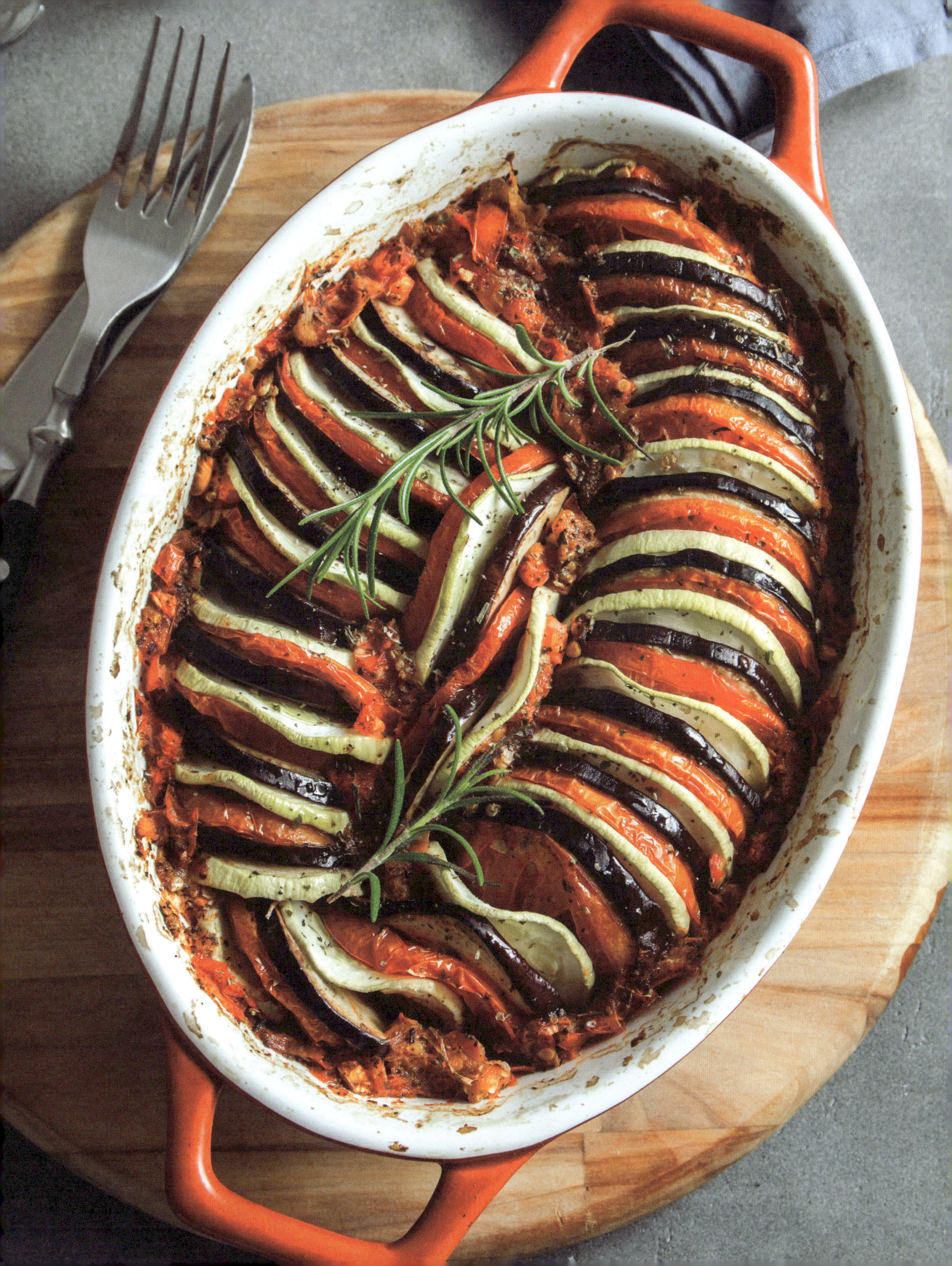

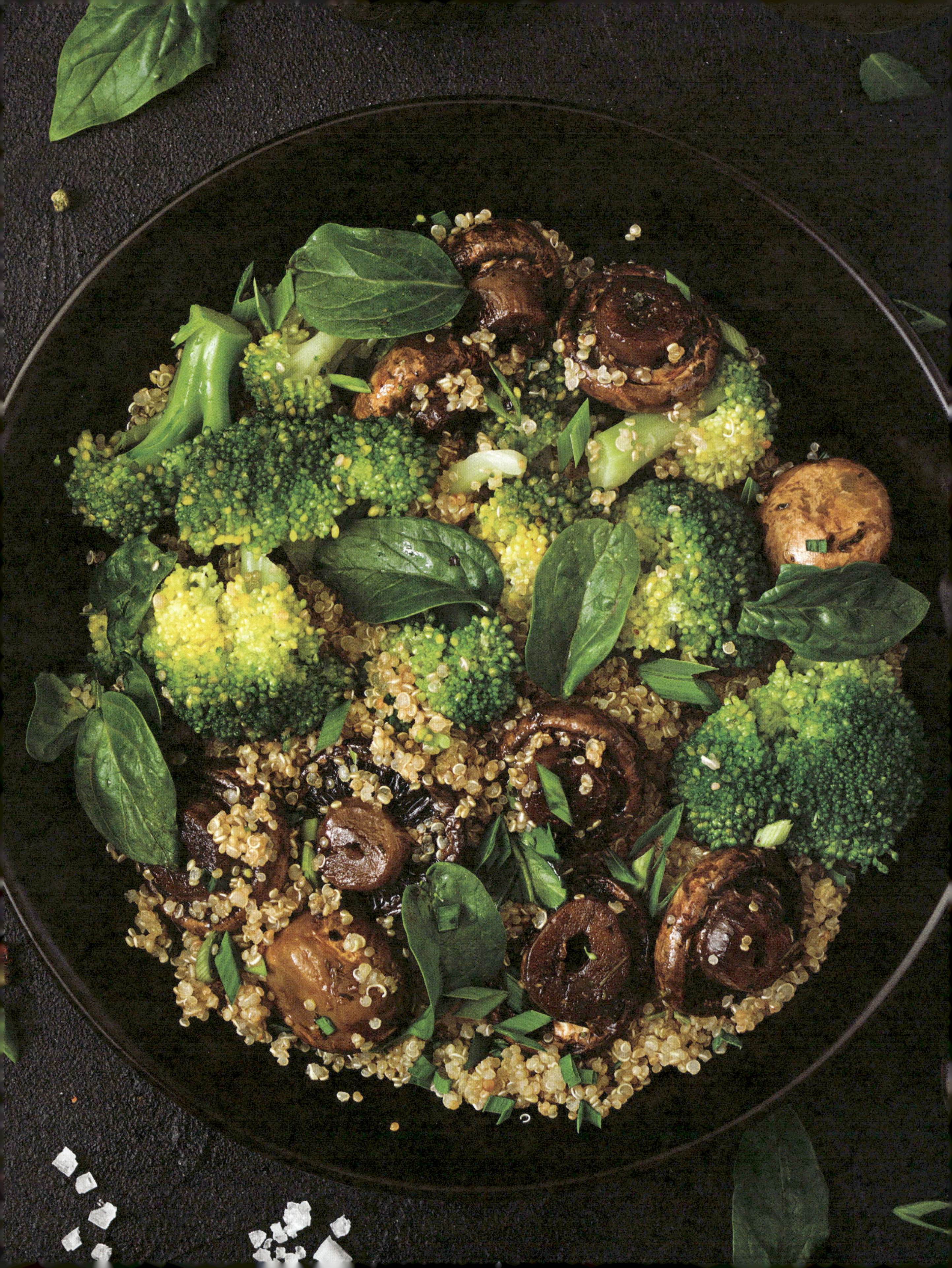

QUINOA WITH BROCCOLI, MUSHROOMS & SPINACH

Nutty-flavored quinoa forms a base for mushrooms and healthy green veggies.

SERVES: 2-4 · PREP TIME: 5 MINUTES · COOK TIME: 25 MINUTES

INGREDIENTS

- 1½ cups (265g) quinoa, rinsed and drained
- 2 tablespoons extra-virgin olive oil
- 1 small onion, chopped
- 2 cloves garlic, minced
- ½ teaspoon salt
- ½ teaspoon black pepper
- 2 dry pints (320g) mushrooms, sliced
- 3 cups broccoli florets
- 3-4 tablespoons fresh basil, finely chopped
- 4 ounces (114g) baby spinach leaves

FREE FROM
- GLUTEN
- NUTS
- SUGAR

METHOD

STOVETOP

DIRECTIONS

- Bring medium saucepan to medium heat to lightly toast the quinoa and remove any excess water, stirring constantly.
- Add water, set burner on high, and bring to a boil. Reduce heat to low, cover, and simmer with the lid slightly ajar for 12 to 15 minutes, or until quinoa is fluffy and all the liquid has been absorbed. Place cooked quinoa in a serving bowl.
- While the quinoa cooks, heat the olive oil over medium heat, and then sauté the onions, garlic, salt, and pepper, until softened and slightly golden, about 2 to 3 minutes.
- Add the mushrooms, and continue cooking until golden, about 2 to 3 minutes.
- Add the broccoli, and cook for about 30 seconds, until its vibrant green and slightly softened with a nice crunch to it.
- Add the mushroom and broccoli mixture to the quinoa.
- Top with fresh spinach leaves, and serve warm or cold as a side dish or salad.

CHEF'S TIPS

- You can store leftovers in the fridge for several days.

TABBOULEH SALAD

The cooling taste of mint makes this traditional Eastern Mediterranean dish a refreshing summer salad.

SERVES: 4–6 · PREP TIME: 20 MINUTES · CHILL TIME: 30 MINUTES

INGREDIENTS

- ½ cup extra fine bulgur wheat
- 4 Roma tomatoes
- 2 bunches parsley
- 12–15 fresh mint leaves,
- 1 red onion
- 3–4 tablespoons lemon juice
- 3–4 tablespoons extra-virgin olive oil
- salt, to taste

DIRECTIONS

- Wash the bulgur wheat, and soak it in water for 5 to 7 minutes. Drain very well, and set aside.
- Very finely chop the tomatoes and onion. Place the tomatoes in a colander to drain excess juice. Wash and thoroughly dry the parsley and mint, remove the stems, and chop very finely.
- Place the chopped vegetables and herbs in a serving bowl, and mix gently. Add the lemon juice and olive oil, and mix again. Cover, and refrigerate for 30 minutes.
- Serve with a side of pita.

FREE FROM

- GLUTEN
- NUTS
- SUGAR

METHOD

ASSEMBLY

TERIYAKI TEMPEH BOWL

The quick and easy meal features tempeh coated in tangy ginger-and-garlic infused teriyaki sauce.

SERVES: 2 · PREP TIME: 10 MINUTES · COOK TIME: 25 MINUTES

INGREDIENTS

- 1 head broccoli, cut into florets
- ⅓ cup (62g) rice
- 2 tablespoons cornstarch
- ¼ cup (60mL) soy sauce
- 1 tablespoon sweet rice wine
- 1 tablespoon brown sugar
- 1 clove garlic, minced
- 1 teaspoon fresh ginger, grated
- 1 8-ounce (277g) package organic tempeh
- 2 tablespoons coconut oil
- 1 scallion, minced
- sesame seeds, for garnish

DIRECTIONS

- Place a steamer insert into a saucepan and fill with water to just below the bottom of the steamer. Bring water to a boil. Add broccoli, cover, and steam until tender, 3 to 5 minutes. Set aside.
- Add rice and ⅓ cups (160 mL) water to a medium saucepan, and bring to a boil over high heat. Lower heat to a simmer, and cover. Simmer until water is completely absorbed and rice is tender, about 15 to 25 minutes. Fluff with a fork, replace the lid, and let rest for about 10 minutes.
- While the rice cooks, in a small bowl, whisk together the cornstarch and ¼ cup(60mL) water. Set aside.
- In a saucepan, add 1 cup (240mL) water, soy sauce, rice wine, brown sugar, garlic, and ginger. Bring to a simmer, and then stir in the cornstarch. Stir for another minute, as the sauce begins to thicken. Turn off heat, and set aside to cool and further thicken.
- As the sauce cools, chop tempeh into small squares. Heat coconut oil in a skillet until melted. Add the tempeh, and stir fry until golden brown. Turn off heat, and add the sauce to the tempeh in the skillet and toss to coat.
- Serve in bowls with rice and broccoli garnished with minced scallions and sesame seeds.

CONTAINS
- SEEDS
- SOY

FREE FROM
- GLUTEN
- NUTS
- SUGAR

METHOD

STOVETOP

BARBEQUE TEMPEH SKEWERS

These sweet and smoky tempeh skewers make a tangy summertime main dish.

SERVES: 4–8 · PREP TIME: 2–24 HOURS · COOK TIME: 8 MINUTES

INGREDIENTS

- 1 8-ounce (277g) package organic tempeh
- 3 tablespoons lemon juice
- 2 tablespoons extra-virgin olive oil
- 2 tablespoons tamari soy sauce
- 1 tablespoon chili powder
- 1 tablespoon smoked paprika
- 2 cloves garlic, minced
- 1 teaspoon dried oregano
- 1 tablespoon hot sauce

DIRECTIONS

- Slice the tempeh into 8 rectangles, and then place them in a medium-sized saucepan with water to cover. Bring to a simmer, and cook for 10 minutes. Drain the tempeh and pat dry. Slide a soaked bamboo or metal skewer into each one, and set aside.
- In a shallow dish, whisk together lemon juice, oil, tamari sauce, chili powder, paprika, garlic, oregano and hot sauce.
- Arrange steamed tempeh skewers in the dish, turn to completely coat with marinade, and then cover and refrigerate, turning halfway through, for at least 2 hours or overnight.
- Prepare a grill for medium-heat cooking. Place tempeh on the grill, and cook for about 4 minutes. Flip and then cook for another 4 minutes until browned and hot throughout.
- Remove from the grill, and transfer to a plate, and serve warm with rice, veggies, and your preferred sauce.

CHEF'S TIPS

- You can also oven bake the tempeh. Heat oven to 350°F (180°C), place on a baking sheet, and bake for 30 minutes until browned and heated through, turning once and basting frequently.

CONTAINS

- CHILIS
- SOY

FREE FROM

- GLUTEN
- NUTS
- SUGAR

METHOD

STOVETOP
GRILL

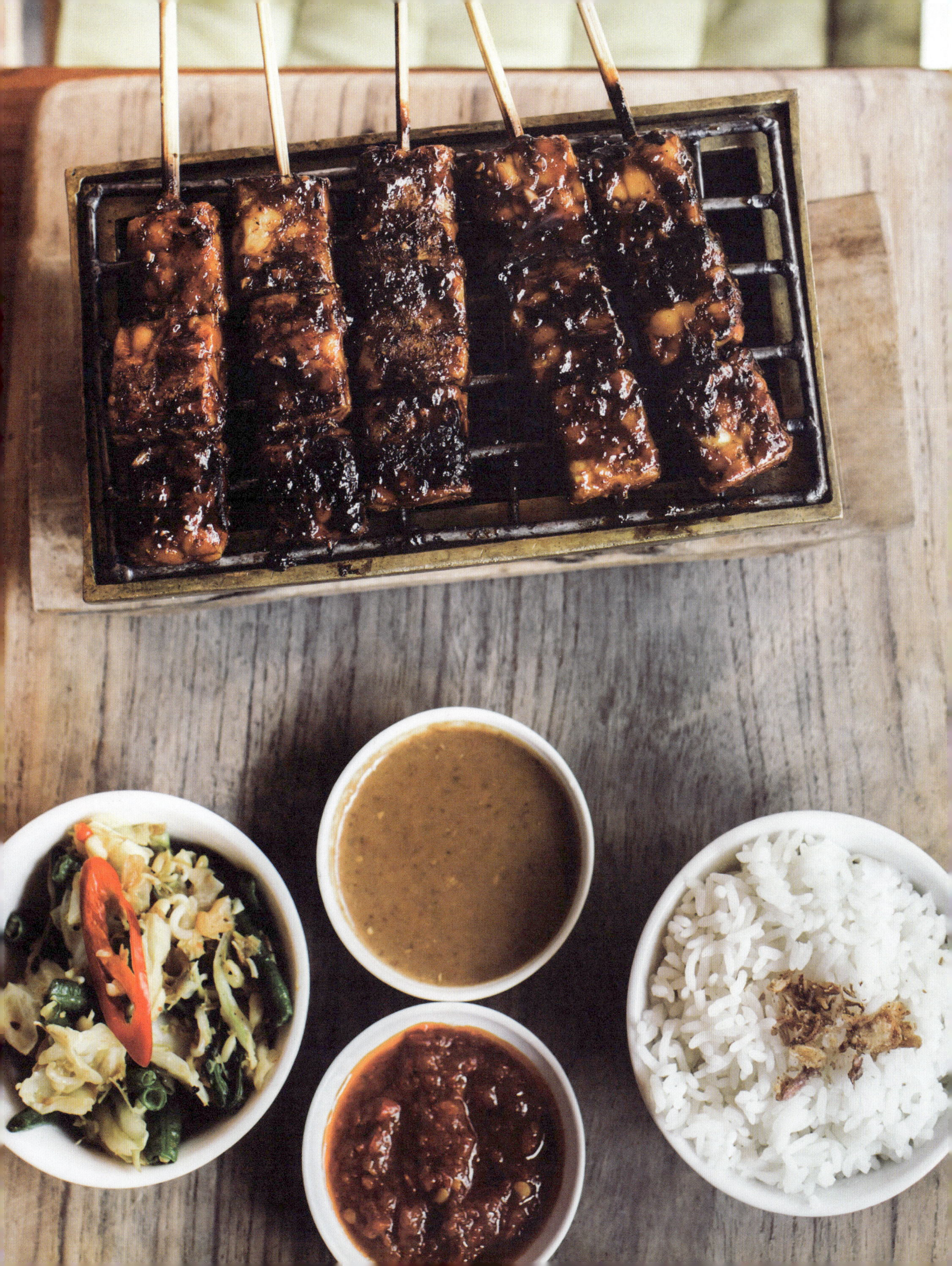

BASIL PESTO

Capture the taste of summertime herbs with this classic Italian pasta sauce.

SERVES: 8 · PREP TIME: 5 MINUTES · TOTAL TIME: 5 MINUTES

INGREDIENTS

- 3 cups (60g) fresh basil leaves
- ½ cup (67g) toasted pine nuts
- 2 cloves garlic, peeled and chopped
- 2 tablespoons white miso paste
- ½ cup (120mL) extra-virgin olive oil
- 2 tablespoons lemon juice
- salt, to taste
- ground black pepper, to taste

DIRECTIONS

- Place all ingredients, except the olive oil, in a blender or food processor. With the motor running, drizzle in the olive oil until you have a coarse but grainy and consistent paste. Taste, and add more salt and pepper, if needed.
- Serve over your favorite pasta or use as a sandwich topping.

CONTAINS
- NUTS

FREE FROM
- GLUTEN
- SUGAR

METHOD
BLENDER

CHEF'S TIPS

- You can store leftovers pesto in an airtight container in the refrigerator for up to 3 days, or you can freeze the pesto for several months.
- You can substitute 2 tablespoons of either nutritional yeast or vegan cashew Parmesan for the white miso paste.
- You can substitute lightly toasted walnuts for the pine nuts.

TAGLIATELLE PASTA WITH SPINACH PESTO & GREEN PEAS

As pretty as it is flavorful, this fast and easy pasta dish makes a satisfyingly hearty main dish.

SERVES: 4–6 · PREP TIME: 10 MINUTES · COOK TIME: 20 MINUTES

INGREDIENTS

- 1 cup (150g) green peas
- 3 cups (90g) raw spinach
- ⅓ cup (50g) raw cashews
- 4 tablespoons nutritional yeast
- 2 cloves garlic
- 3 tablespoons lemon juice
- 12 ounces (336g) tagliatelle
- pinch of salt

DIRECTIONS

- Soak cashews in boiling water for 10 minutes, and then place them with the remaining ingredients in a blender, and blend until creamy.
- Bring a large pot of water to a boil over high heat. Season the boiling water lightly with salt. When the salt dissolves, add the tagliatelle, and cook according to package directions for al dente.
- Just before the pasta is ready, pour the spinach mixture into a skillet, and add the peas. Heat for 3 to 4 minutes. Add the cooked pasta, and stir to coat.
- Season to taste, and serve warm.

CONTAINS
- NUTS

FREE FROM
- GLUTEN
- SUGAR

METHOD
BLENDER
STOVETOP

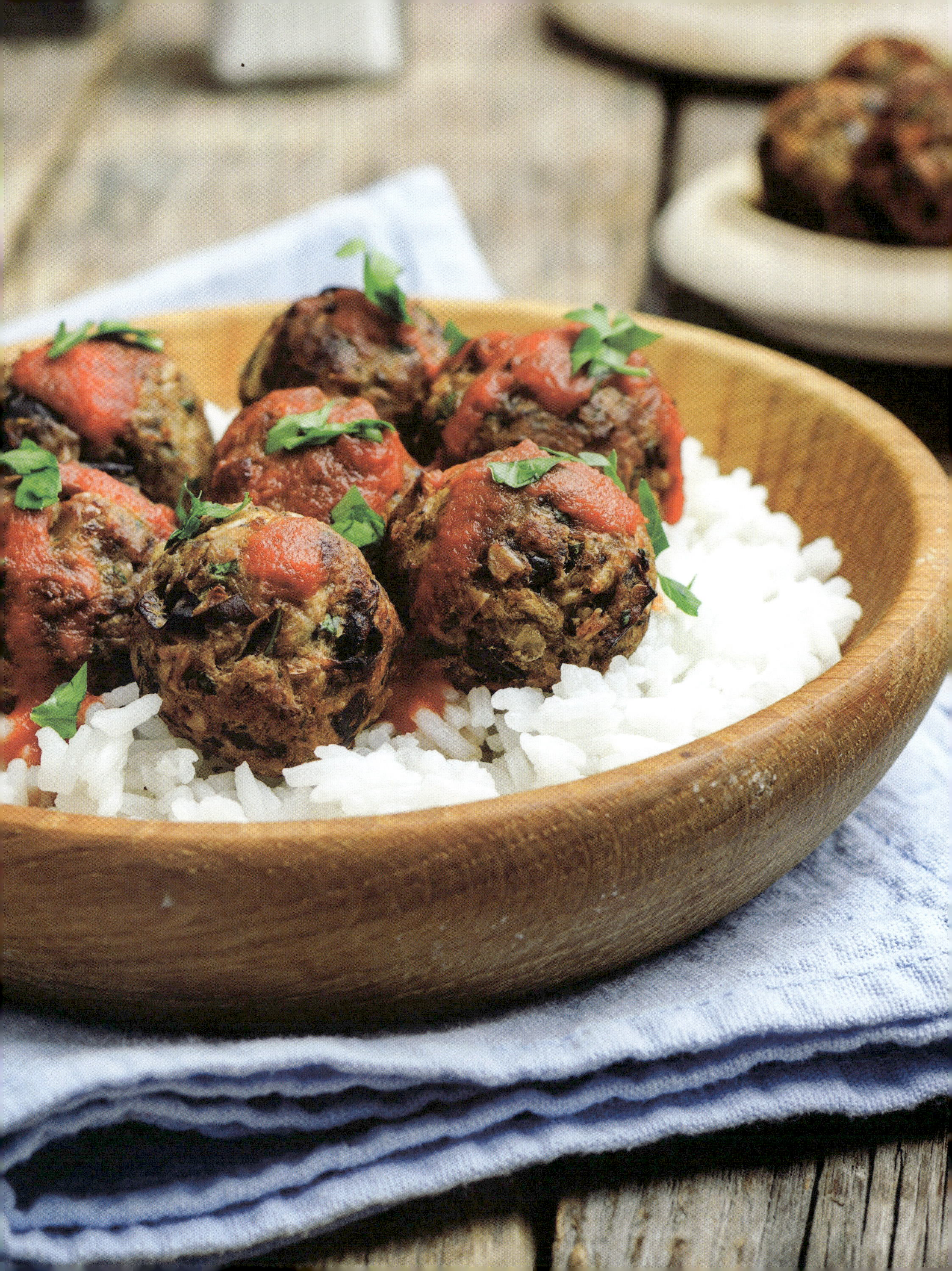

EGGPLANT MEATBALLS

Serve these savory meatballs over rice or with pasta and tomato sauce for a warming and filling supper.

SERVES: 4 · PREP TIME: 10 MINUTES · COOK TIME: 1 HOUR 10 MINUTES

INGREDIENTS

- olive oil cooking spray
- 1 tablespoon olive oil
- 1 large eggplant
- ½ cup (120mL) water
- 1 teaspoon kosher salt
- ½ teaspoon black pepper
- 1 medium onion (chopped)
- 3 cloves garlic minced
- 1 cup canned white beans, drained and rinsed
- ¼ cup fresh flat-leaf parsley
- 2 teaspoons fresh basil
- 1 cup whole-wheat breadcrumbs
- salt, to taste
- pepper, to taste

CONTAINS
GLUTEN

FREE FROM
NUTS
SUGAR

METHOD
BLENDER
STOVETOP
OVEN BAKE

DIRECTIONS

- Preheat the oven to 375°F (190°C). Spray a large rimmed baking sheet with cooking spray.
- Chop the eggplant into small cubes. Dice the onion. Coarsely chop the parsley.
- In a skillet, heat ½ tablespoon of the olive oil over medium-high heat. When hot, add the eggplant and water. Season with salt and pepper and cook, stirring occasionally until tender, about 10 to 15 minutes.
- Transfer to the bowl of a blender or food processor.
- Add the remaining oil to the skillet, and sauté the onion and garlic until the onions are translucent, about 3 to 5 minutes.
- Add the onions and garlic to the blender, along with the drained beans and parsley, and pulse until well combined, but not pureed. Combine the mixture with the breadcrumbs. Taste for salt, and then roll into 12 meatballs.
- Transfer to the prepared baking sheet and bake until firm and browned, about 25 to 30 minutes.
- Serve with rice, pasta, zucchini spirals, or spaghetti squash.

CHEF'S TIPS

- If using dried beans, soak ⅓ cup overnight, Drain and rinse. Add just enough cold water to cover them in a lidded. Bring to a boil, then cover and simmer them gently for 20 to 30 minutes or until the beans are tender but not mushy.

BEETROOT BURGERS

Whether served on a bun with your favorite toppings or with a salad, these colorful patties are sure to please.

SERVES: 8 · PREP TIME: 30 MINUTES · COOK TIME: 20 MINUTES

INGREDIENTS

- ⅓ cup (60g) quinoa
- ⅔ cup (160mL) water
- 1 red onion, diced
- 3 cloves garlic, minced
- 3 small beets, peeled and grated
- 2 green onions, chopped
- 2 tablespoons (12g) ground flax
- 1 cup (90g) oats
- ¼ cup (30g) gluten-free fine breadcrumbs
- 1 tablespoon balsamic vinegar
- 1 teaspoon cumin
- 1 teaspoon coriander
- 1 teaspoon sea salt
- 2 tablespoons olive oil

FREE FROM

- GLUTEN
- NUTS
- SUGAR

METHOD

BLENDER
STOVETOP

DIRECTIONS

- Bring medium saucepan to medium heat to lightly toast the quinoa and remove any excess water, stirring constantly.
- Add water, set burner on high, and bring to a boil. Reduce heat to low, cover, and simmer with the lid slightly ajar for 12 to 15 minutes, or until quinoa is fluffy and all the liquid has been absorbed.
- While the quinoa cooks, heat 1 tablespoon of the oil over medium-high heat in a skillet. When the oil is hot, add the diced onion, garlic, and grated beet to a pan and sauté for 7 to 10 minutes until softened.
- While they're cooking, blend oats in a blender or food processor until they are a grainy powder. Add the rest of the ingredients to the food processor, and pulse until well combined.
- Shape the mixture into 8 patties.
- In a large skillet, heat the other tablespoon of olive oil over medium-low heat. Gently place the patties in the frying pan. Add the patties and cook for about 5 to 10 minutes per side, or until crisp on the outside.
- Serve on hamburger buns or with a side salad.

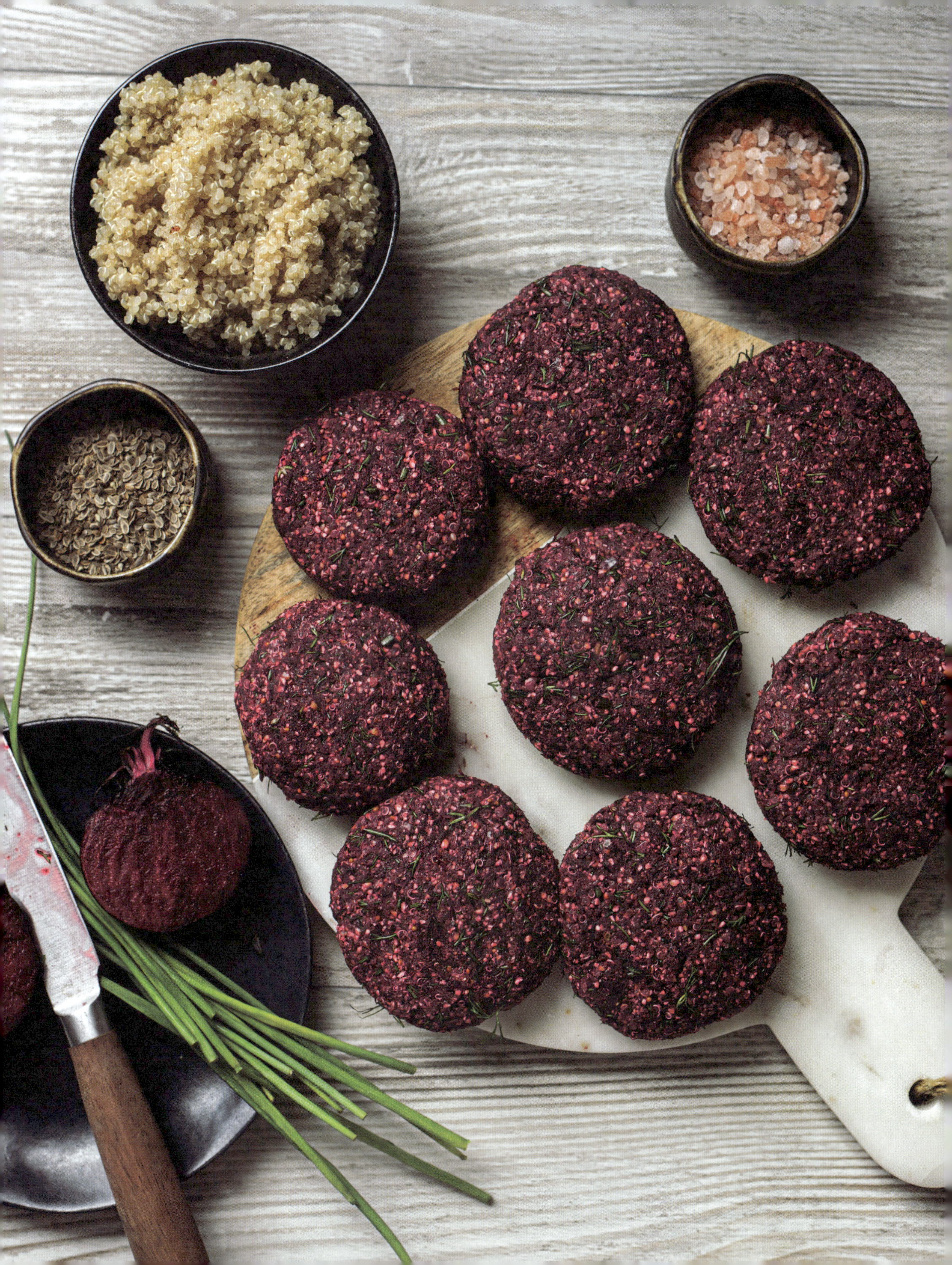

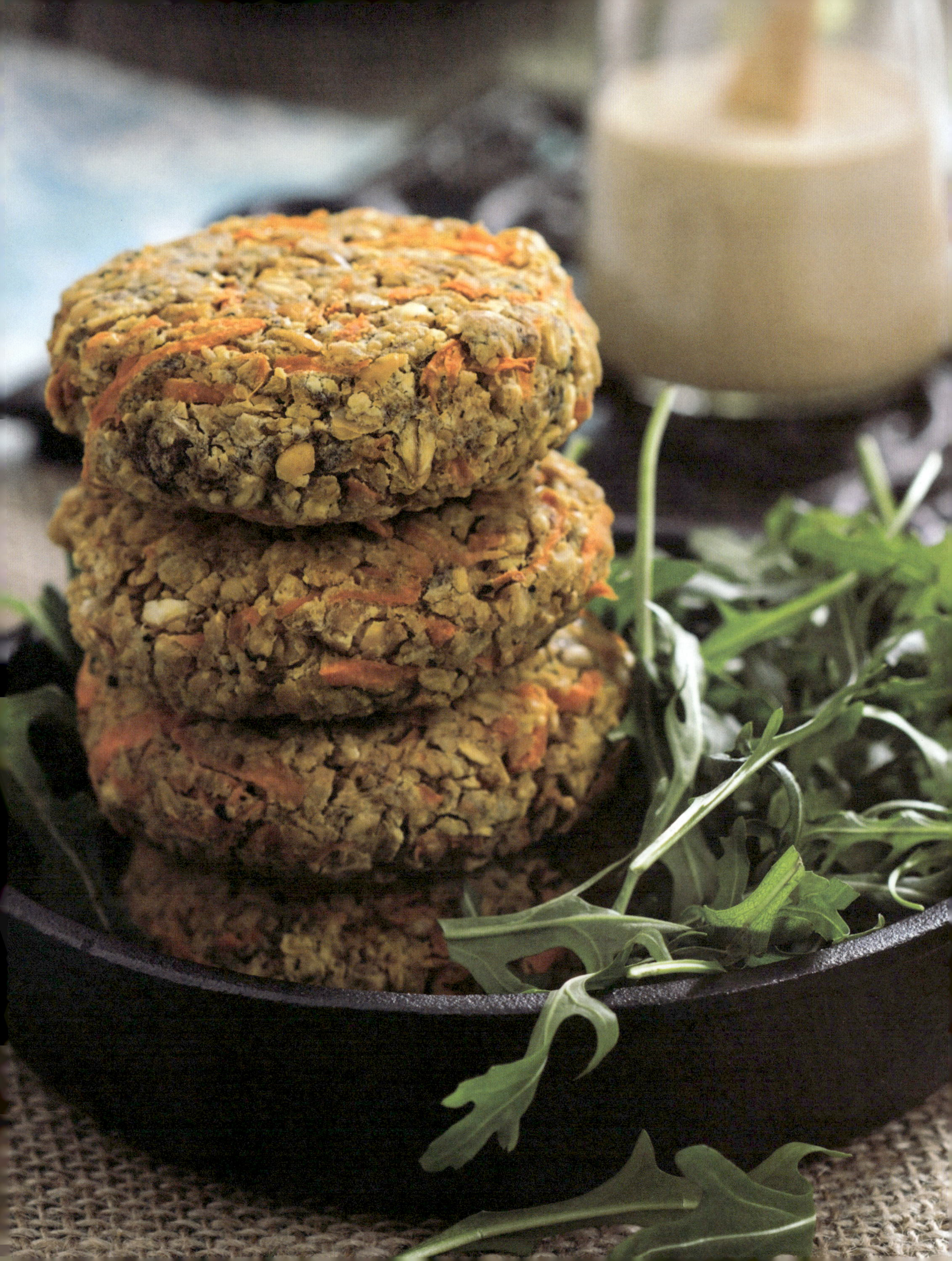

SWEET POTATO BURGERS

Soothe the burger craving with this tasty patties flavored with Indian spices.

SERVES: 4–6 · PREP TIME: 10 MINUTES · COOK TIME: 45 MINUTES

INGREDIENTS

- 1 sweet potato
- 1 15-ounce (425g) can white beans, rinsed and drained
- ½ small red onion, diced
- 1 cup carrots, grated
- ¾ cup (65g) whole oats
- ½ cup cilantro, chopped
- 1–2 tablespoons olive oil
- ¼ teaspoon cumin
- ¼ teaspoon chili powder
- ¼ teaspoon turmeric
- salt, to taste
- pepper, to taste

FREE FROM
- GLUTEN
- NUTS
- SUGAR

METHOD
- BLENDER
- OVEN BAKE
- STOVETOP

DIRECTIONS

- Preheat oven to 400°F (200°C).

- Cut sweet potato in half, and place it cut side down on a baking sheet. Place in oven, and cook for 30 to 40 minutes, or until tender. Once cool, remove skin, chop into pieces, and set aside.

- In a blender or food processor, blend oats until they are a fine powder. Remove, and set aside.

- Add beans, onion, sweet potatoes, carrots, and cilantro, and pulse for 10 seconds. Add in cumin, chili powder, turmeric, salt, and pepper, and pulse for another 5 seconds, until semi-smooth. Slowly pour in ground oats, and blend until mixture holds together.

- Divide mixture into 4 to 6 patties.

- In a skillet, heat 1 to 2 tablespoons of olive oil over medium heat. Once hot, place burger patties in pan, and cook each side for 3 to 4 minutes, or until golden brown.

- Serve with a side salad or place them in hamburger buns with your favorite toppings.

POTATO PANCAKES

Called many names, including latke and draniki, these savory pancakes feature in many national cuisines.

SERVES: 4–6 · PREP TIME: 10 MINUTES · COOK TIME: 45 MINUTES

FREE FROM
- GLUTEN
- NUTS
- SUGAR

METHOD
STOVETOP

INGREDIENTS

- 3 Yukon gold or russet potatoes
- ½ yellow onion, grated
- 2 green onions, chopped
- ½ cup (60g) all-purpose flour
- 3 tablespoons unsweetened nondairy milk
- 1 tablespoon cornstarch
- 1¼ teaspoon salt
- ½ teaspoon baking powder
- ¼ teaspoon black pepper
- ¼ teaspoon baking powder
- light vegetable oil, for frying

DIRECTIONS

- Grate potatoes, and squeeze out as much moisture as you can using paper towel.
- Combine the grated potato, flour, green onion, milk, cornstarch, salt, baking powder, and black pepper. Mix well to develop the gluten in the flour to help with binding.
- In a large skillet, heat a generous amount of vegetable oil over medium-high heat. When the oil is hot, scoop some of the mixture onto spatula, and flatten with your fingers to form a small patty.
- Slide the patty into the hot oil, using a fork to nudge it into the pan. Repeat until the pan is full, but the patties aren't crowded.
- Cook until deeply golden-brown, about 4 to 5 minutes per side. Remove from pan, and drain excess oil on paper towel.
- Serve with your favorite toppings, such as apple sauce.

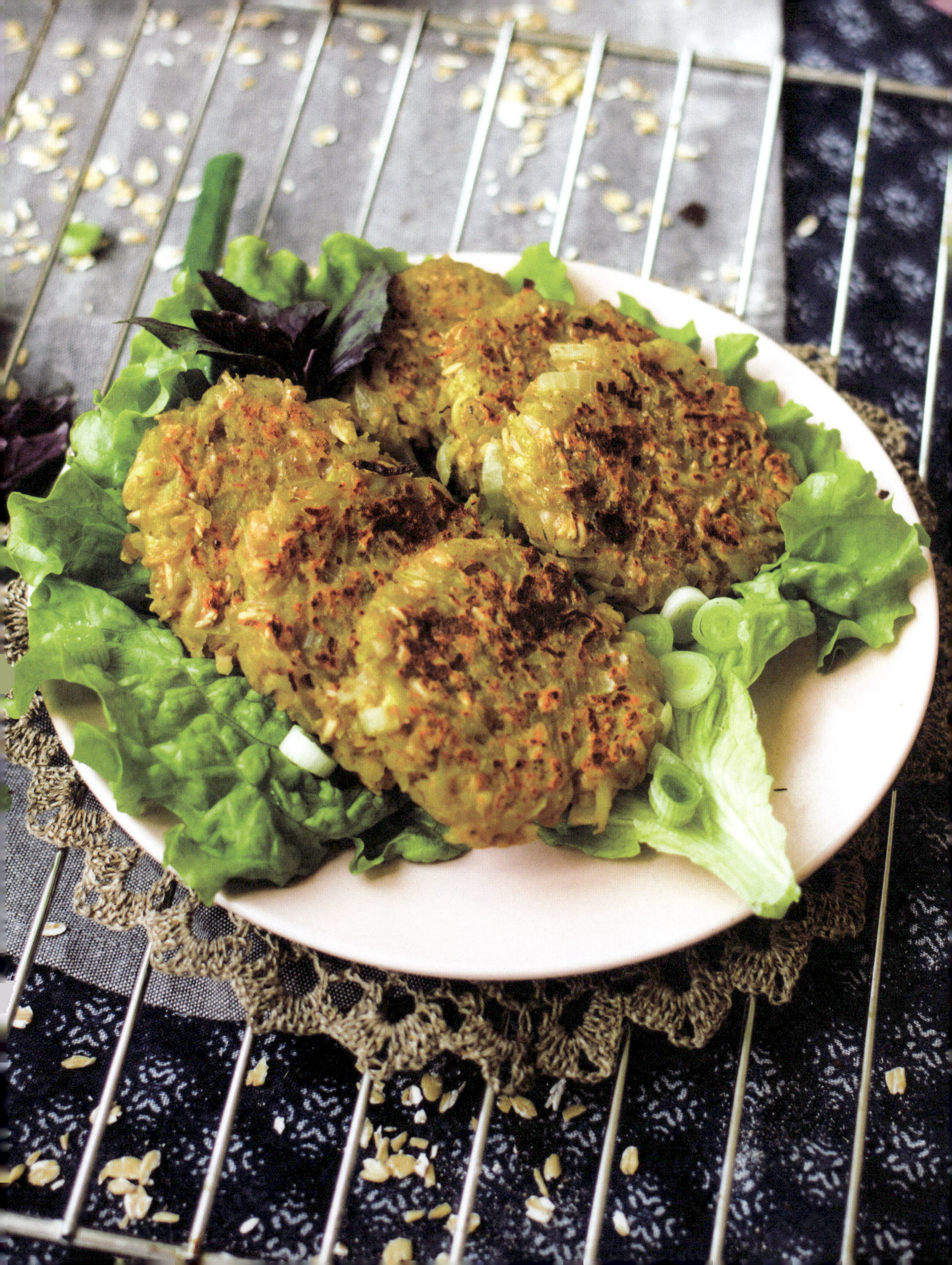

NUTTY CHOCOLATE MOUSSE (*see page 153*)

DESSERTS & SWEETS

WHIPPED COCONUT CREAM

Canned coconut cream will whip up into a smooth and delicious topping for your favorite desserts.

SERVES: 4 · PREP TIME: 5 MINUTES · TOTAL TIME: 5 MINUTES

INGREDIENTS
1 14-ounce (400ml) can coconut cream, chilled overnight
1 teaspoon vanilla extract
3 tablespoons confectioner's sugar

DIRECTIONS
- Open the chilled can of coconut cream—the cream will have separated from the water and risen to the top.
- Scoop the cream into a large bowl. Reserve the water for other uses.
- With a hand mixer, beat on medium speed, gradually increasing to high until you achieve a whipped cream consistency, about 3 to 4 minutes.
- Add the confectioner's sugar and vanilla, and continue to beat for another minute or so.
- Serve immediately.

CONTAINS
SUGAR

FREE FROM
DAIRY
GLUTEN
NUTS

METHOD
MIXER

WHIPPED AQUAFABA TOPPING

This easy vegan version of whipped cream makes a great topping for puddings, pies, and other treats.

SERVES: 4 · PREP TIME: 5 MINUTES · TOTAL TIME: 5 MINUTES

INGREDIENTS

½ cup (120mL) aquafaba (the liquid from 1 15-ounce (400g) can of chickpeas)

⅛ teaspoon cream of tartar

½–¾ (60–90g) cup confectioner's sugar

1 teaspoon pure vanilla extract

DIRECTIONS

- Drain the liquid from the can of chickpeas into a large bowl, reserving the chickpeas for another use.
- Add the cream of tartar, and with a hand mixer, beat on medium speed until the mixture starts to foam. Increase speed to high and continue beating until stiff peaks form, about 3 to 4 minutes.
- Add the confectioner's sugar and vanilla, and continue to beat for another minute or so.
- Serve immediately.

FIVE INGREDIENTS

CONTAINS
- SUGAR

FREE FROM
- DAIRY
- GLUTEN
- NUTS

METHOD

MIXER

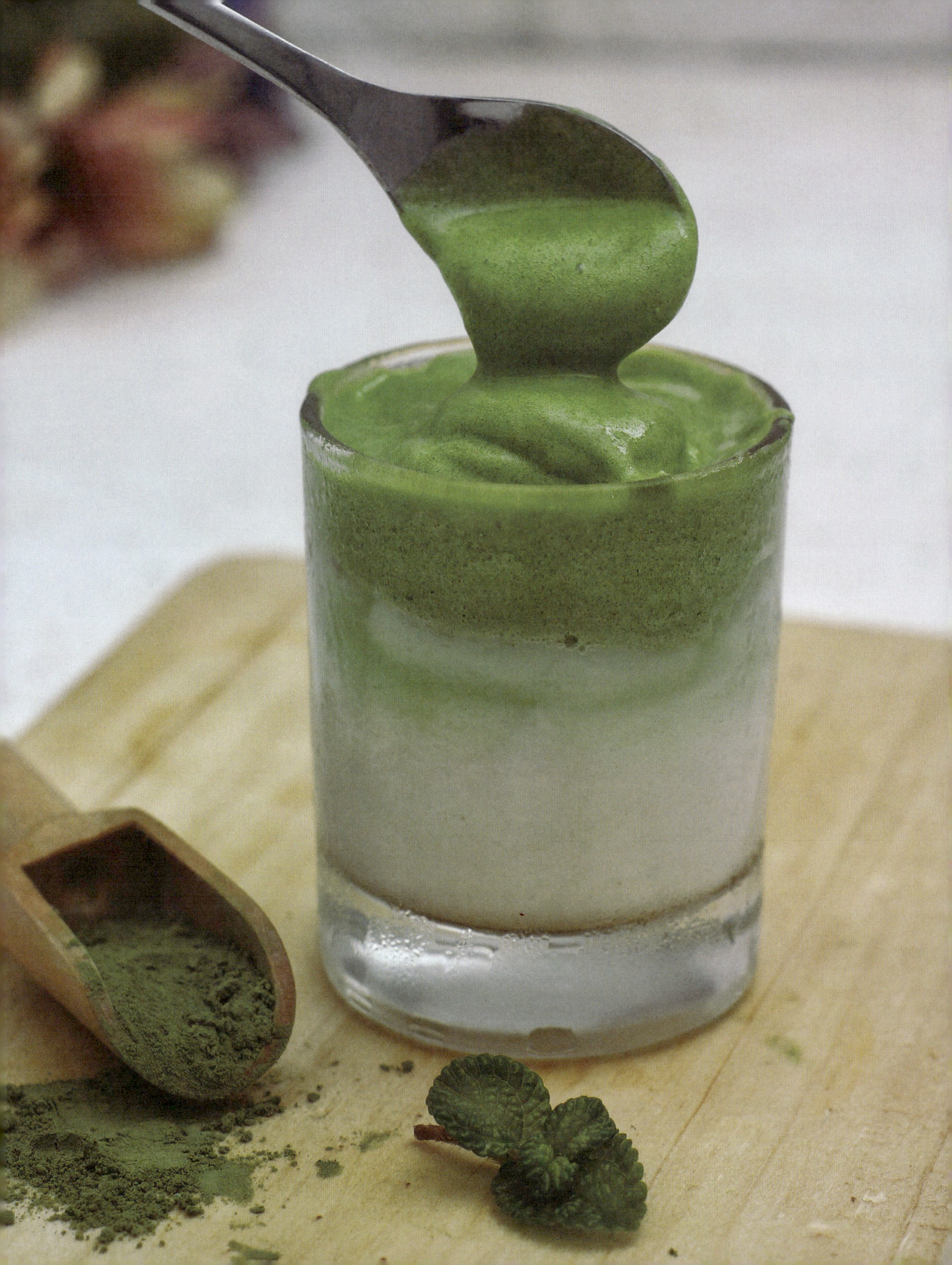

DALGONA MATCHA LATTE

End a meal with this green tea version of Dalgona, a sweet, cold, and creamy whipped beverage.

SERVES: 2 · PREP TIME: 10–15 MINUTES · TOTAL TIME: 10–15 MINUTES

INGREDIENTS

- ¼ cup (60mL) aquafaba
- ¼ teaspoon cream of tartar
- 2–3 tablespoons confectioner's sugar
- 2 teaspoons matcha powder
- 1 cup (240mL) vanilla oat milk (or any plant-based milk of your choice)

DIRECTIONS

- Pour the aquafaba into a large mixing bowl, add the cream of tartar, and using a handheld mixer whip on high until the aquafaba becomes fluffy and thick (which will take about 5 to 8 minutes).
- When the aquafaba has thickened, sift in 1 tablespoon of the confectioner's sugar, and whip it in. Continue adding the remaining sugar, 1 tablespoon at a time, until fully incorporated.
- Sift in the matcha powder, and continue to whip the mixture until it is fully incorporated.
- Fill two glasses with ice, and pour a ½ cup of oat milk in each.
- Top each glass with half of the whipped matcha, and serve immediately.

CONTAINS

- SUGAR

FREE FROM

- DAIRY
- GLUTEN
- NUTS

METHOD

MIXER

CHEF'S TIPS

- Don't just let the viscous liquid in a can of peas dribble down your drain, and save the liquid left over when you soak dried legumes. This liquid, known as aquafaba ("water bean"), will act as an egglike binder in recipes, and it will also whip up into semi-stiff peaks.
- You can use a granulated sugar for this recipe, but the lighter confectioner's sugar will not weight down the peaks of the aquafaba.

MATCHA GREEN TEA BROWNIES WITH WHITE CHOCOLATE DRIZZLE

These sweet treats are paleo friendly and gluten free.

YIELD: 16 · PREP TIME: 20 MINUTES · COOK TIME: 45 MINUTES

INGREDIENTS

- 2 cups (450g) pitted dates
- ⅓ cup (80 mL) unsweetened almond milk
- ¼ cup (60g) almond butter
- 3 cups (330g) ground almonds
- 3 teaspoons matcha powder

For the white chocolate glaze:
- 1 ounce (28g) cacao butter
- 3 tablespoons unsweetened almond milk
- 2 tablespoons maple syrup

DIRECTIONS

- Bring a saucepan full of water to boil, and place the dates inside. Soak for 15 minutes in the boiling water
- Preheat oven to 350°F (180°C). Line a square baking tin with non-stick baking paper.
- Drain the dates and place in a blender or food processor, and ass the almond milk and almond butter. Blend until completely smooth, stirring it around a couple of times if necessary.
- In a large bowl, place ground almonds and matcha powder, and mix to combine thoroughly. Add the date mixture, and mix well, adding a splash more milk if it's looking too dry.
- Transfer into the lined baking tin, and bake for about 20 minutes (the brownies should be firm, but still gooey inside. Remove from the oven, and allow to cool completely.
- To make the glaze, bring water to boil in a saucepan. Place the cacao butter in a bowl, and place it in the boil water to melt it.
- Add the milk and maple syrup, and mix.
- Using a spoon, drizzle the glaze over the brownies. Place in fridge until the glaze has completely set before cutting into squares.

CONTAINS

- NUTS
- SUGAR

FREE FROM

- DAIRY
- GLUTEN

METHOD

STOVETOP

OVEN BAKE

CHEF'S TIPS

- You can keep the brownies for several days in an airtight container in the refrigerator.

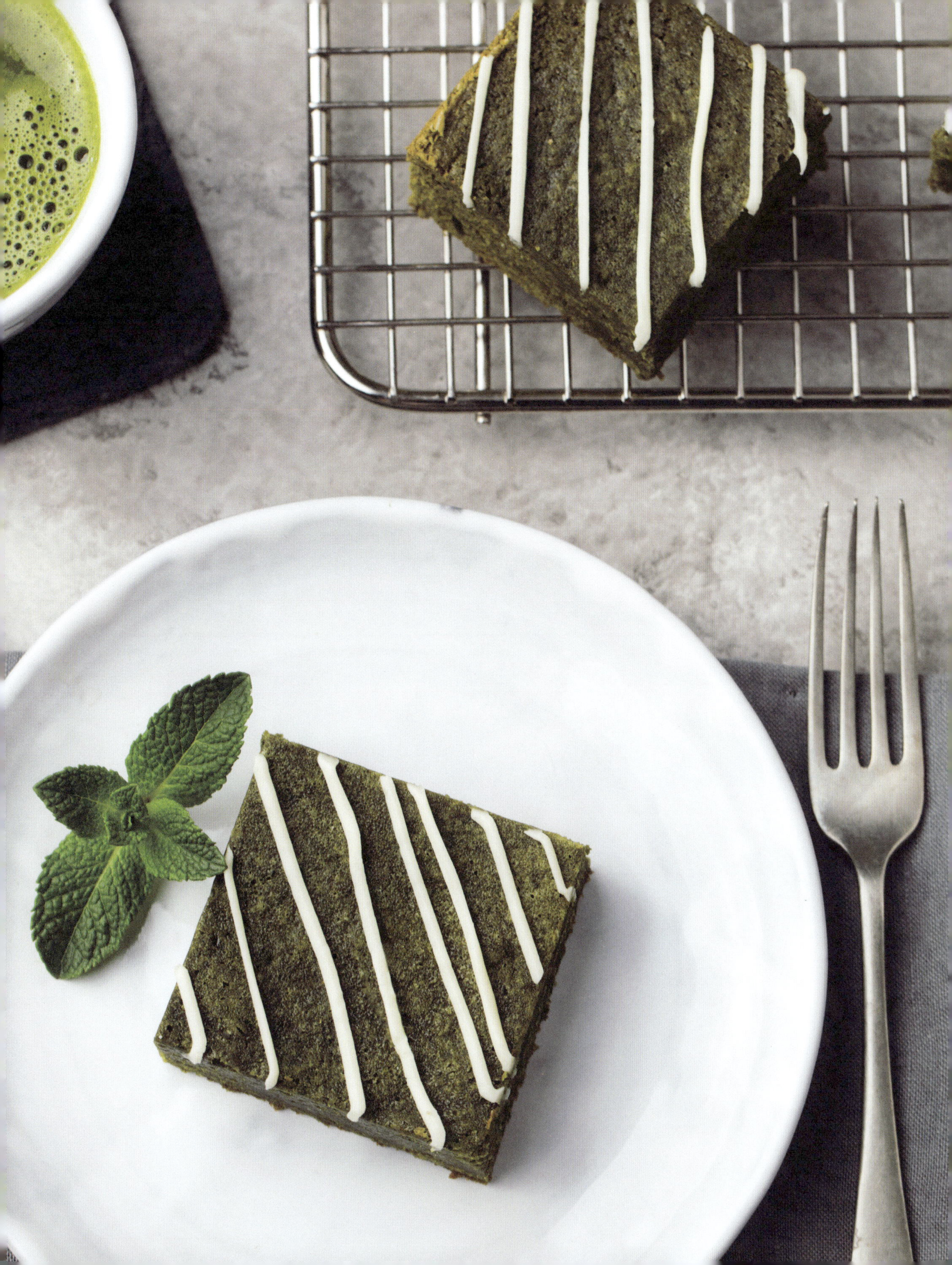

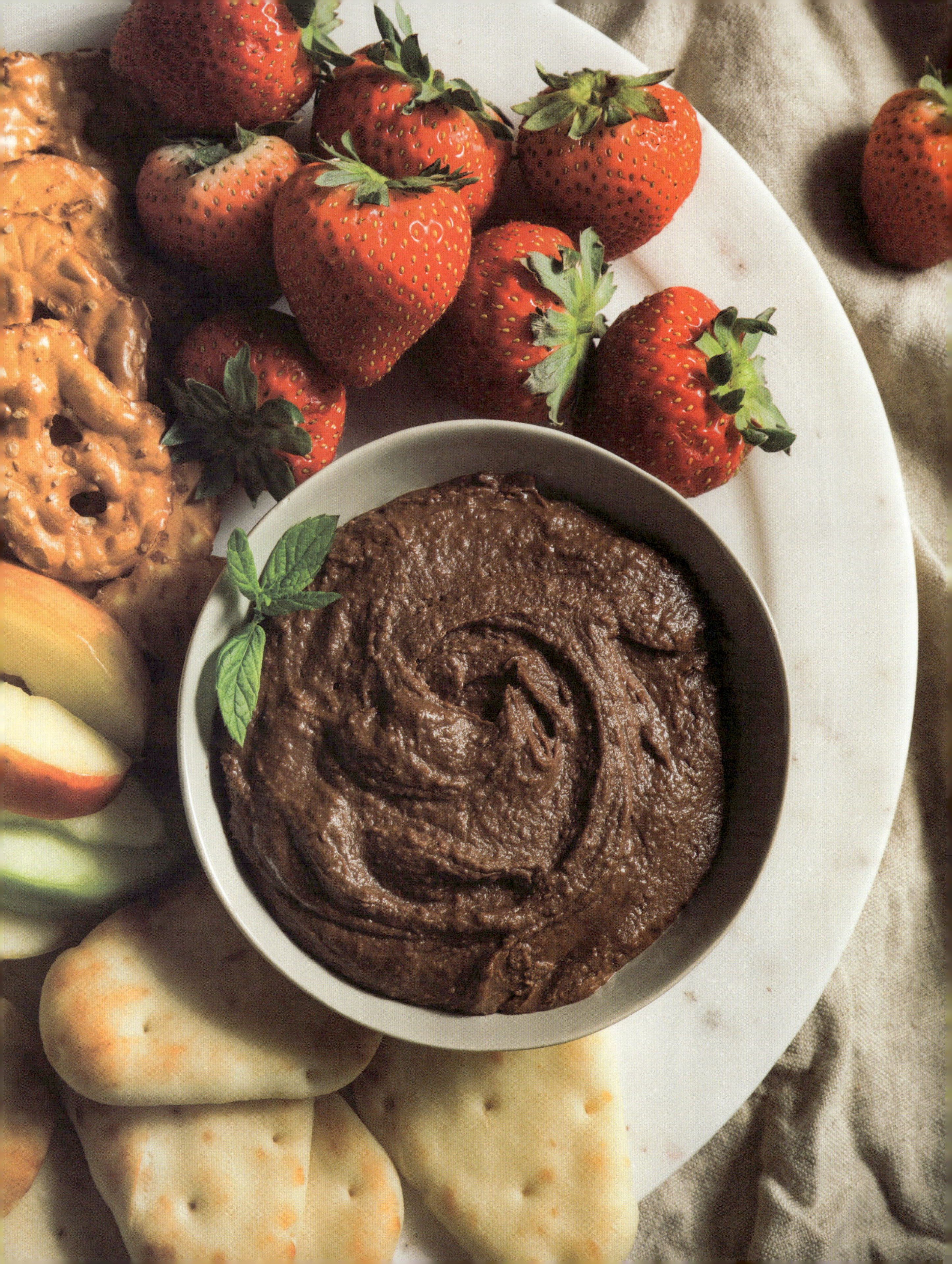

CHOCOLATE HUMMUS

Use this rich and chocolaty spread as a sandwich topper or as a dip for your favorite fruits and crackers.

YIELD: 16–20 · PREP TIME: 15 MINUTES · TOTAL TIME: 15 MINUTES

INGREDIENTS

- 1 14-ounce (400g) can chickpeas, drained and rinsed
- ¼ cup (65g) peanut butter
- 6 tablespoons maple syrup
- ¼ cup (50g) coconut sugar
- 3 tablespoons unsweetened cocoa powder
- 2 tablespoons almond milk
- 2 teaspoons pure vanilla extract
- sea salt, to taste

DIRECTIONS

- Place all ingredients in the order listed into the container of a blender or food processor.
- Starting at low speed, blend for a few seconds, and increase speed to high, about 1 minute, scraping sown sides as needed until the mixture is smooth.
- Transfer the hummus to a serving dish, and serve with your favorite fruits (cut to bite size) and crackers, or you can spread it on toasted bread.

CONTAINS
- NUTS
- SUGAR

FREE FROM
- DAIRY
- GLUTEN

METHOD

BLENDER

CHEF'S TIPS

- This hummus will last in the refrigerator for up to a week stored in an airtight container.

MINT CHOCOLATE AVOCADO PUDDING

Avocado gives this chocolate pudding its silky feel, and mint gives it that extra pizazz.

SERVES: 2 · PREP TIME: 15 MINUTES · SET TIME: 1–2 HOURS

INGREDIENTS

- 2 avocados
- ½ cup (120mL) unsweetened coconut cream
- ⅓ cup (80 mL) unsweetened coconut milk
- ½ cup + 2 tablespoons (125g) sugar
- ¼ teaspoon kosher salt
- ½ cup + 2 tablespoons (55g) unsweetened cocoa powder
- 2 tablespoons honey
- 1 tablespoon vanilla
- ¼ teaspoon peppermint extract

DIRECTIONS

- Place all ingredients in a blender, and puree on high until the mixture is smooth and silky, scraping the sides, as needed.
- Spoon the mixture into dessert cups, and chill for 1 to 2 hours.
- Serve with a garnish of fresh mint.

CONTAINS
- SUGAR

FREE FROM
- DAIRY
- GLUTEN
- NUTS

METHOD
BLENDER

NUTTY CHOCOLATE MOUSSE

Silken tofu gives a light texture to this chocolate mousse flavored with almonds.

SERVES 4 · PREP TIME: 5 MINUTES · COOK TIME: 10 MINUTES

INGREDIENTS

- 1 12.3-ounce (349g) package soft or silken tofu, drained
- ½ cup (43g) unsweetened cocoa powder
- ½ cup (120mL) unsweetened almond milk
- ½ teaspoon pure almond extract
- 2–3 tablespoons agave nectar, to taste
- ¼ cup (42g) dairy-free semi-sweet chocolate chips
- ½ teaspoon vegetable oil
- almonds, coarsely chopped, for garnish

DIRECTIONS

- Add the cocoa powder to a medium bowl, and add the coconut milk a little at a time, whisking until the mixture is smooth.
- Place the tofu in a blender or food processor, and then add the cocoa mixture, almond extract, and 2 tablespoons agave nectar. Blend until smooth. Taste, and add more agave nectar if needed.
- Transfer the mixture to a microwave-safe bowl, and add the chocolate chips and vegetable oil. Microwave in 10-second increments, until the chips have melted, and then stir the mixture to combine well.
- Fold the melted chocolate chips into the blended mixture, and carefully mix to combine.
- Spoon the mixture into dessert cups, and chill for 1 to 2 hours.
- Serve topped with chopped almonds.

CONTAINS
- NUTS
- SUGAR

FREE FROM
- DAIRY
- GLUTEN

METHOD
BLENDER
MICROWAVE

COCOA BANANA-AVOCADO PUDDING

The combination of banana and avocado gives this rich and sweet chocolate pudding a creamy texture.

SERVES: 6 · PREP TIME: 10 MINUTES · SET TIME: 1–2 HOURS

INGREDIENTS

- 2 ripe avocados
- 4 large ripe bananas, sliced
- ½ cup (43g) unsweetened cocoa powder
- 2 teaspoon vanilla extract
- 4 tablespoons honey

DIRECTIONS

- Peel and pit the avocado. Cut into large chunks, and place in blender.
- Reserving a few slices of banana for garnish, place the rest of the ingredients in a blender, and puree on high until the mixture is smooth and silky, scraping the sides, as needed.
- Spoon the mixture into dessert cups, and chill for at least 1 hour.
- Garnish with the reserved banana slices, and sprinkle with chopped nuts, if desired.

CONTAINS
- SUGAR

FREE FROM
- DAIRY
- GLUTEN
- NUTS
- SEEDS

METHOD
BLENDER

CHEF'S TIPS

- You can replace the honey with agave nectar or maple syrup, if desired.

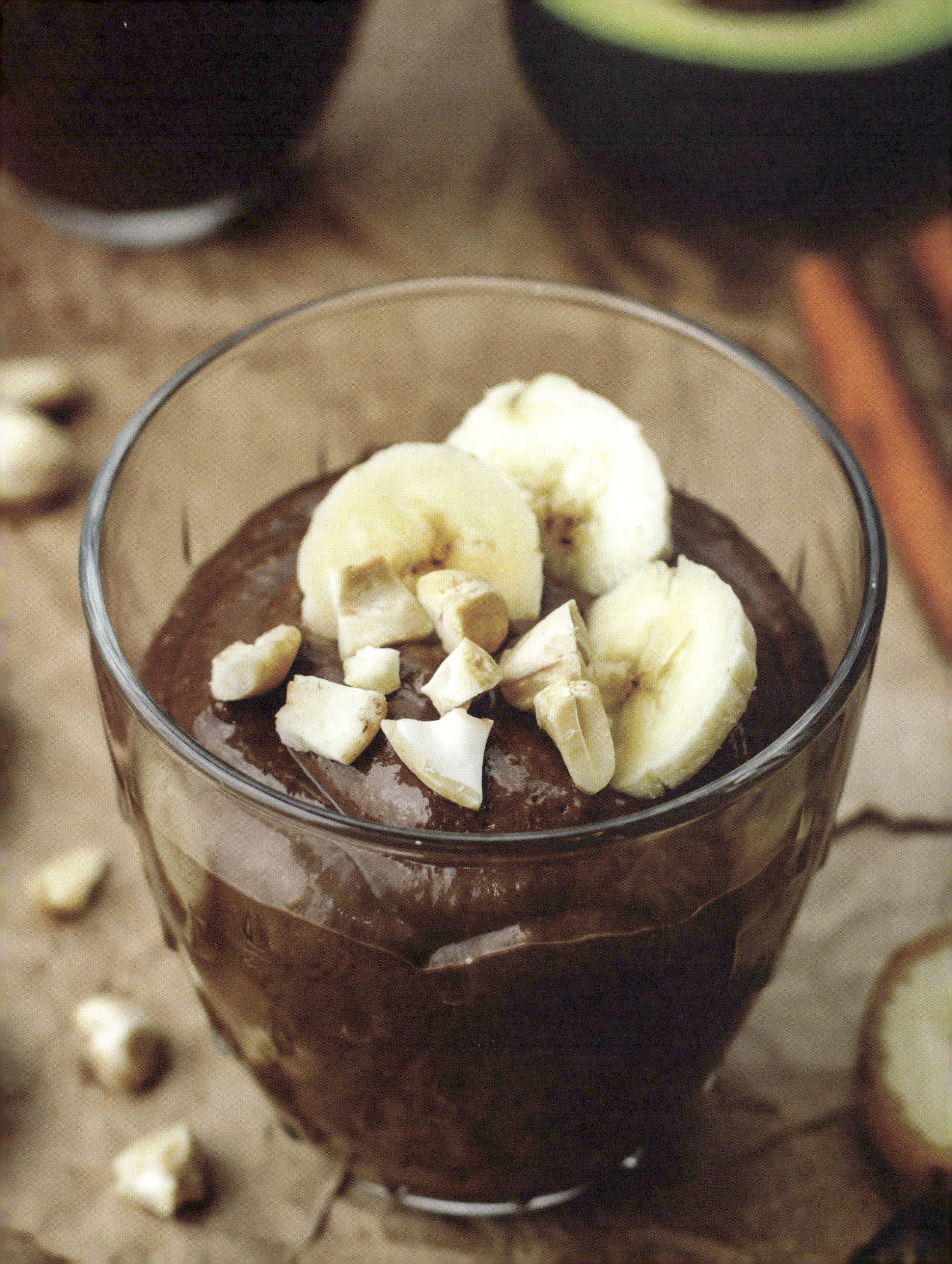

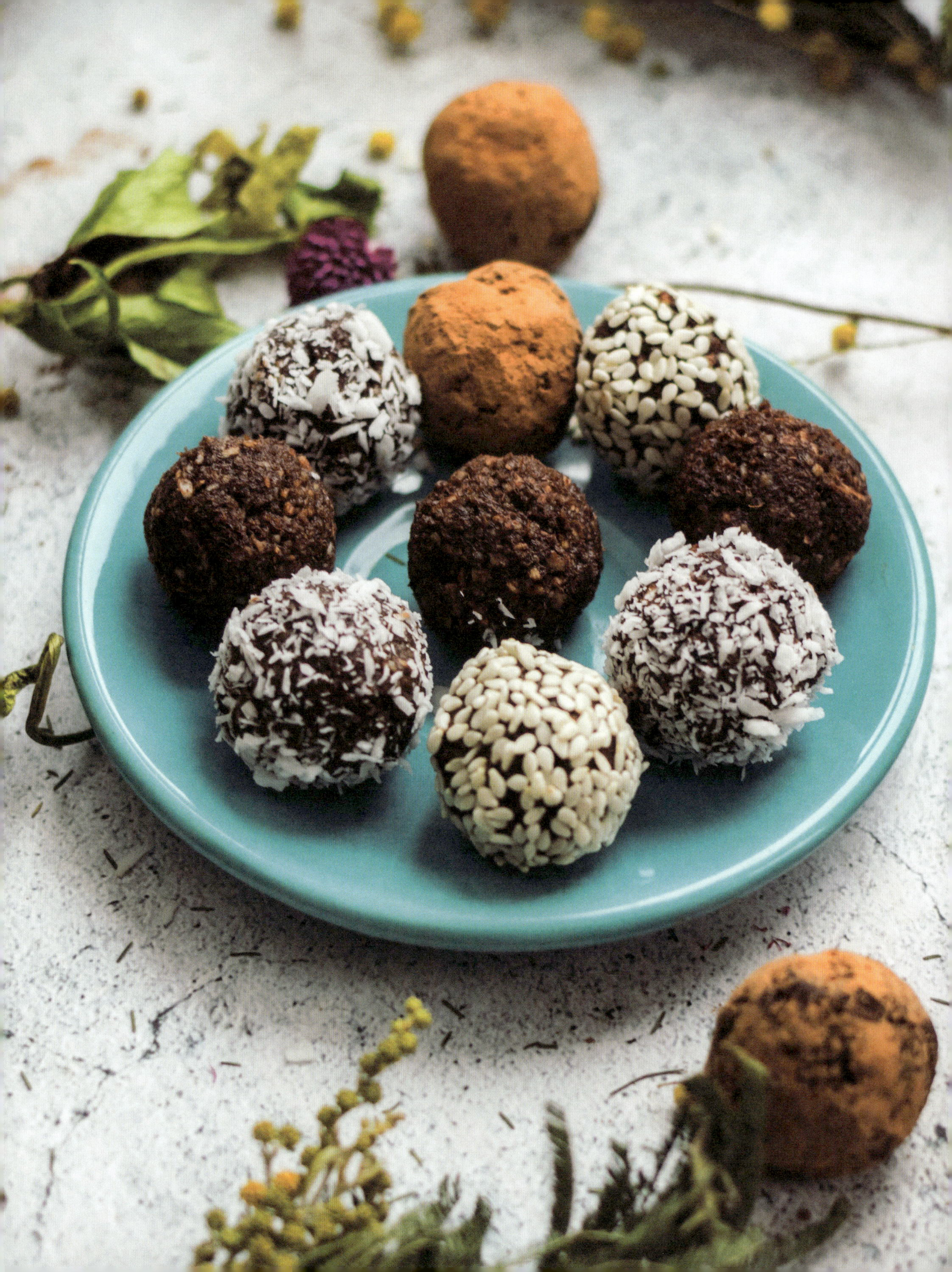

CAROB & DATE BALLS

These healthy treats get their sweetness from sticky Medjool dates and dried prunes.

YIELD: 24 · PREP TIME: 30 MINUTES · CHILL TIME: 3–5 HOURS

INGREDIENTS

- 6 large Medjool dates
- 3 heaped teaspoon cashew butter
- ⅔ cup (57g) desiccated coconut
- 2 tablespoons carob powder
- 1 tablespoon coconut oil
- 100g dried prunes
- ¼ cup (43g) coconut flour
- ½ teaspoon ground vanilla
- unsweetened cocoa or cacao powder, coconut flakes, or sesame seeds, for topping

FREE FROM
- DAIRY
- GLUTEN
- NUTS
- SUGAR

METHOD
BLENDER
ASSEMBLY

DIRECTIONS

- Add all the ingredients into a blender, and blend until the mixture forms a paste (if the mixture is dry add a little more coconut oil, if wet, add a little more coconut flour).
- Place in refrigerator, and chill for 2 to 3 hours, until a knife inserted in the middle of the bowl comes out clean.
- Once the mixture is cool and firm, place your choice of topping in a small dish.
- Use a teaspoon or small melon baller to scoop out a small ball of the chilled mixture, and then gently roll it in your hands.
- Toss it in the topping. Shake off any excess, and place on a parchment-lined serving plate. Continue scooping and rolling until all the chocolate is used up (about 24 balls). If any of the mixture becomes too soft to form, refrigerate until solid enough to again shape.
- Refrigerate for 1 to 2 hours, and then serve chilled.

CHEF'S TIPS

- You can store the balls in an airtight container in the refrigerator for up to a week.

DARK CHOCOLATE TRUFFLES

These easy-to-make sweets are decadently delicious and sure to please the most ardent chocoholic.

YIELD: 16–20 · PREP TIME: 15 MINUTES · CHILL TIME: 3–24 HOURS

INGREDIENTS

1¾ cups (300g) vegan chocolate or chocolate chips

1 cup (240ml) coconut milk

½ teaspoon vanilla extract

¼ cup unsweetened cocoa or cacao powder, for topping

DIRECTIONS

- Place the chocolate chips in a medium-sized bowl (if using bar chocolate, chop it into small pieces).
- Add coconut milk to a small bowl, and heat in the microwave until it is very warm, but not boiling.
- Remove from microwave, and immediately pour the heated coconut milk over the chocolate. Loosely cover the bowl to trap the heat.
- Let sit for about 5 minutes, and then gently stir until the chocolate pieces are completely melted and the mixture is silky smooth.
- Stir in the vanilla extract, and then place the uncovered bowl in the refrigerator. Chill for 2 to 3 hours, until a knife inserted in the middle of the bowl comes out clean.
- Once the mixture is cool and firm, place the cocoa or cacao powder in a small dish.
- Use a tablespoon-sized scoop or a melon baller to scoop out a small ball of the chilled chocolate, and then gently roll it in your hands.
- Toss it in the topping. Shake off any excess, and place on a parchment-lined serving plate. Continue scooping and rolling until all the chocolate is used up (about 16 to 20 balls). If any of the chocolate becomes too soft to form, refrigerate until solid enough to shape.
- Refrigerate for 1 to 2 hours or overnight, and then serve chilled.

FREE FROM

- DAIRY
- GLUTEN
- NUTS
- SUGAR

METHOD

BLENDER

ASSEMBLY

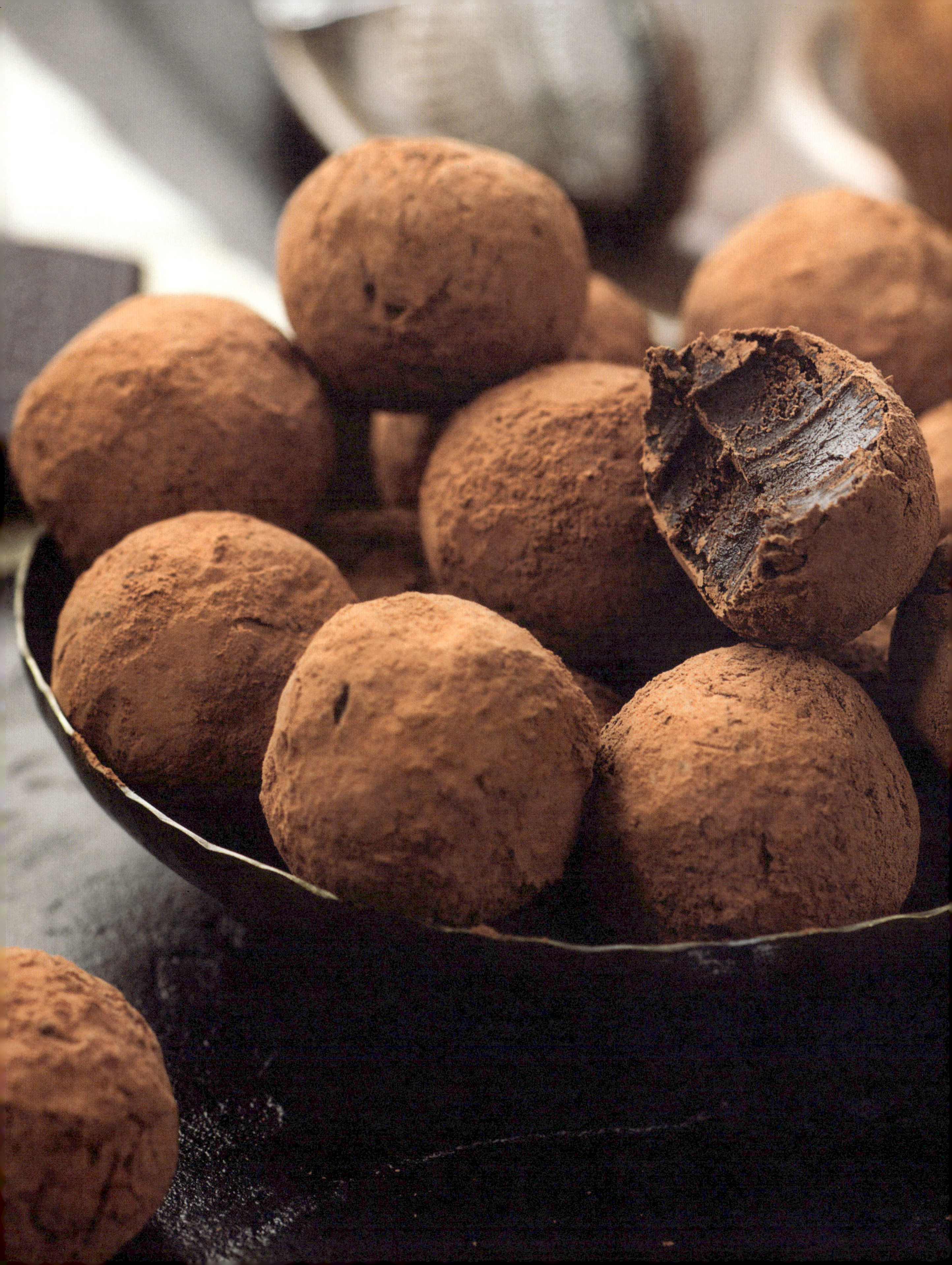

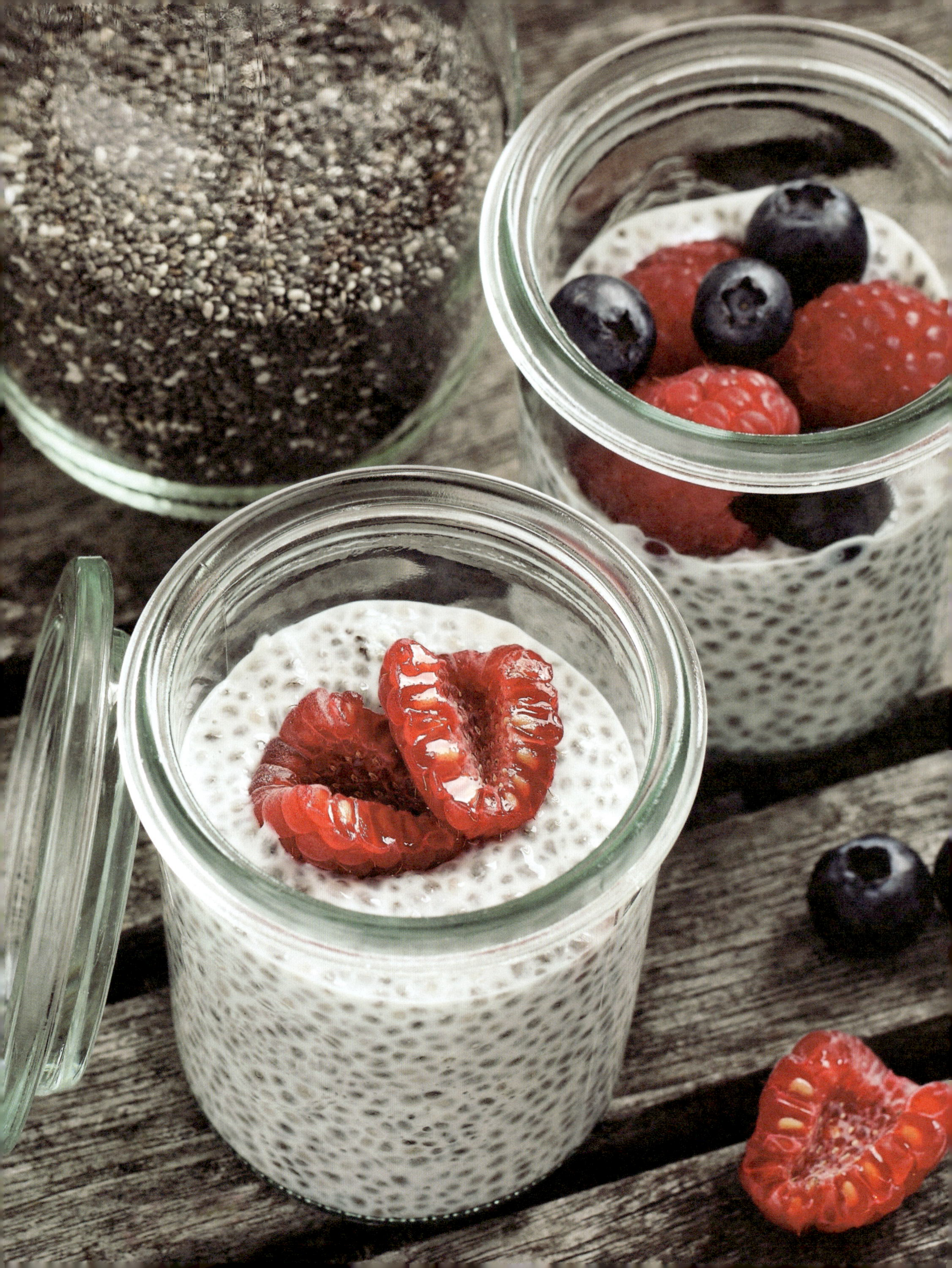

CHIA PUDDING

This creamy and filling vegan dessert is also is paleo, gluten-free, and keto.

SERVES: 2 · PREP TIME: 10 MINUTES · SET TIME: 1–24 HOURS

INGREDIENTS

6–8 tablespoons chia seeds

2 cups (480mL) coconut or nut milk

1 tablespoon maple syrup

½ teaspoon vanilla extract

fresh or frozen berries, for topping

DIRECTIONS

- In a bowl, stir together chia seeds, milk, maple syrup, and vanilla.
- Once the mixture is well combined, let it sit for 5 minutes, and then stir again to break up any clumps of seeds.
- Split mixture between two mason jars or other type of dessert cup, and then refrigerate for 1 to 2 hours or overnight to set. If the pudding isn't thick enough after setting, add another tablespoon or so of chia seeds, stir, and then refrigerate for 30 minutes.
- When the pudding has set to a creamy consistency, top with your favorite berries, and serve.

CONTAINS

SUGAR

FREE FROM

DAIRY

GLUTEN

NUTS

METHOD

ASSEMBLY

BLUE SPIRULINA CHIA PUDDING

Blue spirulina lends this pudding a sky blue color, and maple syrup and vanilla impart rich, subtle sweetness.

SERVES: 4 · PREP TIME: 10 MINUTES · SET TIME: 1–24 HOURS

INGREDIENTS

- 4 cups (960mL) coconut milk
- 12 tablespoons chia seeds
- 1 teaspoon natural blue spirulina powder
- 1 teaspoon vanilla extract
- 2 tablespoon maple syrup
- Whipped Coconut Cream (see page 144), for topping
- blueberries, for garnish
- blackberries, for garnish

DIRECTIONS

- In a bowl, stir together chia seeds, blue spirulina powder, milk, maple syrup, and vanilla.
- Once the mixture is well combined, let it sit for 5 minutes, and then stir again to break up any clumps of seeds.
- Split mixture between two mason jars or other type of dessert cup, and then refrigerate for 1 to 2 hours or overnight to set. If the pudding isn't thick enough after setting, add another tablespoon or so of chia seeds, stir, and then refrigerate for 30 minutes.
- When the pudding has set to a creamy consistency, top with whipped coconut cream, garnish with berries, and serve.

CONTAINS
- SUGAR

FREE FROM
- DAIRY
- GLUTEN
- NUTS

METHOD
ASSEMBLY

CHEF'S TIPS

- You can keep chia pudding for 5 to 7 days in an airtight container in the refrigerator.

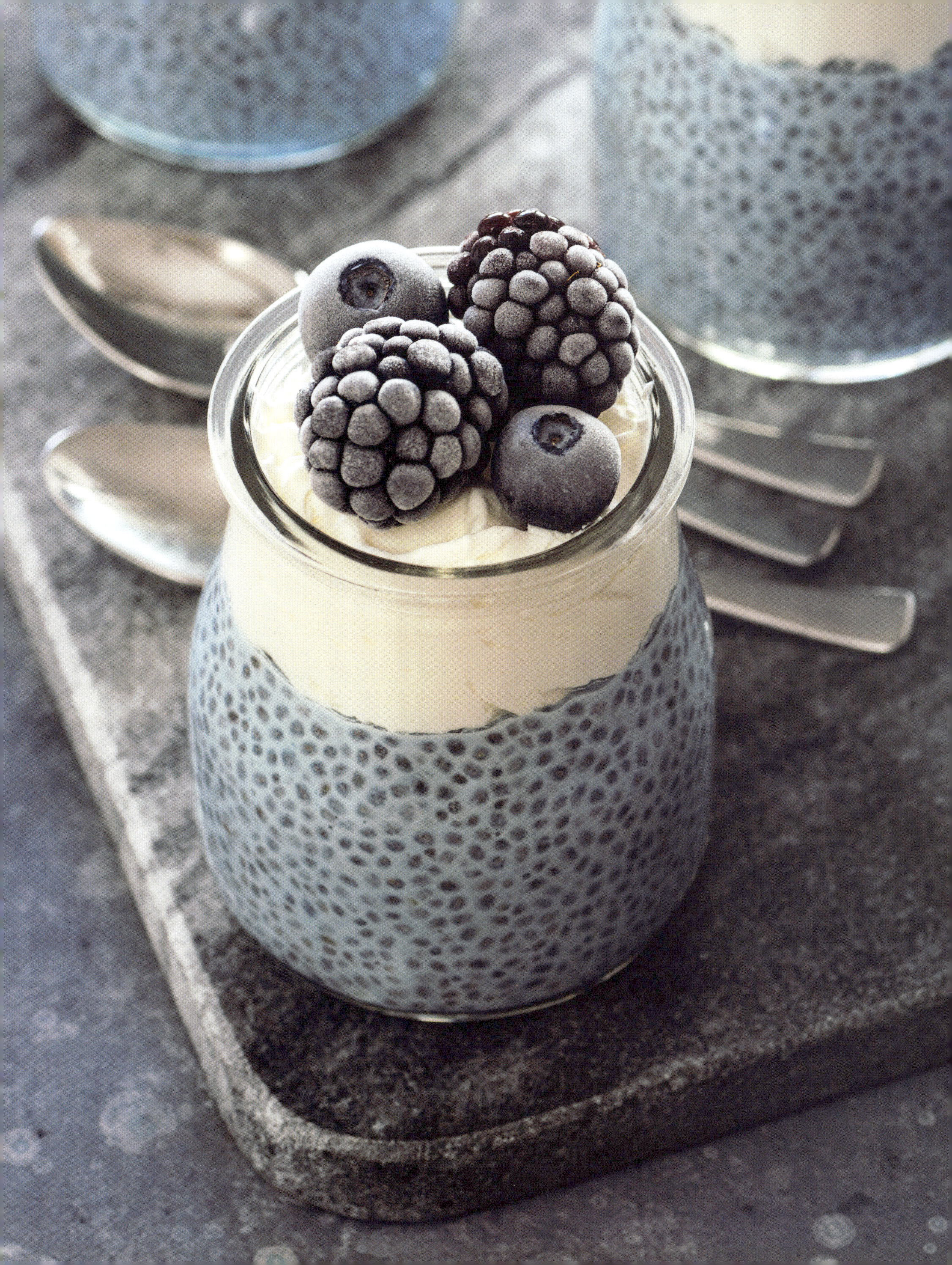

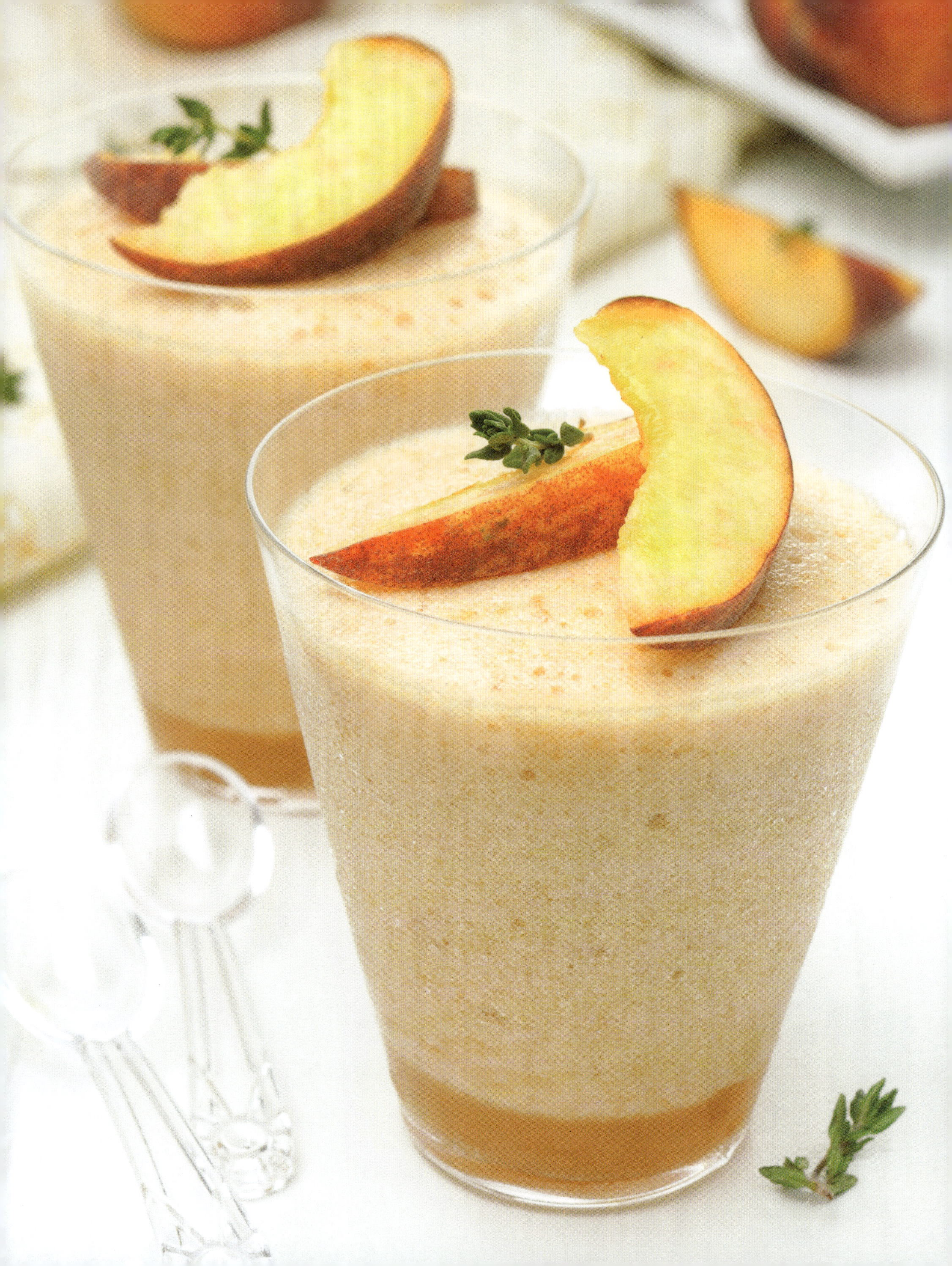

LAYERED PEACH PUDDING

A creamy peach pudding is layered over fresh peach puree to make this delicious summertime treat.

SERVES: 4 · PREP TIME: 15 MINUTES · SET TIME: 1–2 HOURS

INGREDIENTS

- 4 peaches
- 3 tablespoons apple juice
- 1 cup (150g) raw cashews
- 2 tablespoons maple syrup
- 1 teaspoon vanilla extract
- 1 tablespoon fresh lemon juice
- ½ cup (120mL) light coconut cream
- 1 tablespoon lemon zest
- ½ teaspoon pink Himalayan salt

-DIRECTIONS

- In a large pot, pour enough water to fully submerge the peaches, and bring the water to a boil.
- Cut a small X at the bottom of each peach, and using a slotted spoon, lower the peaches into the boiling water, and boil them for 2 minutes.
- While the peaches are boiling, fill a large bowl with ice and water. Put the peaches into an ice bath for 1 minute. You should now be able to simply rub the skin of the peaches. Remove the pit and cut into slices, reserving a few for the garnish.
- Place the peach chunks into a food processor or blender, add the apple juice, and blend until smooth.
- Spoon about 2 tablespoons of the puree into dessert cups.
- Place the rest of the ingredients in the blender, and puree on high until the mixture is smooth and silky, scraping the sides as needed.
- Spoon the mixture into the dessert cups over the puree layer, and chill for 1 to 2 hours.
- Serve with a garnish of peach slices.

CONTAINS

- NUTS
- SUGAR

FREE FROM

- DAIRY
- GLUTEN

METHOD

STOVETOP

BLENDER

CHEF'S TIPS

- To substitute frozen peaches for fresh, just thaw the fruit before adding to the blender.

BERRY MOUSSE

Use the berries of you choice to flavor and color this cool and silky dessert.

SERVES: 4-6 · PREP TIME: 4-8 HOURS · SET TIME: 4 HOURS

INGREDIENTS

- 1 cup cashews
- ⅓ cup (80 mL) coconut cream
- ¼ cups (60mL) coconut water
- ⅓ cup (80mL) virgin coconut oil, melted to room temperature
- ½ cups (85g) strawberries, fresh or thawed frozen
- 1 cup (144g) boysenberries, fresh or thawed frozen
- ¾ cup (105g) raspberries, fresh or thawed frozen
- ½–1 teaspoon berry-flavored stevia, to taste
- 3–4 tablespoons light honey, to taste

FREE FROM

- DAIRY
- GLUTEN
- NUTS
- SUGAR

METHOD

BLENDER

DIRECTIONS

- Soak the cashews for 2 to 8 hours.
- Place the cashews, coconut cream, and coconut water into a blender. Blend until very smooth and very creamy, about 1 to 2 minutes. Bubbles should form throughout.
- Cut the strawberries in half, and add them with the boysenberries raspberries, stevia, and honey, and blend again until very smooth.
- Add the coconut oil, and blend just until incorporated.
- Pour into ramekins or dessert cups, and cover with plastic wrap or fitted ramekin covers. Chill for at least 4 hours.
- Garnish with fresh berries and/or whipped topping, and serve.

CHEF'S TIPS

- You can make this mousse with the berries of your choice. For a bright pink, try any combination of boysenberries and red and black raspberries, as well as pitted cherries. For lavender and purple colors, try blueberries or blackberries. You can also use a tablespoon of a fine berry powder of your choice to enhance the color.
- You can store this mousse covered in the refrigerator for up to 5 days.

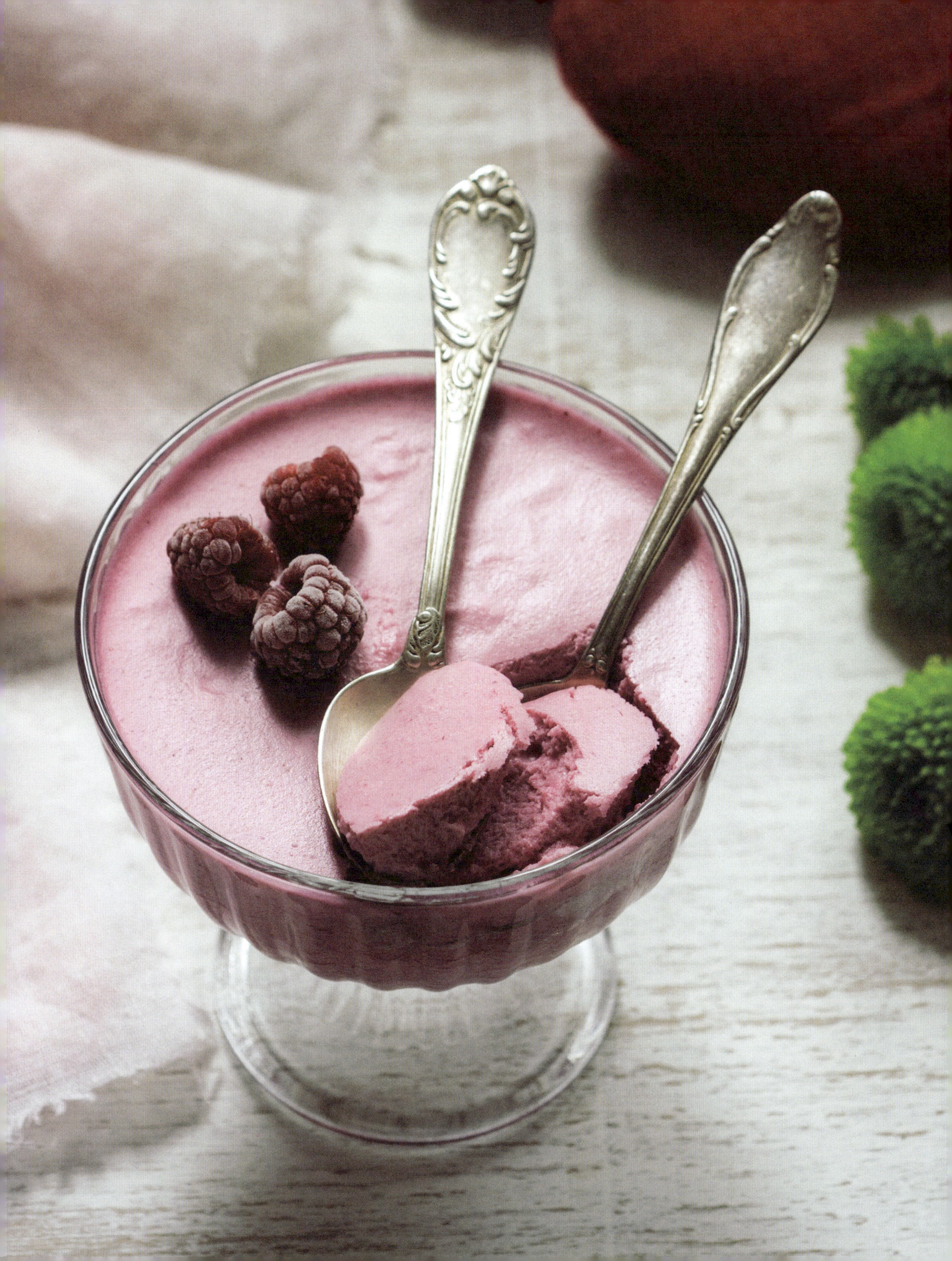

OLD-FASHIONED TAPIOCA PUDDING

This vegan version of a traditional dessert is light and creamy and paleo-friendly.

SERVES: 4–6 · PREP TIME: 15 MINUTES · COOK TIME: 15 MINUTES

INGREDIENTS

½ cup (75g) small pearl tapioca

1½ cup (360 mL) water

1 cup (240mL) dairy-free milk

⅓ cup (65g) granulated sugar

½ teaspoon vanilla extract

DIRECTIONS

- In a large bowl, combine the water and lemon juice, and place the apple slices in the mixture to soak.
- Place the tapioca pearls in a large bowl, and cover with the water. Let them soak at room temperature for 15 minutes.
- Add the soaked tapioca pearls with along with the water to a saucepan, add the milk, and bring the mixture to a boil.
- Reduce heat to medium-low, and stir occasionally until the mixture thickens and reaches a pudding-like consistency, about 15 to 20 minutes.
- Remove from heat, and stir in the sugar and vanilla extract.
- Spoon the mixture into dessert cups, and then chill in refrigerator for 1 hour, or serve warm. Top with your favorite fruits, nuts, or dessert topping.

CONTAINS

SUGAR

FREE FROM

DAIRY

GLUTEN

NUTS

METHOD

STOVETOP

VEGAN RECIPES: DESSERTS & SWEETS

MANGO TAPIOCA PARFAIT

Healthy and colorful, this creamy, easy-to-make dessert is perfect for a summer evening.

SERVES: 4–6 · PREP TIME: 20 MINUTES · TOTAL TIME: 20 MINUTES

INGREDIENTS

3 ripe mangoes, peeled, pitted, and cut into chunks

¼ cup (50g) coconut sugar

2–4 tablespoons water

½ teaspoon vanilla extract

2 cups Old-Fashioned Tapioca Pudding (*see* opposite page)

DIRECTIONS

- Peel and pit the mangoes, and then cut them into chunks, reserving one of the chopped mangoes for topping.
- In a blender, combine mangoes, sugar, vanilla extract, and water, and puree until smooth.
- Divide the puree between 4 to 6 dessert cups. Layer the tapioca pudding over the puree, and then top with the chopped mango.
- Garnish with mint or a dollop of a whipped topping, and serve.

CONTAINS

SUGAR

FREE FROM

DAIRY

GLUTEN

NUTS

METHOD

BLENDER

ASSEMBLY

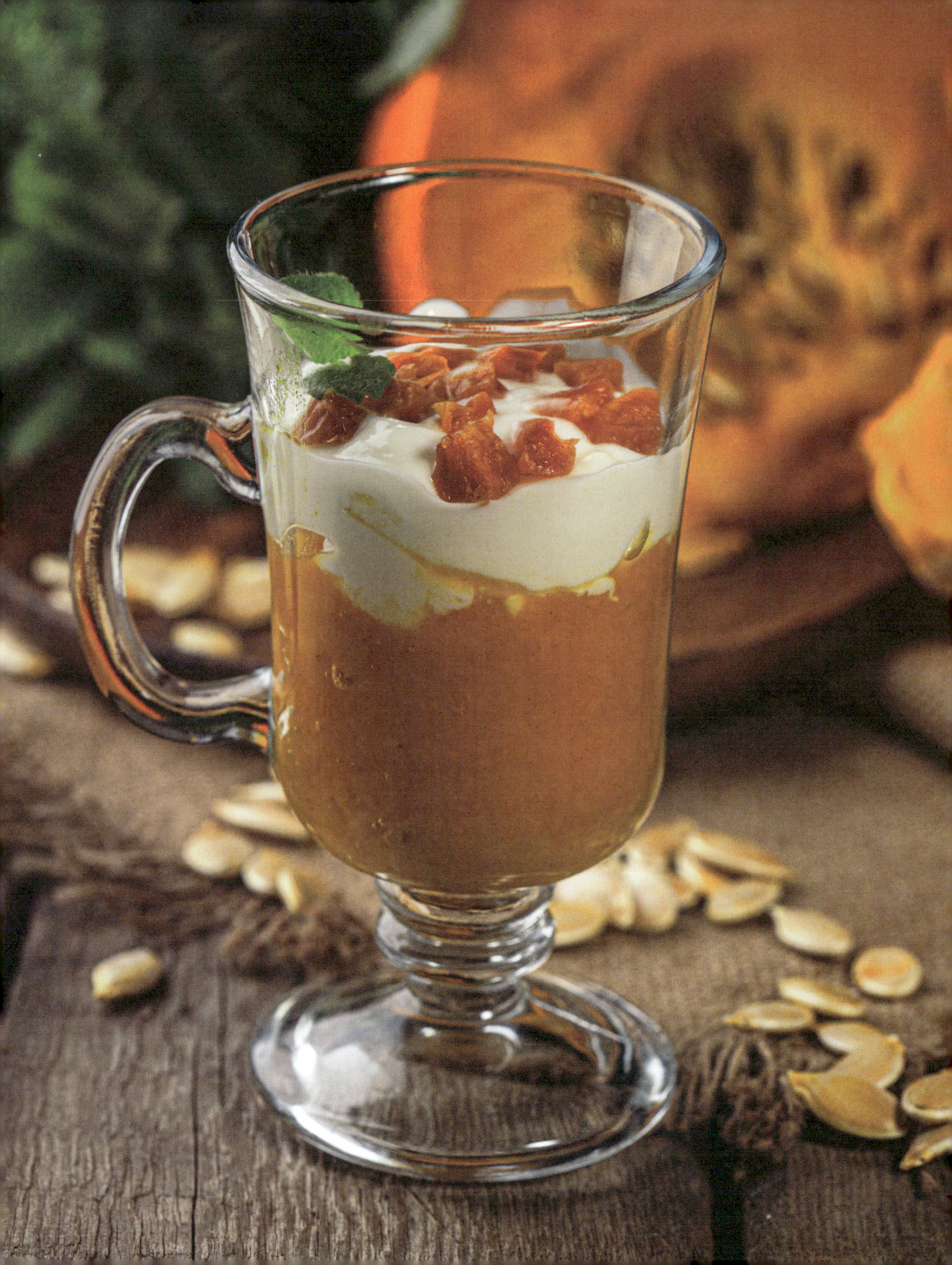

PUMPKIN SPICE PUDDING

With spices that evoke crisp autumn days, this dessert makes a great end to a fall celebration.

SERVES: 4 · PREP TIME: 15 MINUTES · SET TIME: 1–2 HOURS

INGREDIENTS

- 1 13.5 ounce (400g) can full-fat coconut milk, chilled
- ⅓ cup (80 mL) aquafaba (the liquid from a can of chickpeas)
- ¼ cup (30g) confectioner's sugar
- ¼ teaspoon cream of tartar
- ⅔ cup (160g) pumpkin puree, fresh or canned
- 1 teaspoon pumpkin pie spice
- ¼ cup pure maple syrup
- 1 teaspoon vanilla extract
- 1 tablespoon dried apricots, diced fine, for topping

-DIRECTIONS

- Gently remove the solidified pieces of coconut from the can of coconut milk, and place in a large mixing bowl, taking care to not get any of the liquid. Using a stand mixer or hand mixer, whip on medium until it reaches a whipped cream–like texture. Place in the fridge. Wipe out the base of the stand-mixer.
- Place the liquid from the can of chickpeas, confectioner's sugar, and cream of tartar in a large bowl. Whip on medium until at least doubled in volume and able to hold stiff peaks, about 10 to 12 minutes.
- While the aquafaba whips (if using a stand mixer) or after the aquafaba is whipped, mix together in a medium bowl the pumpkin puree, spices, maple syrup, and vanilla until the mixture is smooth.
- Slowly add in pumpkin mixture to the aquafaba, and whip until combined. Add in the coconut cream (save some to top the puddings), and whip again, just to combine.
- Divide the mixture into dessert cups, and layer on the topping of your choice. Place in the refrigerator until well set, about 1 to 2 hours.
- Serve with whipped coconut cream and dried apricot.

CONTAINS
- SUGAR

FREE FROM
- DAIRY
- GLUTEN
- NUTS

METHOD
MIXER

CHEF'S TIPS

- It is essential to chill the coconut milk to ensure that the solids and liquids separate. Too much of the water will prevent the coconut from whipping properly.
- If using canned, be sure it is 100% pumpkin with no added spices.
- For homemade pumpkin spice blends, *see* page 9.

APPLE CRUMBLE

Served warm, this vegan version of the classic dessert is delicious autumn comfort food.

SERVES: 8 · PREP TIME: 15 MINUTES · COOK TIME: 50 MINUTES

INGREDIENTS

For the filling:
- 8 cups (1kg) baking apples, peeled and cubed
- ½ cup (100g) brown sugar
- ¼ cup (30g) all-purpose flour
- 1 teaspoon ground cinnamon
- ½ teaspoon ground nutmeg
- ¼ teaspoon salt
- 1 tablespoon lemon juice
- 1 teaspoon vanilla extract

For the topping:
- 1 cup (120g) all-purpose flour
- 1½ cups (135g) rolled oats
- 1 cup (210g) brown sugar
- 1 teaspoon ground cinnamon
- ¾ cup (180g) vegan butter
- 1 teaspoon vanilla extract

CONTAINS
- GLUTEN
- SUGAR

FREE FROM
- DAIRY
- NUTS

METHOD

OVEN BAKE

DIRECTIONS

- Preheat oven to 350°F (180°C), and spray a 9-x-13 x-2-inch (33-x-23-x-5-cm) baking pan with vegan nonstick spray.
- To prepare the filling, place the peeled and cubed apples in a large mixing bowl, and add the brown sugar, flour, cinnamon, nutmeg, salt, lemon juice, and vanilla extract. Toss together so that all the apples are well coated. Transfer the apple mixture to the baking pan, patting it down evenly so that the top is smooth.
- To prepare the topping, melt the vegan butter, and then place flour, rolled oats, brown sugar, and cinnamon to a mixing bowl. Combine well. Add the melted vegan butter and vanilla, and stir so that a crumbly mixture forms.
- Using your fingers, evenly spread the topping over the apples.
- Place into the oven, and bake for 50 minutes until the apple mixture is buckling at the sides of the pan, and the top is golden brown. Remove from the oven, and cool for 10 minutes.
- Serve with Aquafaba Whipped topping (*see* page 145) or a vegan vanilla ice cream.

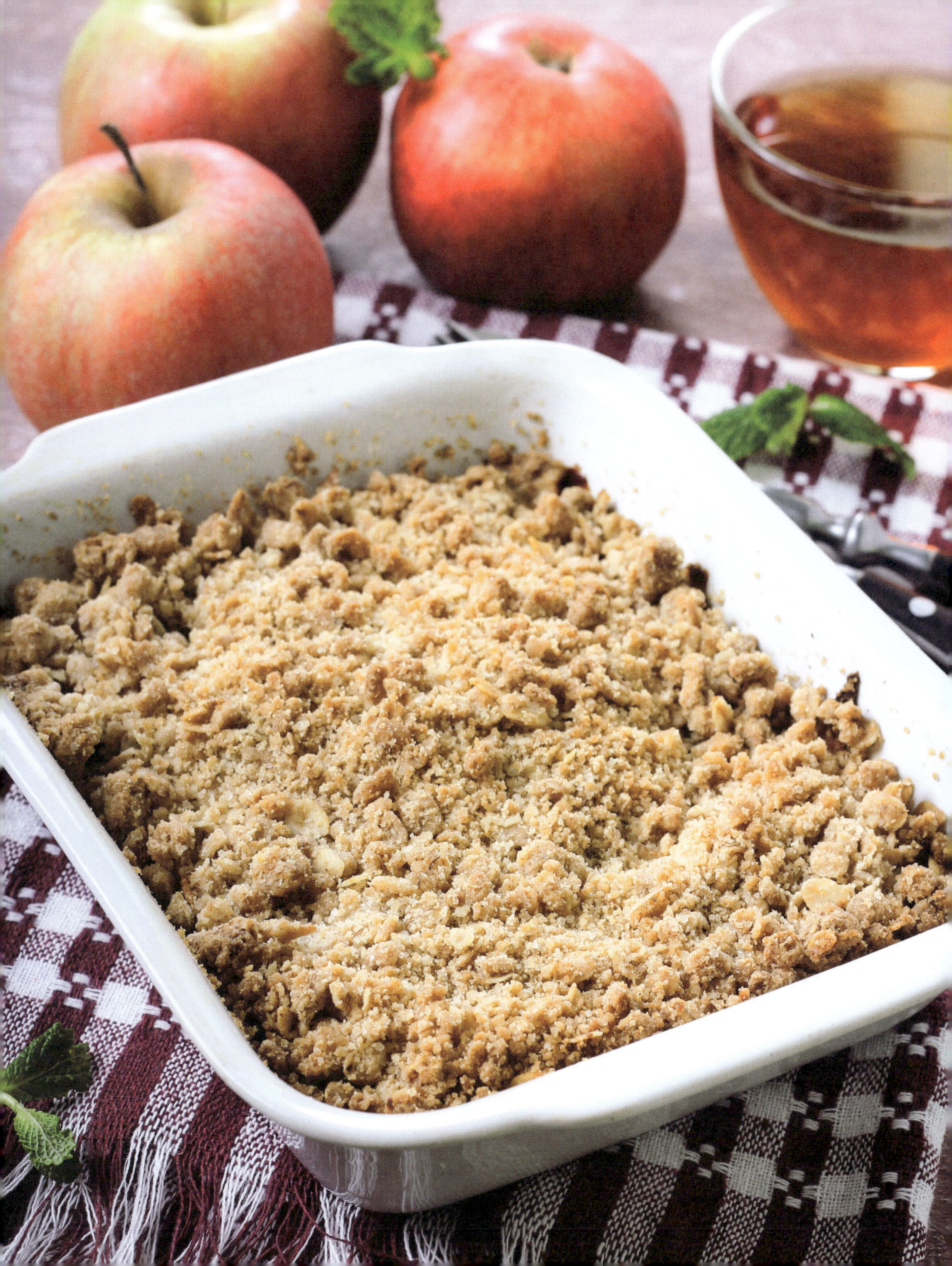

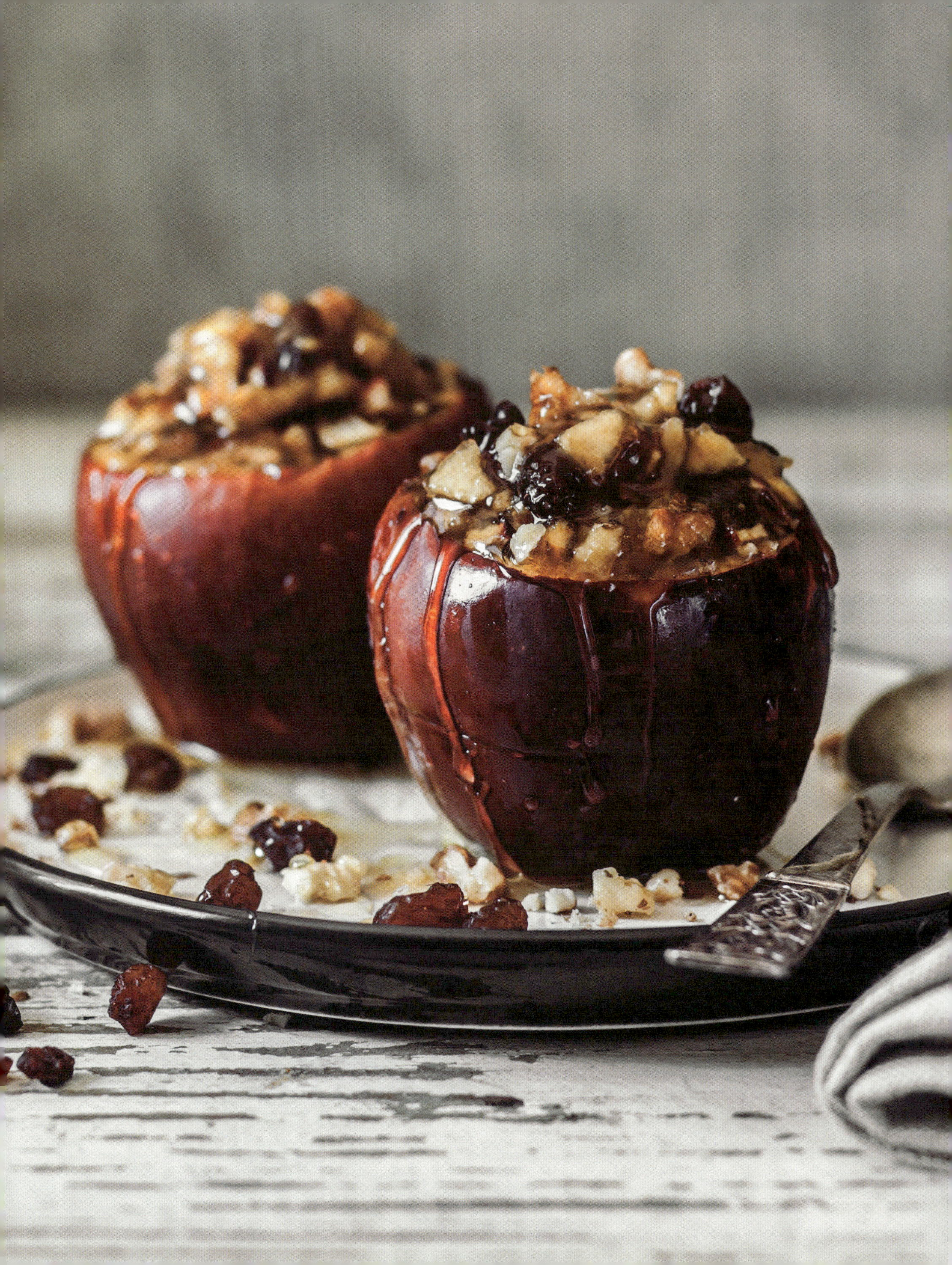

MAPLE WALNUT BAKED APPLES

Enjoy an autumn harvest of maple syrup and apples with these warm and comforting treats.

SERVES 4 · PREP TIME: 10 MINUTES · COOK TIME: 20 MINUTES

INGREDIENTS

4 large apples
¼ cup (60mL) maple syrup
½ cup (60g) walnuts, chopped
¼ cup (40g) raisins
1 teaspoon vanilla extract
1 teaspoon cinnamon

DIRECTIONS

- Preheat oven to 375°F (190°C).
- In a medium bowl, mix together maple syrup, chopped walnuts, vanilla extract, and cinnamon. Set aside.
- Core the apples, making a large well in the centers and leaving the bottoms untouched.
- Place apples in a baking dish, and fill them evenly with the maple walnut filling.
- Bake for 20 minutes, until the apples are soft but still slightly crunchy in the middle.
- Serve warm.

CONTAINS
- NUTS
- SUGAR

FREE FROM
- DAIRY
- GLUTEN

METHOD
OVEN BAKE

VEGAN RECIPES: DESSERTS & SWEETS

CHEF'S TIPS

- Choose apples, such as Jonathan, Honeycrisp, Braeburn, Cortland, or Granny Smith, that hold up to baking.

GRILLED APPLE WITH NUTTY CINNAMON & HONEY DRIZZLE

For a late-summer or early autumn treat, throw some apples slices on the grill.

SERVES 4 · PREP TIME: 5 MINUTES · COOK TIME: 10 MINUTES

INGREDIENTS

- 2 baking apples
- ½ cup (120mL) water
- ¼ cup (60mL) lemon juice
- 1 teaspoon cinnamon
- 2 tablespoons of honey
- ¼ cup (30g) almonds, chopped

DIRECTIONS

- Preheat the grill for medium heat.
- Core the apples, and cut them into ¼-inch slices, leaving peel on.
- In a large bowl, combine the water and lemon juice, and place the apple slices in the mixture to soak.
- In a small bowl, combine the cinnamon and almonds. Set aside
- Place the apples on the grill rack, and cook for 6 to 8 minutes on each side, turning once.
- Remove apples from grill, place them on a serving platter, sprinkle them with the cinnamon-nut mixture, and then drizzle them with honey, and serve immediately.

CONTAINS
- NUTS
- SUGAR

FREE FROM
- DAIRY
- GLUTEN

METHOD
GRILL

CHEF'S TIPS

- You need apples with a firm texture to stand up to grilling. For a sweet apple, try Fuji, Pink Lady, or Honeycrisp, For a tarter taste, go with Granny Smith.

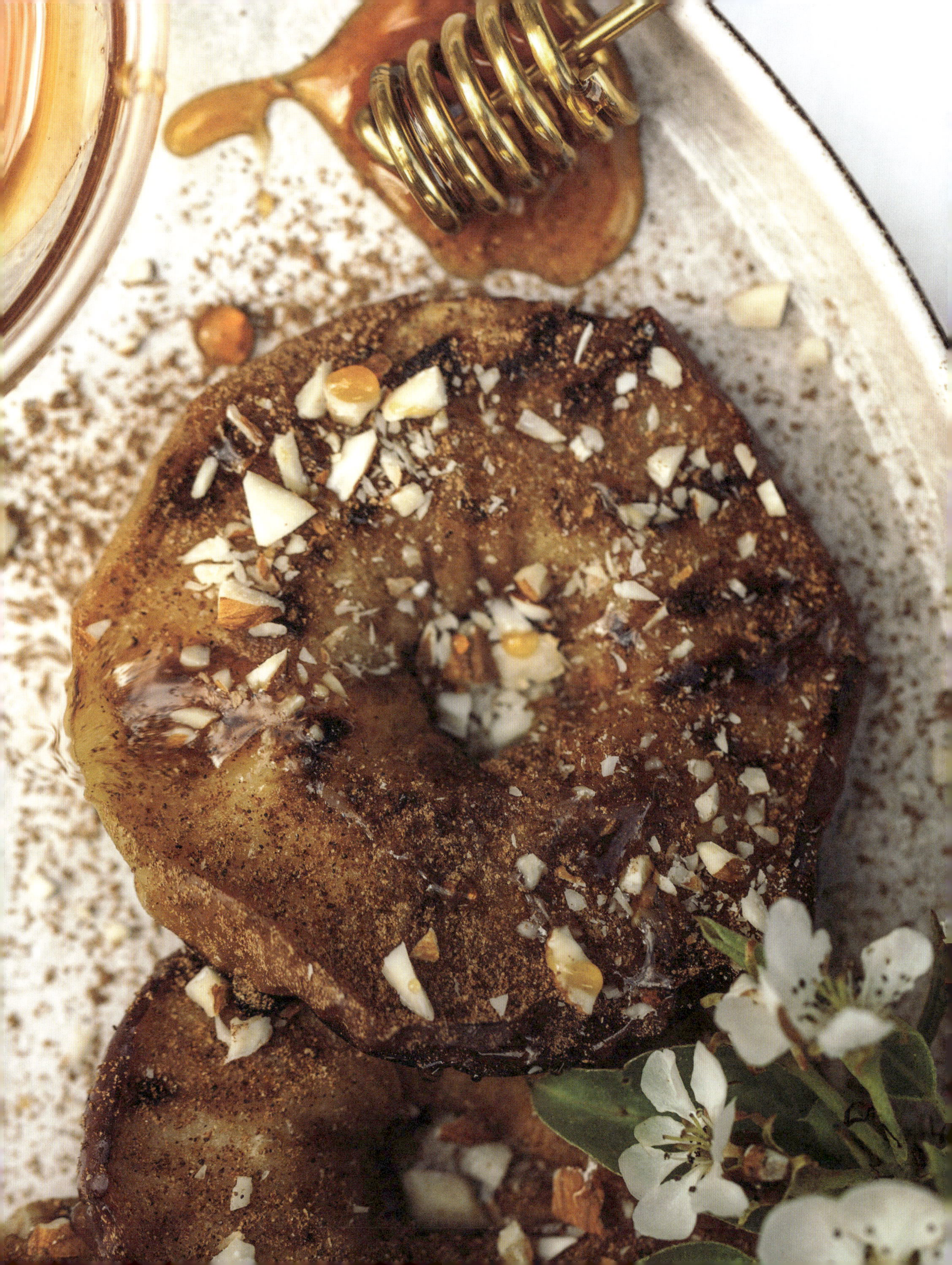

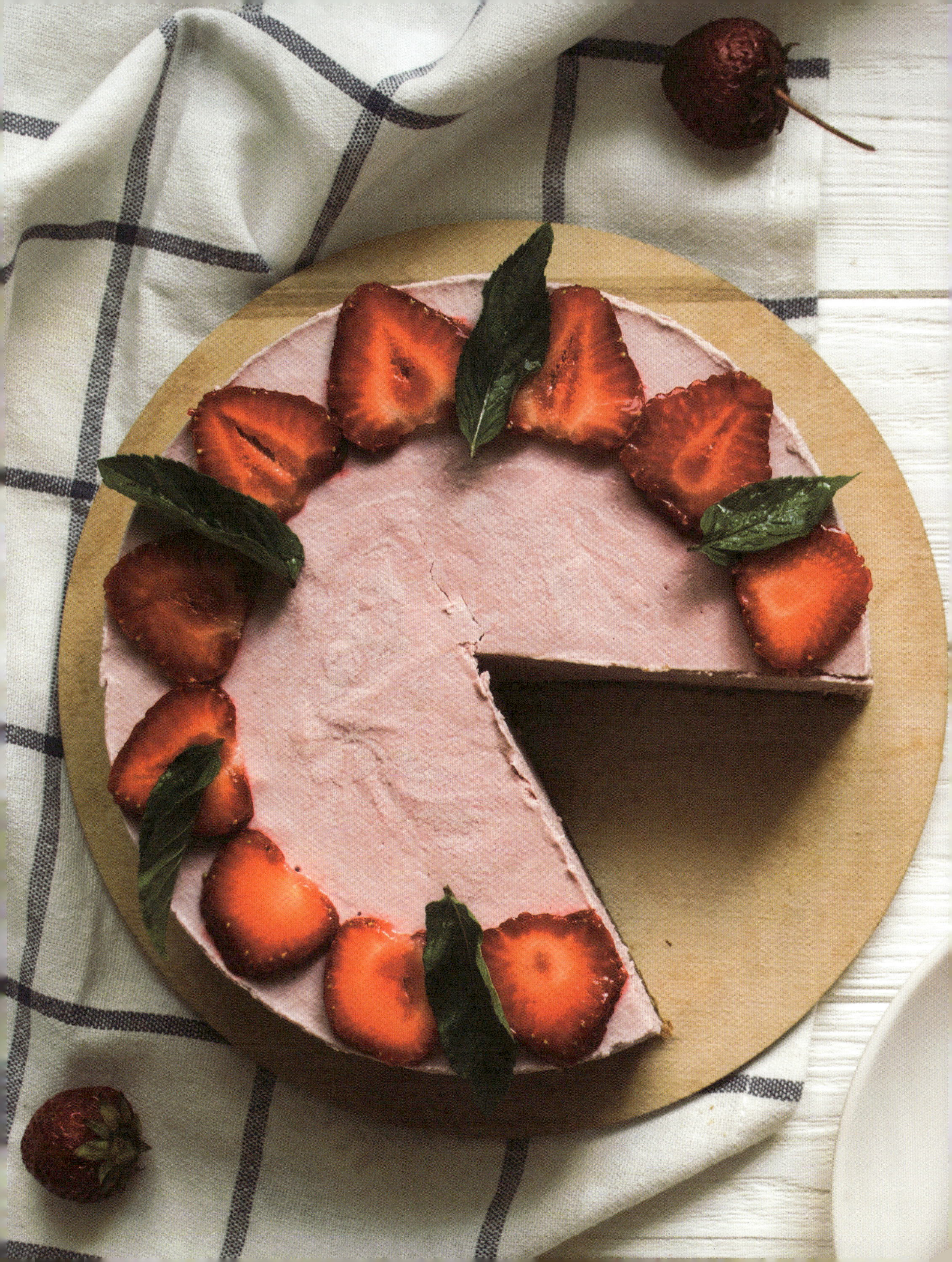

STRAWBERRY FREEZER PIE

With its creamy, cheesecake-like texture, this strawberry pie is great way to finish a summer supper.

SERVES: 6 · PREP TIME: 20 MINUTES · SET TIME: 8 HOURS

INGREDIENTS

For crust:
1 cup (140g) almonds

8 Medjool dates, pitted

Pinch of salt

For filling:
1½ cups (255g) fresh or frozen strawberries, cut into pieces

6 Medjool dates, pitted

¾ cup (190g) raw cashew butter

⅓ cup non-dairy milk

1 tablespoon lemon juice

1 teaspoon vanilla extract

6 fresh strawberries

CONTAINS
- NUTS
- SUGAR

FREE FROM
- DAIRY
- GLUTEN

METHOD

BLENDER

FREEZER

DIRECTIONS

- Line the bottom of a 6-x-3-inch (15-x-8-cm) springform pan with parchment paper.

- To make the crust, place the almonds, 8 Medjool dates, and salt in a blender or food processor, and pulse at low speed until the ingredients clump together. Add 1 to 2 tablespoons water, if the mixture is too dry.

- Press the crust into the pan, and place in the refrigerator to chill while you prepare the filling.

- Place the cut-up strawberries, 6 Medjool dates, raw cashew butter, non-dairy milk, lemon juice, and vanilla extract in a blender or food processor, and blend on high until the mixture is smooth and creamy.

- Remove the pan from the refrigerator, and pour the strawberry mixture over the crust.

- Freeze overnight or for at least 8 hours.

- Thaw for a few minutes, slice the fresh strawberries in half, and then arrange them around the edges of the pie, and serve.

CHEF'S TIPS

- You can freeze this pie for up to a week.

TRI-LAYERED FREEZER CAKE

A stunning cake fit for a celebration, this is a luscious construction of blueberry, white, and green tea layers.

SERVES: 1 · PREP TIME: 30 MINUTES · TOTAL TIME: 6 HOURS

INGREDIENTS

For crust:
1 cup (140g) almonds
8 Medjool dates, pitted
pinch of salt

For layers:
4 cups raw cashews
1 cup (80 mL) full-fat canned coconut milk
9 tablespoons lemon juice
9 tablespoons coconut oil, melted
9 tablespoons pure maple syrup
3 teaspoons pure vanilla extract
3 pinches of salt
2 cups fresh blackberries
1 tablespoon matcha powder
fruit and lower, for garnish

CONTAINS
- NUTS
- SUGAR

FREE FROM
- DAIRY
- GLUTEN

METHOD
BLENDER
FREEZER

DIRECTIONS

- Place 4 cups raw cashews in a large bowl, and cover with water. Soak for 4 hours or overnight. Divide the cashews into thirds, and set aside.

- Line the bottom of a 6-x-3-inch (15-x-6-cm) springform pan with parchment paper.

- To make the crust, place the almonds, Medjool dates, and salt in a blender or food processor, and pulse at low speed until the ingredients clump together. Add 1 to 2 tablespoons water, if the mixture is too dry. Press the crust into the pan, and place in the refrigerator to chill.

- To make the blueberry layer, place ⅓ of the soaked cashews in a blender or food processor, and add ⅓ cup of the coconut milk, 3 tablespoons each of the coconut oil, lemon juice, and maple syrup, 1 tablespoon of the vanilla extract, a pinch of salt, and the blueberries. Blend until completely smooth. Pour the blueberry mixture into the pan on top of the crust. Smooth into an even layer, and then place in the freezer for at least 1 hour.

CHEF'S TIPS

- You can store this cake in the freezer for up to 2 weeks.

- To make the white layer, place the same ingredients as for the blueberry layer (minus the blueberries) in the blender, and blend until completely smooth. Pour the white mixture into the pan on top of the blueberry. Smooth into an even layer, and then place in the freezer for another hour.

- To make the green tea layer, place the same ingredients as for the white layer in the blender, add the matcha powder, and blend until completely smooth. Pour the green tea mixture into the pan on top of the white. Smooth into an even layer. Freeze overnight, or for at least 4 hours.

- To serve, decorate with fresh berries and flowers. Serve frozen or let thaw at room temperature for 10 to 15 minutes before slicing.

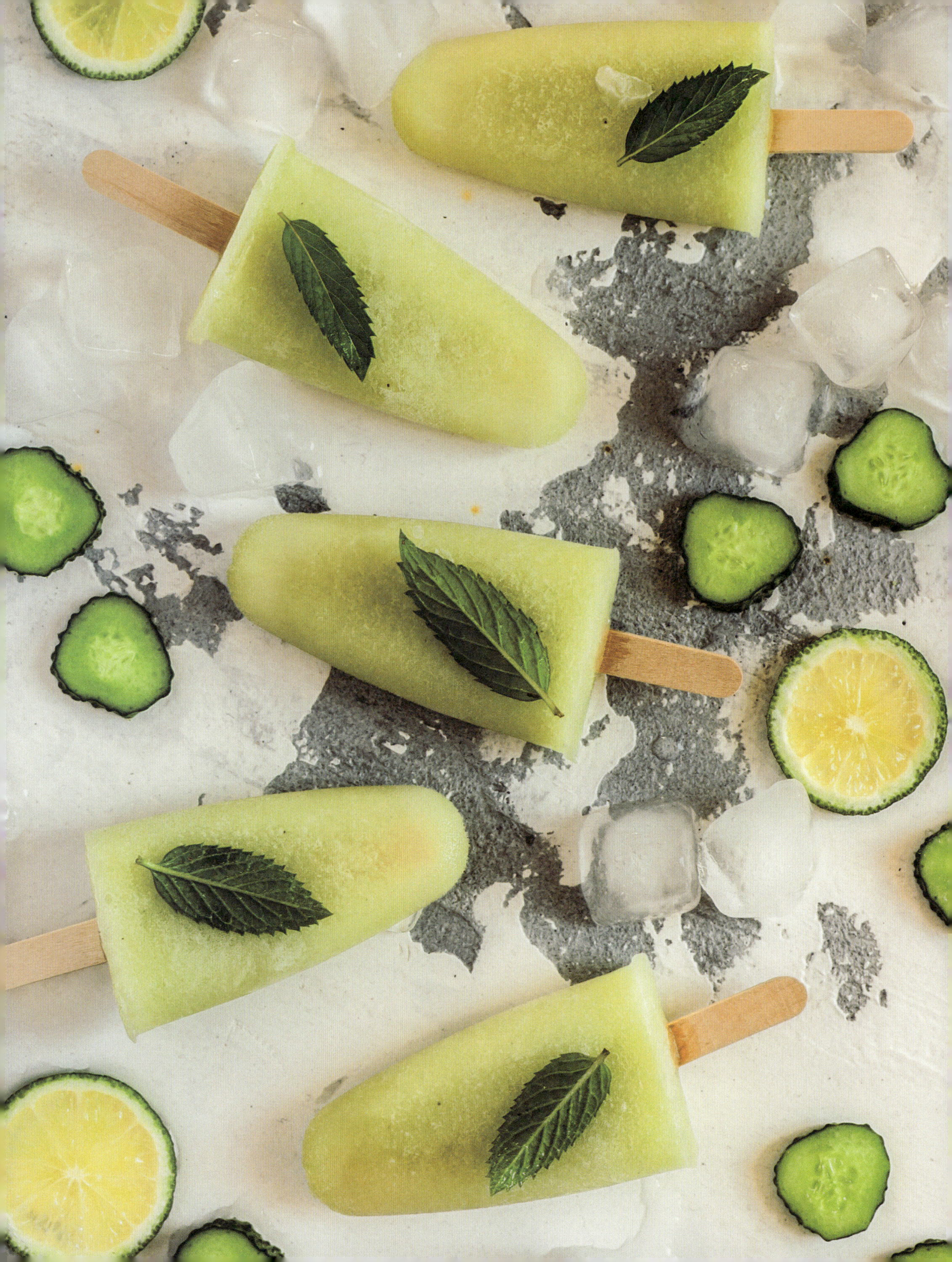

MINTY CUCUMBER, GREEN TEA & LIME POPSICLES

These refreshing popsicles will please both children and adults with their minty, cool taste.

SERVES: 10 · PREP TIME: 10 MINUTES · SET TIME: 4–24 HOURS

INGREDIENTS

- 1¾ cups (420mL) water
- ¾ cup (150g) granulated sugar
- 6 large sprigs of fresh mint
- 2 teaspoons matcha powder
- 3 tablespoons fresh lime juice
- 1 English cucumber, peeled and roughly chopped

DIRECTIONS

- In a small saucepan, bring the sugar and water to a boil. As soon as the sugar is dissolved, remove from the heat, and stir in the mint leaves. Let it steep until it cools, and then strain out the mint leaves, storing them for later use, if desired.
- Add all the green tea, lime juice, mint syrup, and cucumbers to a blender with the liquid in the bottom. Blend until very smooth.
- Pour mixture into popsicle molds, and insert sticks.
- Freeze 4 to 6 hours or overnight.

CONTAINS

- SUGAR

FREE FROM

- DAIRY
- GLUTEN
- NUTS

METHOD

BLENDER

FREEZER

FRUIT PUREE POPSICLES

Nothing beats a fresh fruit popsicle on a blistering hot summer day—just choose your favorite flavor.

SERVES: 6 · PREP TIME: 5 MINUTES · SET TIME: 8 HOURS

INGREDIENTS

¾ cup (180 mL) apple juice

2½ cups fresh or frozen fruit of your choice

4 tablespoons honey

¼ teaspoon vanilla extract

½ teaspoon lemon juice

DIRECTIONS

- If your fruit is frozen, thaw and rinse. Pat dry.
- Place all ingredients in a blender, Reversing some of the fruit or chunks of fruit for later, and blend for 1 or 2 minutes, until the mixture is smooth.
- Evenly distribute the mixture into the six wells of a popsicle mold, and then carefully stir in a nit of the reserved fruit on the top.
- Depending on the type of mold, either secure the lids and sticks on top of the mold, and place it in the freezer, or pour into molds, place in freezer for 30 minutes, then insert popsicle sticks into the molds. Freeze for 8 hours or overnight.
- To release the popsicles, run each one under hot water for 30 seconds, ans serve immediately.

CONTAINS

SUGAR

FREE FROM

DAIRY

GLUTEN

NUTS

METHOD

BLENDER

FREEZER

CHEF'S TIPS

- You can you the fruit of your choice, from fresh or frozen berries to all kinds of sweet melons.
- If you don't own a popsicle mold, you can use small paper cups. Split the mixture between the cups, place in freezer and let chill about 30 to 45 minutes. Insert sticks, and place back in the freezer another 7 hours or overnight.

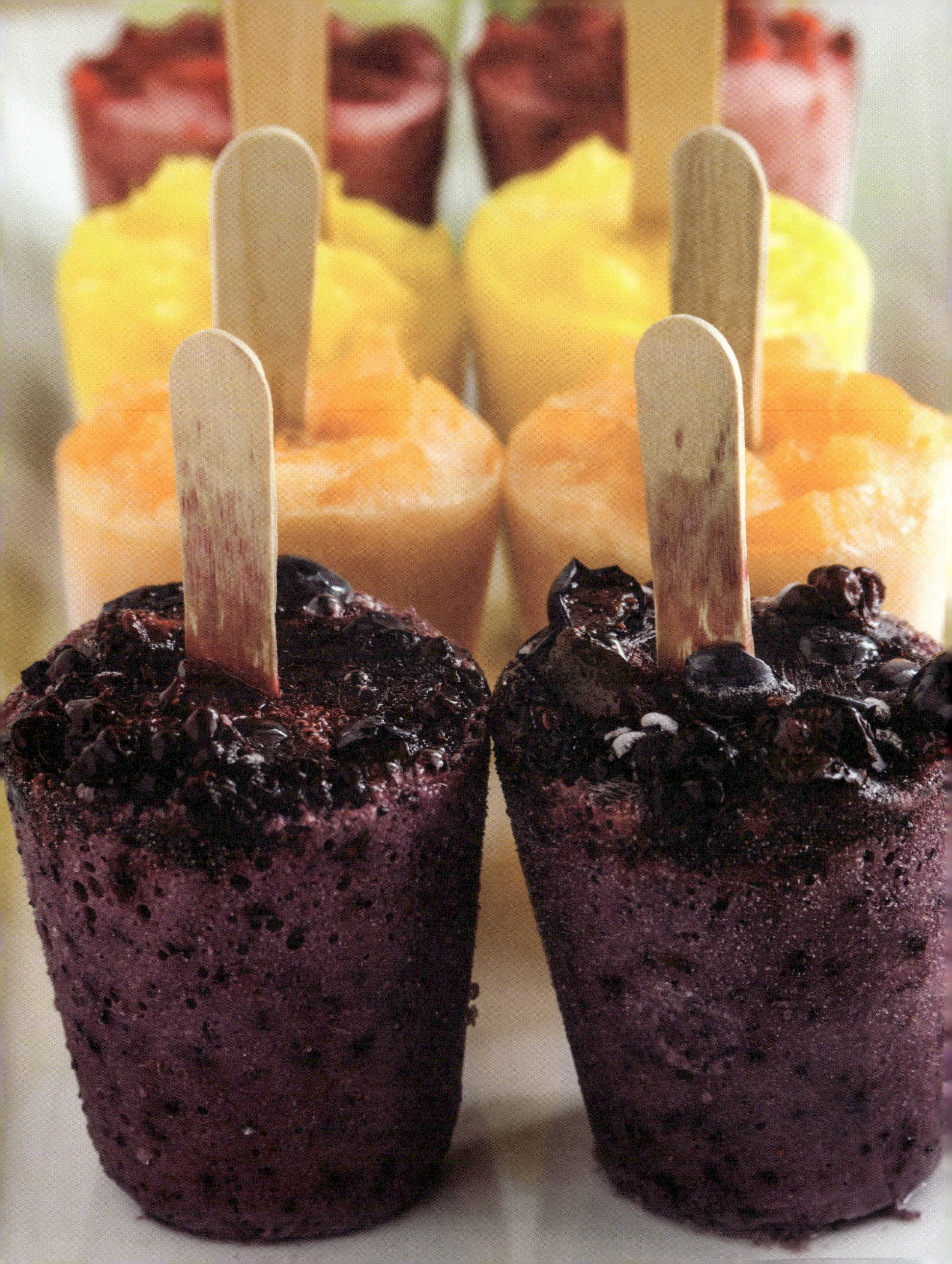

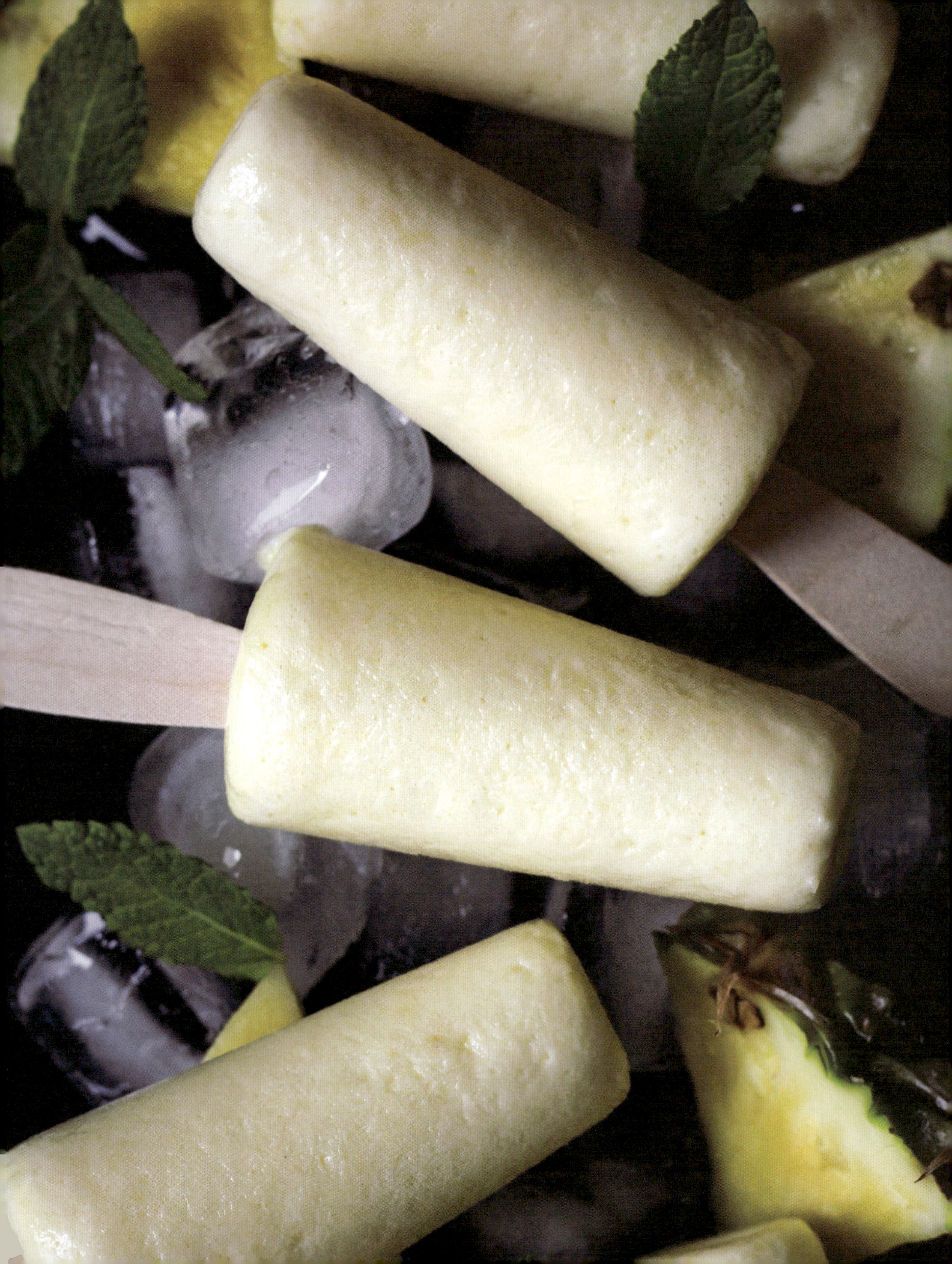

PIÑA COLADA POPSICLES

Evoke the taste of the tropics with these refreshing pineapple-coconut frozen treats.

SERVES: 6 · PREP TIME: 10 MINUTES · SET TIME: 4–24 HOURS

INGREDIENTS

- 1 14-ounce (400mL) can coconut milk
- 1 cup (245g) pineapple, chopped into ½-inch pieces
- 1 whole banana
- 3 tablespoon agave nectar
- 1½ tablespoon vanilla extract
- 2 teaspoon light rum, or ½ teaspoon rum extract
- 1½ tablespoon shredded coconut

DIRECTIONS

- Place all ingredients into a blender (except shredded coconut), and blend until smooth.
- Stir in shredded coconut.
- Pour mixture into popsicle molds, and insert sticks.
- Freeze 4 to 6 hours or overnight.

CONTAINS
- SUGAR

FREE FROM
- DAIRY
- GLUTEN
- NUTS

METHOD
BLENDER
FREEZER

ORANGE GRANITA

Made from fresh oranges—either blood or naval—this icy treat evokes the feeling of long summer days.

SERVES: 4 · PREP TIME: 10 MINUTES · CHILL TIME: 2–3 HOURS

INGREDIENTS

- 3 cups (720 mL) orange juice, freshly squeezed
- ¼ cup (50g) sugar
- 1 tablespoons fresh lemon juice
- ¼ cup (60mL) water
- 2 springs mint

DIRECTIONS

- In a small saucepan, combine the water and sugar. Heat to a boil and cook until the sugar is fully dissolved. Let cool completely.
- In a large bowl, combine the orange juice and sugar syrup.
- Pour the mixture into a roasting pan or baking dish (the container should be large enough so the liquid is no more than 1-inch (24mm) deep). Freeze for 1 hour. Remove from the freezer, and scrape with 2 forks from end to end, breaking up any clumps. Pop it back into the freezer, and give it a scraping every half hour or so, until it is the texture of fluffy icy flakes.
- When the granita is flaky, scoop it into dessert cups, and serve immediately.

CHEF'S TIPS

- You can make granita with just about any fruit, using a blender to combine the whole fruit and sugar syrup. For peach granita, use 4 ripe peaches (peeled, halved, pitted, and coarsely chopped); for watermelon, use ¼ of a whole watermelon, cut into chunks with the peel discarded; for green apple, use about 1 pound (.5kg) of peeled, cored, and diced apples; for strawberry granita, use about 1 quart (1 liters), washed and hulled. You can also switch out the lemon juice for lime, or the mint for basil or lavender. For an adult treat, add a shot of liqueur, such a Grand Marnier or an apple schnapps.

FREE FROM

- DAIRY
- GLUTEN
- NUTS
- SUGAR

METHOD

STOVETOP

FREEZER

ALPHABETICAL LIST OF RECIPES

Air-Fried Falafel, 92

Aloo Gobi, 106

Apple Crumble, 172

Avocado & Roasted Sweet Potato Salad with Spinach & Chickpeas, 88

Avocado-Pomegranate Sweet Potato Toast, 117

Baba Ganoush, 70

Baby Spinach, Plum & Walnut Salad with Honey Mustard Dressing, 76

Banana Bread, 24

Barbeque Tempeh Skewers, 130

Barmbrack, 27

Basil Pesto, 132

Beetroot Burgers, 136

Berry Mousse, 166

Blue Spirulina Chia Pudding, 162

Blueberry Muffins, 31

Bruschetta with Beetroot Hummus, Chopped Nuts & Microgreens, 116

Brussels Sprouts & Kabocha Squash Quinoa Salad, 113

Carob & Date Balls, 157

Cauliflower Hot Wings, 81

Cauliflower Pizza Crust, 36

Chana Masala, 105

Chia Pudding, 161

Chilled Cucumber & Mint Soup, 63

Chocolate Hummus, 151

Cocoa Banana-Avocado Pudding, 154

Cranberry Scones, 21

Cream of Mushroom Soup, 49

Curried Roasted Cauliflower Dip, 78

Dalgona Matcha Latte, 147

Dark Chocolate Truffles, 158

Easy Carrot Potato Soup, 45

Eggplant & Olive Pizza, 39

Eggplant Meatballs, 135

Falafel, Tomato & Cucumber Salad, 94

French Onion Soup, 54

Fruit Puree Popsicles, 184

Gazpacho, 62

Green Spinach Muffins, 32

Grilled Apple with Nutty Cinnamon & Honey Drizzle, 176

Guacamole, 71

Hasselback Potatoes, 103

Hot & Sweet Cauliflower Bites, 79

Kale Potato Soup, 53

Lavender-Lemon Cornbread, 19

Layered Peach Pudding, 165

Lemon & Rosemary Barley Soup, 58

Lentil Loaf with Barbeque glaze, 95

Mango Tapioca Parfait, 169

Maple Walnut Baked Apples, 175

Matcha Green Tea Brownies with White Chocolate Drizzle, 148

Matcha Pistachio Muffins, 28

Melon & Arugula Salad with Watermelon Vinaigrette, 75

Mexican Quinoa Salad with Chili Lime Dressing, 87

Mint Chocolate Avocado Pudding, 152

MInty Cucumber, Green Tea & Lime Popsicles, 183

Mushroom Miso Soup, 47

Nutty Berry Lemon-Poppy Bread, 23

Nutty Chocolate Mousse, 153

Old-Fashioned Tapioca Pudding, 168

Open-Faced Beetroot Hummus Sandwich with Pomegranate & Corn Salsa, 114

Orange Granita, 188

Pad Thai, 110

Peanut Stew, 101

Piña Colada Popsicles, 187

Potato & Corn Chowder, 55

Potato Pancakes, 140

Pumpkin Lentil Curry, 96

Pumpkin Muffins, 35

Pumpkin Spice Pudding, 171

Quick & Easy Miso Soup, 46

Quinoa with Broccoli,

Mushrooms & Spinach, 127

Ratatouille, 124

Red Beet Gazpacho, 65

Red Lentil & Bulgur Wheat Patties, 98

Red Lentil Dal, 99

Roasted Asparagus Soup, 57

Roasted Beetroot Hummus, 66

Roasted Brussels Sprouts, Pecan & Cranberry Quinoa Salad, 120

Roasted Eggplant Rolls with Spinach Hummus, 72

Scones, 20

Sesame Cauliflower, 109

Spinach & Cannelini Soup, 61

Spring Veggie Risotto, 123

Strawberry Freezer Pie, 179

Stuffed Sweet Potato with Arugula, Olives & Guacamole, 102

Sweet Potato Burgers, 139

Sweet Potato Toast with Beetroot Hummus & Roasted Chickpeas, 69

Tabbouleh Salad, 128

Tagliatelle Pasta with Spinach Pesto & Green Peas, 133

Teriyaki Tempeh Bowl, 129

Tofu Breakfast Scramble with Spinach and Tomatoes, 84

Tomato & Avocado Toast, 118

Tomato Soup, 50

Tri-Layered Freezer Cake, 180

Vegetable Broth, 42

Vegetable Soup, 43

Whipped Aquafaba Topping, 145

Whipped Coconut Cream, 144

White Sandwich Loaf, 15

Whole-Wheat Loaf, 16

Zucchini Spiral Noodles with Basil Pesto Salad Bowl, 91

PHOTO CREDITS

All photos copyright Shutterstock.com

Cover photo: Anna Shepulova

Icons: Sylverarts Vectors

THE VEGAN PANTRY

6–7 RONEDYA; 8 MAHATHIR MOHD YASIN; 10 Andrii Horulko

BREADS & MUFFINS

12–13 Charles Brutlag;

14 DOANPHUONG NGUYEN; 17 Duplass; 18 Yulia Davidovich; 20 Sokor Space; 21 MaraZe; 22 Karolsejnova; 25 Irina Rostokina; 26 MShev; 29 Brent Hofacker; 30 YuliiaHolovchenko; 33 nelea33; 34 Rimma Bondarenko; 37 Maren Winter; 38, 39 etorres

SOUPS, STARTERS & SNACKS

40–41 pilipphoto; 42 vilax; 43 Oksana Mizina; 44 Jessica E Marx; 46 Picture Partners; 47 AS Food studio; 48 Dar1930; 51 mythja; 52 New Africa; 54 Lonni; 56 two_meerkats; 59 barbajones; 60 Nataliya Arzamasova; 63 photo-oasis; 64 Kolpakova Svetlana; 67 JeniFoto; 68 zi3000; 70 Anna_Pustynnikova; 71 Pixel-Shot; 73 Viktor Kochetkov; 74 Carey Jaman; 77 DronG; 78 BarthFotografie; 79 Fanfo; 80 JeniFoto

MAIN COURSES & SIDE DISHES

82 Timolina; 85 Lena Novak; 86 AnastasiaKopa; 89 Anna Shepulova; 90 Lapa Smile; 93 Viktoria Hodos; 94 Kiian Oksana; 97 Kiian Oksana; 98 Fanfo; 99 Perutskyi Petro; 100 Rimma Bondarenko; 102 Nina Firsova; 103 Anastasiia Kulikovska; 104 nelea33; 108 Romashko Yuliia; 111 homelesscuisine; 112 IriGri; 115 Tenzen; 116 Nataliia Zhekova; 117 Valentyn Volkov; 119 Ksenija Toyechkina; 121 Nina Firsova; 122 marco mayer; 125 Oksana Mizina; 126 Timolina; 128 Timolina; 129 Natalia Hanin; 131 Breslavtsev Oleg; 132 nelea33; 133 Anna Shepulova; 134 Nataliya Arzamasova; 137 vlasna; 138 Elena Veselova; 141 Viktor Kochetkov

DESSERTS & SWEETS

132–143 Oksana Mizina; 144 shutterstock; 145 chris_tina; 146 Jamilah Pratama; 149 Anna_Pustynnikova; 150 Brent Hofacker; 152 Brent Hofacker; 153 SizeSquares; 155 Nataliya Arzamasova; 156 Viktor Kochetkov; 159 nelea33; 160 Losangela; 163 viennetta; 164 Yulia Davidovich; 167 Danilova Janna; 168 Moving Moment; 169 rontav; 170 Rogozhina Elena; 173 MShev; 174 Tatiana Vorona; 177 Kabachki.photo; 178 Vlad and Juliya Yankovsky; 181 Julia-Bogdanova; 182 Tatiana Vorona; 183 grafvision; 183 Natali Samorod; 185 Teri Virbickis; 186 Marija Stepanovic; 187 OxfordSquare; 189 photosimysia